The World Junior Championships
The Official Book of Team Canada from Eh to Zed

Kevin Gibson

© Copyright 2003 Kevin Gibson. All rights reserved.

No part of this publication may be reproduced, stored in a retrieval system, or transmitted, in any form or by any means, electronic, mechanical, photocopying, recording, or otherwise, without the written prior permission of the author.

Printed in Victoria, Canada

```
National Library of Canada Cataloguing in Publication Data

Gibson, Kevin, 1970-
     The official book of Team Canada from eh to zed / Kevin Gibson.

Contents: Bk. 1.  The World Junior champicnships.
ISBN 1-1420-0162-5 (bk. 1)

     1. Hockey—Canada—History—Miscellanea.  2. Hockey players—Canada—Statistics.  3.
World Junior Championships (Hockey)—Miscellanea.  4. Memorial Cup (Hockey)—Miscella-
nea.  I. Title.

 GV848.4.C3G52 2003        796.962'62'0971         C2003-901744-3
```

TRAFFORD

This book was published *on-demand* in cooperation with Trafford Publishing.
On-demand publishing is a unique process and service of making a book available for retail sale to the public taking advantage of on-demand manufacturing and Internet marketing. **On-demand publishing** includes promotions, retail sales, manufacturing, order fulfilment, accounting and collecting royalties on behalf of the author.

Suite 6E, 2333 Government St., Victoria, B.C. V8T 4P4, CANADA
Phone   250-383-6864   Toll-free 1-888-232-4444 (Canada & US)
Fax   250-383-6804   E-mail   sales@trafford.com
Web site www.trafford.com   TRAFFORD PUBLISHING IS A DIVISION OF TRAFFORD HOLDINGS LTD.
Trafford Catalogue #03-0530   www.trafford.com/robots/03-0530.html

10   9   8   7   6   5   4   3   2   1

Table of Contents

Section
- 1   Dedication
- 2   Acknowledgements and Copyright Disclosures
- 3   Foreword By Bob Nicholson
- 4   Introduction
- 5   Q & A With Szymon Szemberg
- 6   Memorial Cup and NCAA Champions
- 7   All Time Team Canada Results at WJC
- 8   Photo Gallery Part 1
- 9   Player Profiles 1-212
- 10 Photo Gallery Part 2
- 11 Player Profiles 216-424
- 12 Photo Gallery Part 3
- 13 Where They Won and Where They Are From
- 14 Leader Board and Author's All-Star Teams
- 15 Player List
- 16 The End

Dedicated to Nathan, I hope to add your name to this book one day. But if you join the Ballet instead, that's okay too.

Acknowledgements

I would like to thank the following organizations and people for their help in getting this book off the ice. The Canadian Hockey Association specifically Dale Ptycia and Bob Nicholson, the Hockey Hall of Fame specifically Craig Campbell, and the IIHF.
Dan Diamond, Igor Uderian, Trafford Publishing, Scott Morrison, Mike Hogan, Andrea Ruskin, Rick Fournier, Ben Fournier, Helen and Bill Gibson, Sue and Gord Jackson, and a special thanks to my wife Lisa for looking after Nathan while I wrote 400 pages after work, and until 5am on weekends. All information in this book was verified from the following websites, Faceoff.com, LegendsofHockey.net, NHL.com, Hockeydb.com, IIHF.com and CanadianHockey.ca.
"Cover design by Andrea Ruskin"
ANDREA RUSKIN
Communication Designer
Website: http://www.andrearuskin.net
This book and its contents have been copy written, any use without permission in whole or in part without the express written consent of Kevin Gibson, the Canadian Hockey Association and the Hockey Hall of Fame is strictly prohibited. All pictures are courtesy of the Hockey Hall of Fame. The Team Canada logo on the cover is a registered trade mark of the CHA.

Foreword

Firstly, I would like to congratulate Kevin Gibson on spending so much time and energy in compiling a first rate document on Canadian Hockey players representing their country on the International scene. The best resource that Canada has in hockey is its people and the most important people are the players that play the game on the ice. Inside this book you will recognize a lot of the star NHL players that have given back to their country in representing the great game of hockey. Hockey is Canada's game that we have now shared with the world and individuals inside this book are the people that have built the great tradition within our game. Again, congratulations to Kevin on a very well documented book.

Sincerely,
Bob Nicholson
President
Canadian Hockey Association

Introduction

No sport receives more attention in Canada than hockey and what better way to enjoy hockey even more than putting out a series of books on NHL players who have represented Canada. Book one is on the World Junior Championships, book two the Olympics, book three the Summit Series/Canada/World Cup and finally book four will be on the World Championships. Why four books? Doing one book of over 800 players would be costly to print, costly to buy and would weigh about 100 pounds, by doing the four books fans can pick which ones they want or buy the whole set.

To be eligible to have your name in these books you must have played at least one NHL game and have been on the roster of one of the above-mentioned, Team Canada teams. Why must you have played at least one NHL game? I figure if you are tied with me in NHL games played than the reader won't be too interested in your statistics. Therefore I decided on Canada's NHLers.

Book one is on the World Junior Championships, which unofficially commenced in 1974, officially commenced in 1977. Reason being, the International Ice Hockey Federation (see page two for IIHF information) had the first three tournaments as exhibition only, although there were medals won. The players from those teams are in this book; if statistics were kept and medals were given out then I figure it counts. In 1974 the Peterborough Petes of the Ontario Hockey League represented Canada. The Petes also had twelve players represent Canada in 1980. In 1975 a collection of Western Hockey League All-Stars represented Canada. In 1976 the final unofficial tournament the Sherbrooke Beavers of the Quebec Major Junior Hockey League laced up the skates for the Maple Leaf. For four out of the first five official tournaments, Canada sent the majority of the players from the defending Memorial Cup Champion, except for 1978 when an all-star junior team played for Canada. In 1977 eleven players from the St. Catharines Fincups and ten other players from around the CHL represented Canada. In 1979 eleven players from the New Westminster Bruins and nine others from the CHL played for Canada. In 1981 it was ten players from the Cornwall Royals and ten players from the CHL who played at the World Juniors. Since 1982 (the first time Canada won Gold) the best Canadian junior players (ALA 1978) in the world have represented Canada at this IIHF annual event.

What is the Memorial Cup? it is a trophy that has been awarded in Canada for junior hockey supremacy since 1919 and has been the Championship trophy of the Canadian Hockey League since 1972, the Champions of the Ontario Hockey League (OHL), the Western Hockey League (WHL), the Quebec Major Junior Hockey League (QMJHL) and the events host city play for the Memorial Cup to determine Canada's junior champion. I do realise that the three major junior hockey leagues had different names over the year's i.e. Western Canadian Hockey League, Ontario Major Junior Hockey League etc. To make things simpler I just used the current names and initials in this book.

The NCAA since 1948 holds a tournament each spring called the Frozen Four to determine their champion, teams are broken into four groups by geographical region and they play to determine four finalists who then play elimination games to determine a Champion. When you see that a player was selected in the "Supplemental Draft" that was a draft that came about so that NCAA players would not lose their playing eligibility in College that draft was cancelled in 1995.

Who is the International Ice Hockey Federation? They were and are the governing body of hockey in Europe and they are presently responsible for running the World Juniors, the Worlds and the Olympics. The IIHF or "Ligue Internationale de Hockey sur Glace" (LIHG) was founded in May of 1908 in Paris, France. (The name changed in 1954 to the IIHF). A French Journalist named Louis Magnus who became the LIHG's first President started up the LIHG. The originating countries at inception were France, Belgium, Switzerland, Great Britain and Bohemia. Russia and Germany refused an invitation to join. There are presently 50 countries as members of the IIHF. Canada joined the LIHG on April 26, 1920. Canada boycotted IIHF events from 1970-1974, because they were not allowed to use NHL players from non-playoff teams at the World Championships.

Finally, I will say that no one is perfect so if I have missed any players than I would be happy to add them to updated versions of this book. All statistics are updated through the conclusion of the 2002-03 NHL and CHL regular seasons. Feel free to contact me via e-mail thefanswriter@hotmail.com.

Thank You
Kevin Gibson
Author

Q & A With Szymon Szemberg of the IIHF

Q. How did the first World Juniors come about? Whose idea was it? And why Did they decide to do it?

A. There was general interest from the national associations to start a Tournament for juniors and after three unofficial tournaments it was decided To give them official IIHF-status.

Q. What teams played in the first ever tournament and how were they Chosen?

A. Soviet Union, Finland, Canada, Sweden, USA and Czechoslovakia took part in the first unofficial tournament in 1974. They were invited as the top six Ranked countries.

Q. How are the teams selected each year to play in the tournament?
A. Everything goes by ranking. Basically, the bottom teams from each tournament get relegated to a lower division while the top teams get promoted. Thus, Ukraine and Austria were promoted to the 2004 IIHF World U20 Championship in Finland Because they won the Division I groups. Belarus and Germany were relegated.

Q. Can a player play for more than one country? I know there was Controversy about 10 years ago around Adam Deadmarsh.

A. According to IIHF rules a player who has represented a country in an IIHF Tournament after his/hers 18th birthday, he/she cannot play for another Country after that. See case Evgeni Nabokov (San José). He represented Kazakhstan in an U20 tournament some years ago and could thus not play for Russia in the Salt Lake City Olympics.

Memorial Cup Champions Since 1974

1974	Regina Pats
1975	Toronto Marlboros
1976	Hamilton Fincups
1977	New Westminster Bruins
1978	New Westminster Bruins
1979	Peterborough Petes
1980	Cornwall Royals
1981	Cornwall Royals
1982	Kitchener Rangers
1983	Portland Winter Hawks
1984	Ottawa 67's
1985	Prince Albert Raiders
1986	Guelph Platers
1987	Medicine Hat Tigers
1988	Medicine Hat Tigers
1989	Swift Current Broncos
1990	Oshawa Generals
1991	Spokane Chiefs
1992	Kamloops Blazers
1993	Sault Ste. Marie Greyhounds
1994	Kamloops Blazers
1995	Kamloops Blazers
1996	Granby Predateurs
1997	Hull Olympiques
1998	Portland Winter Hawks
1999	Ottawa 67's
2000	Rimouski Oceanic
2001	Red Deer Rebels
2002	Kootenay Ice
2003	Kitchener Rangers

NCAA Champions Since 1974

1974	Minnesota
1975	Michigan Tech
1976	Minnesota
1977	Wisconsin
1978	Boston University
1979	Minnesota
1980	North Dakota
1981	Wisconsin
1982	North Dakota
1983	Wisconsin
1984	Bowling Green (Minnesota)
1985	RPI (New York)
1986	Michigan State
1987	North Dakota
1988	Lake Superior State (Michigan)
1989	Harvard (Massachusetts)
1990	Wisconsin
1991	Northern Michigan
1992	Lake Superior State (Michigan)
1993	Maine
1994	Lake Superior State (Michigan)
1995	Boston University
1996	Michigan
1997	North Dakota
1998	Michigan
1999	Maine
2000	North Dakota
2001	Boston College
2002	Minnesota
2003	Minnesota

All Time Team Canada World Junior Championship Records

YEAR	GP	W	L	T	GF	GA	RANK
2003	6	5	1	0	26	13	2nd
2002	7	5	2	0	40	14	2nd
2001	7	4	2	1	26	16	3rd
2000	7	4	3	0	23	14	3rd
1999	7	4	2	1	30	15	2nd
1998	7	2	5	0	13	18	8th
1997	7	5	0	2	27	13	1st
1996	6	6	0	0	27	8	1st
1995	7	7	0	0	49	21	1st
1994	6	6	0	1	39	20	1st
1993	7	6	1	0	37	17	1st
1992	7	2	3	2	21	30	6th
1991	7	5	1	1	40	18	1st
1990	7	5	1	1	36	18	1st
1989	7	4	2	1	31	23	4th
1988	7	6	0	1	37	16	1st
1987	6	4	1	1	41	23	DQ*
1986	7	5	2	0	54	21	2nd
1985	7	5	0	2	44	14	1st
1984	7	4	2	1	39	17	4th
1983	7	4	2	1	39	24	3rd
1982	7	6	0	1	45	14	1st
1981	5	1	3	1	26	25	7th
1980	5	3	2	0	25	18	5th
1979	5	3	2	0	23	10	5th
1978	6	4	2	0	36	18	3rd
1977	7	5	1	1	50	20	2nd
1976	4	2	2	0	12	27	2nd
1975	5	4	1	0	27	10	2nd
1974	5	3	2	0	17	23	3rd
TOTALS	**193**	**129**	**45**	**19**	**980**	**538**	

Tournaments	Gold	Silver	Bronze
30	10	7	5

*Canada Was Disqualified in 1987 for a Bench Clearing Brawl Against the Soviet Union

Photo Gallery Part One
"All Photos are Courtesy of the Hockey Hall of Fame Collection"

Picture one is from the 1993 World Juniors in Sweden of a tournament program. Jpeg 3

Picture two is a poster from the 1995 World Juniors. Jpeg 4

Pictures three and four are from Wendel Clark`s jersey from the 1985 World Juniors. Jpeg 5 and 6

Picture five is a jersey worn by a Team Canada player at the 1976 World Juniors. Jpeg7

Picture one is from the 1993 World Juniors in Sweden of a tournament program.

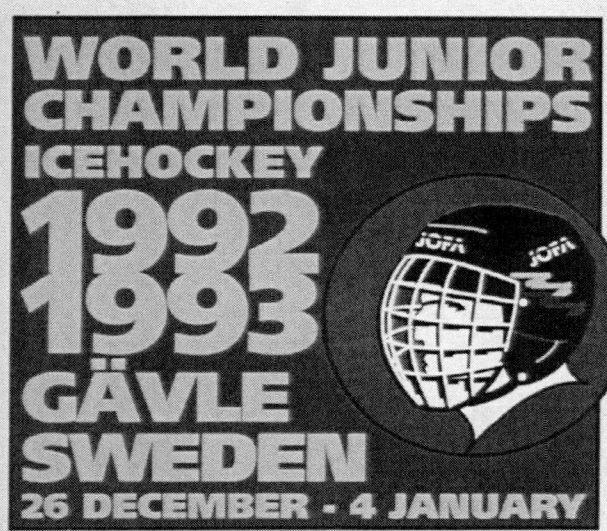

Picture two is a poster from the 1995 World Juniors.

Pictures three and four are from Wendel Clark`s jersey from the 1985 World Juniors.

Picture five is a jersey worn by a Team Canada player at the 1976 World Juniors.

Allen, Bryan

Born: August 21, 1980 in Kingston, Ontario
Drafted: By the Vancouver Canucks from the Oshawa Generals in 1998, 1st round, 4th overall.

Career Junior, NHL and World Junior Statistics

	GP	G	A	PTS	PIM
OHL Regular Season 1996-2000	148	15	36	51	291
OHL Playoffs	51	1	11	12	83
Memorial Cup 1999	4	0	0	0	8
NHL Regular Season 2000-Present	65	5	3	8	79
NHL Playoffs	3	0	0	0	4
Canada 1999 World Juniors *in Winnipeg*	7	1	2	3	2

Junior Highlights

Won Silver Medal at World Junior Championships in 1999
OHL First Team All-Star in 1999

Around the Rink

Allen missed the majority of 1999-2000 season recovering from knee injury suffered in training camp on September 21, 1999. He fully recovered five months later and made his professional debut with Syracuse of the AHL on Feb. 18, 2000. He scored his first professional goal the following night vs. Cincinnati.

Allison, Jason

Born: May 29, 1975 in North York, Ontario
Drafted: By the Washington Capitals from the London Knights in 1993, 1st round 17th overall.

Career Junior, NHL and World Junior Statistics

	GP	G	A	PTS	PIM
OHL Regular Season 1991-95	202	123	203	326	176
OHL Playoffs	24	9	26	35	21
NHL Regular Season 1993-Present	486	137	288	425	365
NHL Playoffs	25	7	18	25	14
Canada 1994 World Juniors *in Czech Republic*	7	3	6	9	2
Canada 1995 World Juniors *in Alberta*	7	3	12	15	6
Canada Totals	**14**	**6**	**18**	**24**	**8**

Junior Highlights

OHL First All-Star Team in 1994
OHL MVP in 1994
Canadian Major Junior First All-Star Team in 1994
Canadian Major Junior Player of the Year in 1994
Won Gold Medal at World Junior Championships in 1994 and 1995
World Junior Championship All-Star Team in 1995

Around the Rink

Allison was traded to Boston with Jim Carey, Anson Carter and Washington's 3rd round choice (Lee Goren) in 1997 Entry Draft for Bill Ranford, Adam Oates and Rick Tocchet, March 1, 1997. Missed majority of 1999-2000 season recovering from thumb injury suffered in game vs. NY Islanders, January 8, 2000. Traded to LA Kings by Boston with Mikko Eloranta for Jozef Stumpel and Glen Murray, October 24, 2001

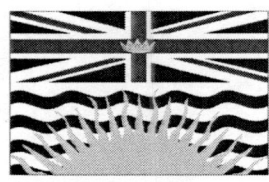

Allison, Ray

Born: March 4, 1959 in Cranbrook, B.C.
Drafted: By the Hartford Whalers from the Brandon Wheat Kings in 1979, 1st round, 18th overall.

Career Junior, NHL and World Junior Statistics

	GP	G	A	PTS	PIM
WHL Regular Season 1974-79	242	188	288	476	693
WHL Playoffs	49	36	39	75	100
Memorial Cup 1979	5	5	3	8	8
NHL Regular Season 1979-87	238	64	93	157	223
NHL Playoffs	12	2	3	5	20
Canada 1979 World Juniors *in Sweden*	5	0	5	5	4

Junior Highlights

WHL First All-Star Team in 1979
Memorial Cup All-Star Team in 1979

Around the Rink

Allison was traded to Philadelphia by Hartford with Fred Arthur and Hartford's 1st (Ron Sutter) and 3rd (Miroslav Dvorak) round choices in 1982 Entry Draft for Rick MacLeish, Blake Wesley, Don Gillen and Philadelphia's 1st (Paul Lawless), 2nd (Mark Paterson) and 3rd (Kevin Dineen) round choices in 1982 Entry Draft, July 3, 1981. Retired in 1990 after three seasons in the minors with Hershey (AHL).

Anderson, John

Born: March 28, 1957 in Toronto, Ontario
Drafted: By the Toronto Maple Leafs from the Toronto Marlboros in 1977, 1st round, 11th overall. Also drafted by the Quebec Nordiques of the WHA in 1977, 2nd round, 14th overall.

Career Junior, NHL and World Junior Statistics

	GP	G	A	PTS	PIM
OHL Regular Season 1973-77	211	154	173	327	98
OHL Playoffs	38	26	23	49	21
Memorial Cup 1975	4	4	6	10	2
NHL Regular Season 1977-89	814	282	349	631	263
NHL Playoffs	37	9	18	27	2
Canada 1977 World Juniors *in Czech Republic*	7	10	5	15	6

Junior Highlights

Memorial Cup All-Star Team in 1975
Memorial Cup Champion in 1975
Won SilverMedal at World Junior Championships in 1977
OHL First All-Star Team in 1977
CHL Second All-Star Team in 1978

Around the Rink

Anderson was traded to Quebec by Toronto for Brad Maxwell, August 21, 1985. Traded to Hartford by Quebec for Risto Siltanen, March 8, 1986. Signed as a free agent with Milan of the Italian league in 1989. Signed as a free agent with Fort Wayne (IHL) in 1990. Signed as a free agent with San Diego (IHL) in 1992. Retired from playing in 1993. Head Coach of the Chicago Wolves (IHL/AHL) 1997-Present.

Andreychuk, Dave

Born: September 29, 1963 in Hamilton, Ontario
Drafted: By the Buffalo Sabres from the Oshawa Generals in 1982, 1st round, 16th overall.

Career Junior, NHL and World Junior Statistics

	GP	G	A	PTS	PIM
OHL Regular Season 1980-83	148	87	89	176	157
OHL Playoffs	13	4	6	10	36
NHL Regular Season 1982-Present	1515	613	668	1281	1067
NHL Playoffs	132	40	41	81	138
Canada 1983 World Juniors *in Russia*	7	6	5	11	14

Junior Highlights

Won Bronze Medal at World Junior Championships in 1983

Around the Rink

Andreychuk was traded to Toronto by Buffalo with Daren Puppa and Buffalo's 1st round choice (Kenny Jonsson) in 1993 Entry Draft for Grant Fuhr and Toronto's 5th round choice (Kevin Popp) in 1995 Entry Draft, February 2, 1993. Traded to New Jersey by Toronto for New Jersey's 2nd round choice (Marek Posmyk) in 1996 Entry Draft and New Jersey's 3rd round choice (later traded back to New Jersey - New Jersey selected Andre Lakos) in 1999 Entry Draft, March 13, 1996. Signed as a free agent by Boston, July 29, 1999. Traded to Colorado by Boston with Raymond Bourque for Brian Rolston, Martin Grenier, Sami Pahlsson and New Jersey's 1st round choice (previously acquired, Boston selected Martin Samuelsson) in 2000 Entry Draft, March 6, 2000. Signed as a free agent by Buffalo, July 13, 2000. Signed as a free agent by Tampa Bay, July 13, 2001.

Armstrong, Chris

Born: June 26, 1975 in Regina, Saskatchewan
Drafted: By the Florida Panthers from the Moose Jaw Warriors in 1993, 3rd round, 57th overall.

Career Junior, NHL and World Junior Statistics

	GP	G	A	PTS	PIM
WHL Regular Season 1991-95	240	41	151	192	238
WHL Playoffs	14	2	12	14	22
NHL Regular Season 2000-2002	3	0	0	0	0
NHL Playoffs	0	0	0	0	0
Canada 1994 World Juniors *in Czech Republic*	7	0	1	1	0

Junior Highlights

Won Gold medal at World Junior Championships in 1994
WHL East First All-Star Team in 1994
Canadian Major Junior Second All-Star Team in 1994
WHL East Second All-Star Team in 1995

Around the Rink

Armstrong was claimed by Nashville from Florida in Expansion Draft, June 26, 1998. Signed as a free agent by San Jose, September 2, 1999. Selected by Minnesota from San Jose in Expansion Draft, June 23, 2000. Signed as a free agent by NY Islanders, August 8, 2001. Signed as a free agent by EV Zug (Swiss), June 14, 2002.

Arniel, Scott

Born: September 7, 1962 in Kingston, Ontario
Drafted: By the Winnipeg Jets from the Cornwall Royals in 1982, 2nd round, 22nd over all

Career Junior, NHL and World Junior Statistics

	GP	G	A	PTS	PIM
QMJHL/OHL Regular Season 1979-82	153	92	125	217	196
QMJHL/OHL Playoffs	22	14	20	34	24
Memorial Cup 1980, 1981	10	6	4	10	6
NHL Regular Season 1981-92	730	149	189	338	599
NHL Playoffs	34	3	3	6	39
Canada 1981 World Juniors *in Germany*	5	3	1	4	4
Canada 1982 World Juniors *in U.S.A.*	7	5	6	11	4
Canada Totals	12	8	7	15	8

Junior Highlights

Won Memorial Cup in 1980 and 1981
Won Gold Medal at World Junior Championships in 1982

Around the Rink

Arniel played three playoff games for Kingston of the (OHL) in 1979 before joining Cornwall of the (QMJHL) for the 1979-80 season. Cornwall moved to the (OHL) for the 1981-82 season. He was traded to Buffalo by Winnipeg for Gilles Hamel, June 21, 1986. Traded to Winnipeg by Buffalo with Phil Housley, Jeff Parker and Buffalo's 1st round choice (Keith Tkachuk) in 1990 Entry Draft for Dale Hawerchuk and Winnipeg's 1st round choice (Brad May) in 1990 Entry Draft, June 16, 1990. Traded to Boston by Winnipeg for future considerations, November 22, 1991. Officially announced retirement and named Assistant Coach of Manitoba (IHL), July 15, 1999. Named Assistant Coach of Buffalo July 26, 2002.

Arthur, Fred

Born: March 6, 1961 in Toronto, Ontario
Drafted: By the Hartford Whalers from the Cornwall Royals in 1980, 1st round, 8th overall.

Career Junior, NHL and World Junior Statistics

	GP	G	A	PTS	PIM
QMJHL Regular Season 1977-81	243	16	176	192	552
QMJHL Playoffs	37	3	23	26	89
Memorial Cup 1980, 1981	10	0	8	8	23
NHL Regular Season 1980-83	80	1	8	9	49
NHL Playoffs	4	0	0	0	2
Canada 1981 World Juniors *in Germany*	5	0	2	2	10

Junior Highlights

QMJHL First All-Star Team in 1980
Won Memorial Cup in 1980 and 1981
Memorial Cup All-Star Team in 1981

Around the Rink

Arthur was traded to Philadelphia by Hartford with Ray Allison and Hartford's 1st (Ron Sutter) and 3rd (Miroslav Dvorak) round choices in 1982 Entry Draft for Rick MacLeish, Blake Wesley, Don Gillen and Philadelphia's 1st (Paul Lawless), 2nd (Mark Patterson) and 3rd (Kevin Dineen) round choices in 1982 Entry Draft, July 3, 1981. Officially announced retirement to attend medical school, October 20, 1982.

Aucoin, Adrian

Born: July 3, 1973 in Ottawa, Ontario
Drafted: By the Vancouver Canucks from Boston University in 1992, 5th round, 117th overall.

Career Junior, NHL and World Junior Statistics

	GP	**G**	**A**	**PTS**	**PIM**
NCAA 1991-92	32	2	10	12	60
NHL Regular Season 1994-Present	521	70	131	201	402
NHL Playoffs	22	4	7	11	10
Canada 1993 World Juniors *in Sweden*	7	0	1	1	8

Junior Highlights

Won Silver Medal at World Junior Championships in 1993

Around the Rink

Aucoin missed majority of 1997-98 season recovering from ankle injury suffered in game vs. Anaheim (October 4, 1997) and groin injury suffered in game vs. Pittsburgh (November 1, 1997). Traded to Tampa Bay by Vancouver with Vancouver's 2nd round choice (Alexander Polushin) in 2001 Entry Draft for Dan Cloutier, February 7, 2001. Traded to NY Islanders by Tampa Bay with Alexander Kharitonov for Mathieu Biron and NY Islanders' 2nd round choice (later traded to Washington - later traded to Vancouver - Vancouver selected Denis Grot) in 2002 Entry Draft, June 22, 2001.

Auld, Alexander

Born: January 7, 1981 in Cold Lake, Alberta
Drafted: By the Florida Panthers from the North Bay Centennials in 1999, 2nd round, 40th overall.

Career Junior, NHL and World Junior Statistics

	GP	W	L	T	SO	AVG
OHL Regular Season 1997-2001	138	52	61	12	4	3.12
OHL Playoffs	13	2	11	0	0	2.83
NHL Regular Season 2001-Present	8	4	3	0	1	1.62
Playoff Games	0	0	0	0	0	0.00
Canada 2001 World Juniors *in Russia*	1	0	1	0	0	12.00

Junior Highlights

Won Bronze Medal at World Junior Championships in 2001

Around the Rink

Auld was traded to Vancouver by Florida for Vancouver's compensatory 2nd round choice (later traded to New Jersey - New Jersey selected Tuomas Pihlman) in 2001 Entry Draft and 3rd round choice (later traded to Atlanta - later traded to Buffalo - Buffalo selected John Adams) in 2002 Entry Draft, May 31, 2001.

Aulin, Jared

Born: March 15, 1982 in Calgary, Alberta
Drafted: By the Colorado Avalanche from the Kamloops Blazers in 2000, 2nd round, 47th overall.

Career Junior, NHL and World Junior Statistics

	GP	G	A	PTS	PIM
WHL Regular Season 1997-2002	230	88	168	256	235
WHL Playoffs	25	2	8	10	10
NHL Regular Season 2002-Present	17	2	2	4	0
NHL Playoffs	0	0	0	0	0
Canada 2000 World Juniors *in Sweden*	7	4	5	9	4

Junior Highlights

Won Bronze Medal at World Junior Championships in 2000
Finished Third in WHL Scoring in 2000-01

Around the Rink

Aulin was traded from Colorado to Los Angeles with Adam Deadmarsh, Aaron Miller, Colorado's first choice in the 2001 NHL Entry Draft and future considerations for Rob Blake and Steve Reinprecht on Feb. 21, 2001. Played first NHL game on December 17, 2002 versus St.Louis. Recorded first NHL point with an assist against Dallas on January 7, 2003. Scored first NHL goal on February 7, 2003 against Carolina.

Babe, Warren

Born: September 7, 1968 in Medicine Hat, Alberta
Drafted: By the Minnesota North Stars from the Lethbridge Broncos in 1986, 1st round, 12th overall.

Career Junior, NHL and World Junior Statistics

	GP	G	A	PTS	PIM
WHL Regular Season 1984-88	233	93	114	207	444
WHL Playoffs	22	6	12	18	49
NHL Regular Season 1987-1991	21	2	5	7	23
NHL Playoffs	2	0	0	0	0
Canada 1988 World Juniors *in Russia*	7	0	2	2	10

Junior Highlights

Won Gold Medal at World Junior Championships in 1988

Around the Rink

Babe played with the Broncos from 1984 to 1986, the team moved to Swift Current, Saskatchewan for the 1986-87 season. Swift Current traded him to the Kamloops Blazers after 16 games in 1986. Missed entire 1989-90 season recovering from head injury suffered during playoff game vs. Flint (IHL), April 1990. Retired from playing in 1991.

Babych, Wayne

Born: June 6, 1958 in Edmonton, Alberta
Drafted: By the St. Louis Blues from the Portland Winter Hawks in 1978, 1st round, 3rd overall.

Career Junior, NHL and World Junior Statistics

	GP	**G**	**A**	**PTS**	**PIM**
WHL Regular Season 1973-78	269	151	197	348	549
WHL Playoffs	26	8	11	19	52
NHL Regular Season 1978-87	519	192	246	438	498
NHL Playoffs	41	7	9	16	24
Canada 1978 World Juniors *in Montreal*	6	5	5	10	4

Junior Highlights

WHL First All-Star Team in 1977 and 1978
Won Bronze Medal at World Junior Championships in 1978

Around the Rink

Babych played for the Edmonton Oil Kings for one game in the 1973-74 season, he followed that up with two full seasons with the Oil Kings, then on June 11, 1976 the Oil Kings were moved to Portland, Oregon becoming the first U.S. based team in WHL history, the Portland Winter Hawks finished third in their division in their inaugural season. Claimed by Pittsburgh from St. Louis in Waiver Draft, October 9, 1984. Traded to Quebec by Pittsburgh for future considerations, October 20, 1985. Traded to Hartford by Quebec for Greg Malone, January 17, 1986. Retired from playing in 1987.

Bannister, Drew

Born: April 9, 1974 in Belleville, Ontario
Drafted: By the Tampa Bay Lightning from the Sault Ste. Marie Greyhounds in 1992, 2nd round, 26th overall.

Career Junior, NHL and World Junior Statistics

	GP	G	A	PTS	PIM
OHL Regular Season 1990-94	222	18	100	118	395
OHL Playoffs	52	11	26	37	68
Memorial Cup 1991, 1992 and 1993	9	1	6	7	10
NHL Regular Season 1995-2002	164	5	25	30	161
NHL Playoffs	12	0	0	0	30
Canada 1994 World Juniors *in Czech Repuplic*	7	0	4	4	10

Junior Highlights

Memorial Cup All-Star Team in 1993
Won Memorial Cup in 1993
Won Gold Medal at World Junior Championships in 1994
OHL Second All-Star Team in 1994

Around the Rink

Bannister was traded to Edmonton by Tampa Bay with Tampa Bay's 6th round choice (Peter Sarno) in 1997 Entry Draft for Jeff Norton, March 18, 1997. Traded to Anaheim by Edmonton for Bobby Dollas, January 9, 1998. Traded to Tampa Bay by Anaheim for Tampa Bay's 5th round choice (Peter Podhradsky) in 2000 Entry Draft, December 10, 1998. Signed as a free agent by NY Rangers, October 3, 1999. Signed as a free agent by Anaheim, July 27, 2001. Missed majority of 2001-02 season, recovering from shoulder injury suffered in game vs. Utah (AHL), November 30, 2001. Signed as a free agent with Karpat in the Finnish league in 2002.

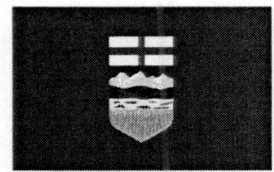

Barnes, Stu

Born: December 25, 1970 in Spruce Grove, Alberta
Drafted: By the Winnipeg Jets from the Tri-City Americans in 1989, 1st round, 4th overall.

Career Junior, NHL and World Junior Statistics

	GP	G	A	PTS	PIM
WHL Regular Season 1987-90	204	148	238	386	370
WHL Playoffs	19	8	13	21	42
NHL Regular Season 1991-Present	820	210	274	484	310
NHL Playoffs	84	25	27	52	18
Canada 1990 World Juniors *in Finland*	7	2	4	6	6

Junior Highlights

WHL West Second All-Star Team in 1988 and 1989
WHL Rookie of the Year in 1988
WHL MVP in 1989
Won Gold Medal at World Junior Championships in 1990

Around the Rink

Barnes played for New Westminster in 1987-88, the team moved for the following season to Tri-City which is made up of three cities in Washington State, Richland, Kennewick and Pasco. Traded to Florida by Winnipeg with St. Louis' 6th round choice (previously acquired, later traded to Edmonton - later traded back to Winnipeg - Winnipeg selected Chris Kibermanis) in 1994 Entry Draft for Randy Gilhen, November 25, 1993. Traded to Pittsburgh by Florida with Jason Woolley for Chris Wells, November 19, 1996. Traded to Buffalo by Pittsburgh for Matthew Barnaby, March 11, 1999. Traded to Dallas by Buffalo for Mike Ryan and Dallas's 2nd round pick in 2003 entry draft.

Bassen, Bob
Born: May 6, 1965 in Calgary, Alberta
Not Drafted: Signed as a Free Agent by the New York Islanders in 1984

Career Junior, NHL and World Junior Statistics

	GP	G	A	PTS	PIM
WHL Regular Season 1982-85	141	65	81	146	145
WHL Playoffs	27	7	19	26	55
NHL Regular Season 1986-2000	765	88	144	232	1004
NHL Playoffs	93	9	15	24	134
Canada 1985 World Juniors *in Finland*	7	2	0	2	8

Junior Highlights

WHL East First All-Star Team in 1985
Won Gold Medal at World Junior Championships in 1985

Around the Rink

Bassen played three seasons of junior hockey with the Medicine Hat Tigers. Signed as a free agent by NY Islanders, October 19, 1984. Traded to Chicago by NY Islanders with Steve Konroyd for Marc Bergevin and Gary Nylund, November 25, 1988. Claimed by St. Louis from Chicago in NHL Waiver Draft, October 1, 1990. Traded to Quebec by St. Louis with Garth Butcher and Ron Sutter for Steve Duchesne and Denis Chasse, January 23, 1994. Signed as a free agent by Dallas, August 10, 1995. Traded to Calgary by Dallas for Aaron Gavey, July 14, 1998. Signed as a free agent by Dallas, December 9, 1999. Claimed on waivers by St. Louis from Dallas, December 11, 1999. Signed as a free agent with Frankfurt in the German league in 2000. Retired from playing in 2000. Assistant Coach with the Utah Grizzlies (AHL) 2001-02.

Baumgartner, Nolan

Born: March 23, 1976 in Calgary, Alberta
Drafted: By the Washington Capitals from the Kamloops Blazers in 1994, 1st round, 10th overall.

Career Junior, NHL and World Junior Statistics

	GP	G	A	PTS	PIM
WHL Regular Season 1992-96	202	34	98	132	255
WHL Playoffs	67	9	37	46	75
Memorial Cup 1994 and 1995	8	0	8	8	10
NHL Regular Season 1995-Present	34	1	4	5	12
NHL Playoffs	1	0	0	0	10
Canada 1995 World Juniors *in Alberta*	7	0	1	1	4
Canada 1996 World Juniors *in United States*	6	1	1	2	22
Canada Totals	**13**	**1**	**2**	**3**	**26**

Junior Highlights

Memorial Cup All-Star Team in 1994 and 1995
Memorial Cup Champion in 1994 and 1995
WHL West First All-Star Team in 1995 and 1996
Won Gold Medal at World Junior Championships in 1995 and 1996
Canadian Major Junior First All-Star Team in 1995
Canadian Major Junior Defenseman of the Year in 1995
World Junior Championships All-Star Team in 1996

Around the Rink

Baumgartner was traded to Chicago by Washington for Remi Royer, July 20, 2000.
Signed as a free agent by Vancouver, July 11, 2002.

Beaudoin, Yves

Born: January 7, 1965 in Pointe-aux-Trembles, Quebec
Drafted: By the Washington Capitals from the Shawinigan Cataractes in 1983, 10th round, 195th overall.

Career Junior, NHL and World Junior Statistics

	GP	G	A	PTS	PIM
QMJHL Regular Season 1981-85	238	48	124	172	270
QMJHL Playoffs	25	7	11	18	51
Memorial Cup 1985	4	0	1	1	6
NHL Regular Season 1985-88	11	0	0	0	5
NHL Playoffs	0	0	0	0	0
Canada 1985 World Juniors *in Finland*	7	0	3	3	4

Junior Highlights

QMJHL First All-Star Team in 1985
Won Gold Medal at World Junior Championships in 1985
Memorial Cup All-Star Team in 1985

Around the Rink

Beaudoin played for a season plus six games for the Hull Olympiques before being traded to Shawinigan in 1982 where he finished his junior career. Signed as a free agent with Innsbruck of the Austrian league in 1988 and played there for one season. Joined Nottingham of the British league in 1989 and retired at the end of that season. Returned to hockey in the Quebec Senior league in 1987 and once again retired in 2001.

Begin, Steve

Born: June 14, 1978 in Trois Rivieres, Quebec
Drafted: By the Calgary Flames from the Val-d'Or Foreurs in 1996, 2nd round, 40th overall.

Career Junior, NHL and World Junior Statistics

	GP	G	A	PTS	PIM
QMJHL Regular Season 1995-98	157	44	73	117	498
QMJHL Playoffs	38	3	18	21	75
Memorial Cup 1998	3	0	1	1	4
NHL Regular Season 1999-Present	123	11	7	18	192
NHL Playoffs	0	0	0	0	0
Canada 1998 World Juniors *in Finland*	7	0	0	0	10

Junior Highlights

Won QMJHL Championship in 1998

Around the Rink

Begin split the 1996-97 season between Val-d'Or (QMJHL) and Saint John of the (AHL). Played first NHL game October 1, 1997 against Detroit. First NHL point was an assist versus Vancouver October 16, 1999. First NHL goal came against Phoenix, February 12, 2000. He joined Calgary for five games in 1997-98 as well as playing the majority of the season with Val d'Or. From 1998-2001, Begin bounced back and forth between Calgary and Saint John. He made the Flames full time at the start of the 2001-02 season.

Belanger, Alain

Born: January 18, 1956 in St. Janvier, Quebec
Drafted: By the Toronto Maple Leafs from the Sherbrooke Beavers in 1976, 3rd round, 48th overall. Also Drafted by the Calgary Cowboys (WHA) in 1976, 4th round, 43rd overall.

Career Junior, NHL and World Junior Statistics

	GP	G	A	PTS	PIM
QMJHL Regular Season 1973-76	144	44	46	90	720
QMJHL Playoffs	0	0	0	0	0
Memorial Cup 1975	3	0	0	0	27
NHL Regular Season 1977-78	9	0	1	1	6
NHL Playoffs	0	0	0	0	0
Canada 1976 World Juniors *in Finland*	4	0	0	0	0

Junior Highlights

Won Silver Medal at World Junior Championships in 1976

Around the Rink

Belanger was traded from Drummondville to Sherbrooke in 1974. Played all nine of his NHL games with Toronto. Played for the New Brunswick Hawks (AHL) from 1978-80 and then retired. Made a come back in 1982 with Sherbrooke (AHL) and retired once again at the end of that season.

Bell, Mark

Born: August 5, 1980 in St. Paul's, Ontario
Drafted: By the Chicago Black Hawks from the Ottawa 67's in 1998, 1st round, 8th overall.

Career Junior, NHL and World Junior Statistics

	GP	G	A	PTS	PIM
OHL Regular Season 1996-2000	212	119	102	211	291
OHL Playoffs	48	16	18	34	35
Memorial Cup 1999	5	2	6	8	8
NHL Regular Season 2000-Present	175	26	32	58	241
NHL Playoffs	5	0	0	0	8
Canada 2000 World Juniors *in Sweden*	7	2	0	2	8

Junior Highlights

Won Memorial Cup in 1999
Won Bronze Medal at World Juniors in 2000

Around the Rink

Bell played the majority of the 2000-01 season with Norfolk (AHL). Made his NHL debut on December 13, 2000 at Atlanta, he played thirteen games with Chicago the rest of the season. First NHL point was an assist against Phoenix on December 27, 2000. He made Chicago full time in 2001-02 scoring his first NHL goal on Patrick Roy on October 21, 2001.

Bernhardt, Tim

Born: January 17, 1958 in Sarnia, Ontario
Drafted: By the Atlanta Flames from the Cornwall Royals in 1978, 3rd round, 47th overall.

Career Junior, NHL and World Junior Statistics

	GP	W	L	T	SO	AVG
QMJHL Regular Season 1975-78	149	Not Available			4	3.64
QMJHL Playoffs	29	13	13	3	2	3.57
NHL Regular Season 1982-87	67	17	36	7	0	4.27
NHL Playoffs	0	0	0	0	0	0.00
Canada 1978 World Juniors *in Montreal*	3	2	1	0	0	2.00

Junior Highlights

QMJHL West Second All-Star Team in 1976
QMJHL First All-Star Team in 1977, 1978
Won Bronze Medal at World Junior Championships in 1978
Around the Rink
Bernhardt was transferred to Calgary after Atlanta franchise relocated, June 24, 1980. Signed as a free agent by Toronto, December 5, 1984. Retired from playing in 1990 after nearly four full seasons in the minors with Newmarket (AHL).

Berry, Brad

Born: April 1, 1965 in Bashaw, Alberta
Drafted: By the Winnipeg Jets from the University of North Dakota in 1983, 2nd round, 29th overall.

Career Junior, NHL and World Junior Statistics

	GP	G	A	PTS	PIM
NCAA 1983-1986	112	12	62	74	60
NHL Regular Season 1985-94	241	4	28	32	323
NHL Playoffs	13	0	1	1	16
Canada 1985 World Juniors *in Finland*	7	0	1	1	2

Junior Highlights

Won Gold Medal at World Junior Championships in 1985

Around the Rink

Berry was signed as a free agent by Minnesota, October 4, 1991. Transferred to Dallas after Minnesota franchise relocated, June 9, 1993. Officially announced retirement from playing, October 25, 1998. Assistant coach at University of North Dakota, 2000-2002.

Bester, Allan

Born: March 26, 1964 in Hamilton, Ontario
Drafted: By the Toronto Maple Leafs from the Brantford Alexanders in 1983, 3rd round, 48th overall.

Career Junior, NHL and World Junior Statistics

	GP	W	L	T	SO	AVG
OHL Regular Season 1981-84	98	45	42	4	4	3.59
OHL Playoffs	9	3	4	0	1	2.77
NHL Regular Season 1983-92	219	73	99	17	7	4.01
NHL Playoffs	11	2	6	0	0	4.37
Canada 1984 World Juniors *in Sweden*	2	2	0	0	1	1.00

Junior Highlights

OHL First All-Star Team in 1983

Around the Rink

Bester was traded to Detroit by Toronto for Detroit's 6th round choice (Alexander Kuzminsky) in 1991 Entry Draft, March 5, 1991. Signed as a free agent by Anaheim, September 9, 1993. Signed as a free agent by Dallas, January 21, 1996. Officially announced retirement, August 5, 1998 after spending two seasons in the IHL with Orlando.

Betts, Blair

Born: February 16, 1980 in Edmonton, Alberta
Drafted: By the Calgary Flames from the Prince George Cougars in 1998, 2nd round, 33rd overall.

Career Junior, NHL and World Junior Statistics

	GP	G	A	PTS	PIM
WHL Regular Season 1996-2000	215	91	116	207	134
WHL Playoffs	46	20	21	41	28
NHL Regular Season 2001-Present	15	2	3	5	2
NHL Playoffs	0	0	0	0	0
Canada 1999 World Juniors *in Winnipeg*	5	0	0	0	2

Junior Highlights

Won Silver Medal at World Junior Championships in 1999

Around the Rink

Betts played his first NHL game on February 4, 2001 versus Minnesota. He also recorded his first NHL goal in that game with a goal against Manny Fernandez.

Beukeboom, Jeff

Born: March 28, 1965 in Ajax, Ontario
Drafted: By the Edmonton Oilers from the Saul Ste. Marie Greyhounds in 1983, 1st round, 19th overall.

Career Junior, NHL and World Junior Statistics

	GP	G	A	PTS	PIM
OHL Regular Season 1982-85	168	19	75	94	406
OHL Playoffs	48	6	17	23	136
Memorial Cup 1985	4	1	1	2	13
NHL Regular Season 1985-99	804	30	129	159	1890
NHL Playoffs	99	3	16	19	197
Canada 1985 World Juniors *in Finland*	3	1	0	1	4

Junior Highlights

OHL First All Star Team in 1985
Won Gold Medal at World Junior Championships in 1985
Won OHL Championship in 1985

Around the Rink

Beukeboom was traded to the NY Rangers by Edmonton for David Shaw to complete transaction that sent Mark Messier to NY Rangers for Bernie Nicholls, Steven Rice and Louie DeBrusk (October 4, 1991), November 12, 1991. Suffered eventual career-ending head injury in game vs. LA Kings, November 19, 1998. Announced retirement July 15, 1999.

Billington, Craig

Born: September 11, 1966 in London, Ontario
Drafted: By the New Jersey Devils from the Belleville Bulls in 1984, 2nd round, 23rd overall.

Career Junior, NHL and World Junior Statistics

	GP	W	L	T	SO	AVG
OHL Regular Season 1983-86	94	49	39	0	2	4.18
OHL Playoffs	35	16	11	0	1	3.68
NHL Regular Season 1985-2002	327	109	146	30	9	3.61
NHL Playoffs	8	0	2	0	0	4.23
Canada 1985 World Juniors *in Finland*	5	3	0	2	1	2.60
Canada 1986 World Juniors *in Hamilton*	5	4	1	0	0	2.80
Canada Totals	**10**	**7**	**1**	**2**	**1**	**2.70**

Junior Highlights

Named Best Goaltender at World Junior Championships in 1985
Won Gold Medal at World Junior Championships in 1985
OHL First All-Star Team in 1985
Won Silver Medal at World Junior Championships in 1986

Around the Rink

Billington was traded to Ottawa by New Jersey with Troy Mallette and New Jersey's 4th round choice (Cosmo Dupaul) in 1993 Entry Draft for Peter Sidorkiewicz and future considerations (Mike Peluso, June 26, 1993), June 20, 1993. Traded to Boston by Ottawa for NY Islanders' 8th round choice (previously acquired, Ottawa selected Ray Schultz) in 1995 Entry Draft, April 7, 1995. Signed as a free agent by Florida, September 5, 1996. Claimed by Colorado from Florida in Waiver Draft, September 30, 1996. Traded to Washington by Colorado for future considerations, July 16, 1999. Retired after playing 5 games at the start of the 2002-03 season.

Biron, Martin

Born: August 15, 1977 in Lac St. Charles, Quebec
Drafted: By the Buffalo Sabres from the Beauport Harfangs in 1995, 1st round, 16th overall.

Career Junior, NHL and World Junior Statistics

	GP	W	L	T	SO	AVG
QMJHL Regular Season 1994-97	135	75	46	18	7	2.81
QMJHL Playoffs	41	23	15	0	4	3.05
NHL Regular Season 1995-Present	182	73	78	19	16	2.44
NHL Playoffs	0	0	0	0	0	0.00
Canada 1997 World Juniors *in Switzerland*	1	0	0	0	0	0.00

Junior Highlights

QMJHL All-Rookie Team in 1995
QMJHL Defensive Rookie of the Year in 1995
Canadian Major Junior First All-Star Team in 1995
Canadian Major Junior Goaltender of the Year in 1995
Won Gold Medal at World Junior Championships in 1997

Around the Rink

Biron played his first two and half seasons of junior hockey with the Beauport Harfangs (QMJHL), the team moved to Quebec City for the start of the 1997-98 season. He was traded to the Hull Olympiques after 18 starts in 1996. Played one minute at the World Junior Championships and faced zero shots.

Biron, Mathieu

Born: April 29, 1980 in Lac St. Charles, Quebec
Drafted: By the Los Angeles Kings from the Shawinigan Cataractes in 1998, 1st round, 21st overall.

Career Junior, NHL and World Junior Statistics

	GP	G	A	PTS	PIM
QMJHL Regular Season 1997-99	128	21	60	81	176
QMJHL Playoffs	12	0	3	3	16
NHL Regular Season 1999-Present	144	5	13	18	76
NHL Playoffs	0	0	0	0	0
Canada 2000 World Juniors *in Sweden*	7	0	0	0	8

Junior Highlights

World Junior Championships All-Star Team in 2000
Won Bronze Medal at World Junior Championship in 2000

Around the Rink

Biron was traded to NY Islanders by LA Kings with Olli Jokinen, Josh Green and LA Kings' 1st round choice (Taylor Pyatt) in 1999 Entry Draft for Ziggy Palffy, Brian Smolinski, Marcel Cousineau and New Jersey's 4th round choice (previously acquired, LA Kings selected Daniel Johansson) in 1999 Entry Draft, June 20, 1999. Traded to Tampa Bay by NY Islanders with NY Islanders' 2nd round choice (later traded to Washington - later traded to Vancouver - Vancouver selected Denis Grot) in 2002 Entry Draft for Adrian Aucoin and Alexander Kharitonov, June 22, 2001.

Blight, Rick

Born: October 17, 1955 in Portage La Prairie, Manitoba
Drafted: By the Vancouver Canucks from the Brandon Wheat Kings in 1975, 1st round, 10th overall. Also drafted by the Michigan Stags (WHA) in 1974, 2nd round, 19th overall.

Career Junior, NHL and World Junior Statistics

	GP	G	A	PTS	PIM
WHL Regular Season 1971-75	201	141	195	336	257
WHL Playoffs	28	5	6	11	14
NHL Regular Season 1975-83	326	96	125	221	170
NHL Playoffs	5	0	5	5	2
Canada 1975 World Juniors *in Winnipeg/Brandon*	6	2	2	4	4

Junior Highlights

WHL Rookie of the Year in 1973
Won Silver Medal at World Junior Championships in 1975

Around the Rink

Blight signed as a free agent by Toronto, August 31, 1981. Signed as a free agent by Edmonton, October 25, 1982. Traded to LA Kings by Edmonton for Alan Hangsleben, December 7, 1982. Retired from playing in 1983.

Boimistruck, Fred

Born: January 14, 1962 in Sudbury, Ontario
Drafted: By the Toronto Maple Leafs from the Cornwall Royals in 1980, 3rd round, 43rd overall.

Career Junior, NHL and World Junior Statistics

	GP	G	A	PTS	PIM
QMJHL Regular Season 1979-81	138	34	82	116	257
QMJHL Playoffs	29	4	19	23	67
Memorial Cup 1980 and 1981	10	6	2	8	8
NHL Regular Season 1981-83	83	4	14	18	45
NHL Playoffs	0	0	0	0	0
Canada 1981 World Juniors *in Germany*	5	3	0	3	8

Junior Highlights

Won Memorial Cup in 1980 and 1981
QMJHL First All-Star Team in 1981

Around the Rink

Boimistruck played only two NHL seasons, both with Toronto. Signed as a Free Agent with Fort Wayne (IHL) in 1984, released after two games and signed as a Free Agent with Langnau (Swiss League). Signed as a Free Agent with Flint (IHL) in 1985. Signed as a Free Agent with Brantford (OHA SR. League) in 1986. Retired from playing in 1987. Became assistant coach with the Belleville Bulls from 1997-99.

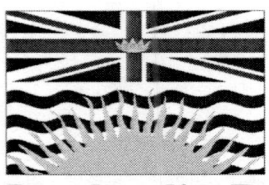

Bombardir, Brad

Born: May 5, 1972 in Powell River, B.C.
Drafted: By the New Jersey Devils from the University of North Dakota in 1990, 3rd round, 56th overall.

Career Junior, NHL and World Junior Statistics

	GP	G	A	PTS	PIM
NCAA 1990-94	144	19	52	71	144
NHL Reg. Season 1997-Present	287	7	44	51	102
NHL Playoffs	6	0	0	0	0
Canada 1992 World Juniors *in Germany*	7	0	3	3	4

Junior Highlights

Bombardir was part of history when he scored at 0:19 of the third period in a 5-1 win at Michigan Tech. Greg Johnson assisted on the goal making Johnson the WCHA's all-time assists leader and UND's all-time leading scorer on Feb. 26, 1993

Around the Rink

Bombardir missed the majority of the 1999-2000 season recovering from esophagus injury suffered in game vs. Philadelphia, October 30, 1999. Traded to Minnesota by New Jersey for Chris Terreri and Minnesota's 9th round choice (later traded to Tampa Bay - Tampa Bay selected Thomas Ziegler) in 2000 Entry Draft, June 23, 2000. Missed majority of 2001-02 season recovering from ankle injury suffered in game vs. San Jose, October 16, 2001.

Botterill, Jason

Born: May 19, 1976 in Edmonton, Alberta
Drafted: By the Dallas Stars from the University of Michigan in 1994, 1st round, 20th overall.

Career Junior, NHL and World Junior Statistics

	GP	G	A	PTS	PIM
NCAA 1993-97	150	104	82	186	483
NHL Regular Season 1997-Present	69	3	8	11	75
NHL Playoffs	0	0	0	0	0
Canada 1994 World Juniors *in Czech Republic*	7	1	0	1	8
Canada 1995 World Juniors *in Alberta*	7	0	4	4	6
Canada 1996 World Juniors *in United States*	6	1	3	4	6
Canada Totals	**20**	**2**	**7**	**9**	**20**

Junior Highlights

Won Gold Medal at World Junior Championships in 1994, 1995 and 1996
Central Collegiate Hockey Association (NCAA) Second All-Star Team in 1996
Won NCAA Championship in 1996
NCAA West Second All-American Team in 1997

Around the Rink

Botterill was traded to Atlanta by Dallas for Jamie Pushor, July 15, 1999. Traded to Calgary by Atlanta with Darryl Shannon for Hnat Domenichelli and Dmitri Vlasenkov, February 11, 2000. Signed as a free agent by Buffalo, August 12, 2002.

Bouchard, Joel

Born: January 23, 1974 in Montreal, Quebec
Drafted: By the Calgary Flames from the Verdun College Francais in 1992, 6th round, 129th overall.

Career Junior, NHL and World Junior Statistics

	GP	**G**	**A**	**PTS**	**PIM**
QMJHL Regular Season 1990-94	243	37	160	197	277
QMJHL Playoffs	36	4	9	13	41
Memorial Cup 1992	2	0	0	0	0
NHL Regular Season 1994-Present	311	20	38	58	231
NHL Playoffs	0	0	0	0	0
Canada 1993 World Juniors *in Sweden*	7	0	0	0	0
Canada 1994 World Juniors *in Czech Republic*	7	0	1	1	10
Canada Totals	**14**	**0**	**1**	**1**	**10**

Junior Highlights

Won Gold Medal at World Junior Championships in 1993 and 1994
QMJHL First All-Star Team in 1994

Around the Rink

Bouchard played the 1990-91 season for Longueil College Francais (QMJHL) and then played his final three seasons of Junior with Verdun College Francais (QMJHL). Claimed by Nashville from Calgary in Expansion Draft, June 26, 1998. Claimed on waivers by Dallas from Nashville, March 14, 2000. Signed as a free agent by Phoenix, August 31, 2000. Signed as a free agent by New Jersey, October 25, 2001. Signed as a free agent by NY Rangers, August 5, 2002. Acquired from New York Rangers with Rico Fata, Mikael Samuelsson and Richard Lintner for Alexei Kovalev, Dan LaCouture, Janne Laukkanen, Mike Wilson and future considerations, February 10, 2003

Bouchard, Pierre-Marc

Born: April 27, 1984 in Sherbrooke, Quebec
Drafted: By the Minnesota Wild from the Chicoutimi Sagueneens in 2002, 1st round, 8th overall.

Career Junior, NHL and World Junior Statistics

	GP	G	A	PTS	PIM
QMJHL Regular Season 2000-2002	136	84	151	235	74
QMJHL Playoffs	10	7	11	18	4
NHL Regular Season 2002-Present	50	7	13	20	18
NHL Playoffs	2	0	0	0	2
Canada 2003 World Juniors *in Nova Scotia*	6	2	3	5	2

Junior Highlights

Won Scoring Title in QMJHL in 2001-2002
QMJHL Offensive Player of the Year in 2001-02
QMJHL First Team All-Star in 2001-02
Canadian Hockey League Player of the Year in 2001-02
Won Silver Medal at World Junior Championships in 2003

Around the Rink

Bouchard made Minnesota's starting line up in his first season as a professional. Played first NHL game October 11, 2002 against Boston, also recorded his first NHL point in that game with an assist on Minnesota's first goal of the game. Scored first NHL goal, November 9, 2002 versus San Jose.

Bouck, Tyler

Born: January 13, 1980 in Camrose, Alberta
Drafted: By the Dallas Stars from the Prince George Cougars in 1998, 2nd round, 57th overall.

Career Junior, NHL and World Junior Statistics

	GP	G	A	PTS	PIM
WHL Regular Season 1995-2000	197	65	87	152	466
WHL Playoffs	26	7	15	22	67
NHL Regular Season 2000-Present	55	2	5	7	33
NHL Playoffs	1	0	0	0	0
Canada 1999 World Juniors *in Winnipeg*	5	0	0	0	2
Canada 2000 World Juniors *in Sweden*	7	1	2	3	20
Canada Totals	12	1	2	3	22

Junior Highlights

Won Silver Medal at World Junior Championships in 1999
Won Bronze Medal at World Junior Championships in 2000
WHL West First All-Star Team in 2000

Around the Rink

Bouck was traded to Phoenix by Dallas for Jyrki Lumme, June 23, 2001. Traded to Vancouver by Phoenix with Todd Warriner, Trevor Letowski and Phoenix's 3rd round choice in 2003 Entry Draft for Drake Berehowsky and Denis Pederson, December 28, 2001. Did not play an NHL game in 2002-03, spent the season in the AHL with Springfield and Manitoba.

Boutilier, Paul

Born: May 3, 1963 in Sydney, Nova Scotia
Drafted: By the New York Islanders from the Sherbrooke Beavers in 1981, 1st round, 21st overall.

Career Junior, NHL and World Junior Statistics

	GP	G	A	PTS	PIM
QMJHL Regular Season 1980-83	151	35	103	138	187
QMJHL Playoffs	35	10	38	48	12
Memorial Cup 1982	5	2	8	10	2
NHL Regular Season 1982-89	288	27	83	110	358
NHL Playoffs	41	1	9	10	45
Canada 1982 World Juniors *in United States*	7	2	5	7	4
Canada 1983 World Juniors *in Russia*	7	2	3	5	2
Canada Totals	**14**	**4**	**8**	**12**	**6**

Junior Highlights

Won Gold Medal at World Junior Championships in 1982
QMJHL First All-Star Team in 1982
Memorial Cup All-Star Team in 1982
Won Bronze Medal at World Junior Championships in 1983

Around the Rink

Boutilier was transferred to Boston by the New York Islanders as compensation for the Islanders signing of free agent Brian Curran, August 6, 1986. Traded to Minnesota by Boston for Minnesota's 4th round choice (Darwin McPherson) in 1987 Entry Draft, March 10, 1987. Traded to the New York Rangers by Minnesota with Jari Gronstrand for Jay Caufield and Dave Gagner, October 8, 1987. Traded to Winnipeg by NY Rangers for future considerations, December 16, 1987, only played three games with Winnipeg spent most of his time with their AHL affiliate in Moncton. Played in the Swiss league from 1989-91 and then retired from playing.

Bouwmeester, Jay

Born: September 27, 1983 in Edmonton, Alberta
Drafted: By the Florida Panthers from the Medicine Hat Tigers in 2002, 1st round, 3rd overall.

Career Junior, NHL and World Junior Statistics

	GP	G	A	PTS	PIM
WHL Regular Season 1998-2002	194	40	111	151	114
WHL Playoffs	0	0	0	0	0
NHL Regular Season 2002-Present	82	4	12	16	14
NHL Playoffs	0	0	0	0	0
Canada 2000 World Juniors *in Sweden*	7	0	0	0	2
Canada 2001 World Juniors *in Russia*	7	0	2	2	2
Canada 2002 World Juniors *in Czech Republic*	7	0	2	2	10
Canada Totals	**21**	**0**	**4**	**4**	**14**

Junior Highlights

Won Bronze Medal at World Junior Championships in 2000 and 2001
Won Silver Medal at World Junior Championships in 2002
WHL Eastern Conference First All-Star Team in 2001-02
Won the Fastest Skater award at the Top Prospects Skills Competition in 2002

Around the Rink

Bouwmeester has never played in a playoff game, in Junior or the NHL. He made Florida's starting line up in his first season. First NHL game was against Tampa on October 10, 2002, also recorded his first NHL point in that game with an assist. Scored first NHL goal on November 11, 2002 against Chicago.

Bradley, Brian

Born: January 21, 1965 in Kicthener, Ontario
Drafted: By the Calgary Flames from the London Knights in 1983, 3rd round, 51st overall.

Career Junior, NHL and World Junior Statistics

	GP	G	A	PTS	PIM
OHL Regular Season 1981-1985	210	138	235	373	117
OHL Playoffs	19	8	15	23	10
NHL Regular Season 1985-98	651	182	321	503	528
NHL Playoffs	13	3	7	10	16
Canada 1985 World Juniors *in Finland*	7	9	5	14	2

Junior Highlights

Won Gold Medal at World Junior Championships in 1985

Around the Rink

Bradley was traded to Vancouver by Calgary with Peter Bakovic and Kevan Guy for Craig Coxe, March 6, 1988. Traded to Toronto by Vancouver for Tom Kurvers, January 12, 1991. Claimed by Tampa Bay from Toronto in Expansion Draft, June 18, 1992. Missed majority of 1997-98 and entire 1998-99 seasons recovering from head injury suffered in game vs. LA Kings, November 11, 1997. Officially announced retirement, October 23, 1999.

Bradley, Matt

Born: June 13, 1978 in Stittsville, Ontario
Drafted: By the San Jose Sharks from the Kingston Frontenacs in 1996, 4th round, 102nd overall.

Career Junior, NHL and World Junior Statistics

	GP	G	A	PTS	PIM
OHL Regular Season 1995-98	175	67	88	155	82
OHL Playoffs	19	3	9	12	15
NHL Regular Season 2000-Present	121	12	17	29	99
NHL Playoffs	10	0	0	0	0
Canada 1998 World Juniors *in Finland*	7	1	1	2	4

Junior Highlights

Won William Hanley Award (Most Gentlemanly Player - OHL) in 1998
OHL Eastern Conference All-Star Team in 1997-98

Around the Rink

Bradley played his first NHL game Oct. 6, 2000. He scored his first goal Nov. 9, 2000, against the St. Louis Blues. Traded to Pittsburgh for Wayne Primeau, March 11, 2003.

Brewer, Eric

Born: April 17, 1979 in Vernon, B.C.
Drafted: By the New York Islanders from the Prince George Cougars in 1997, 1st round, 5th overall.

Career Junior, NHL and World Junior Statistics

	GP	G	A	PTS	PIM
WHL Regular Season 1995-98	168	14	62	76	76
WHL Playoffs	26	6	6	12	35
NHL Regular Season 1998-Present	327	27	61	88	195
NHL Playoffs	12	2	8	10	8
Canada 1998 World Juniors *in Finland*	7	0	2	2	8

Junior Highlights

Played in CHL Top Prospects Game in 1997
WHL West Second All-Star Team in 1998

Around the Rink

Brewer was traded to Edmonton by NY Islanders with Josh Green and NY Islanders' 2nd round choice (Brad Winchester) in 2000 Entry Draft for Roman Hamrlik, June 24, 2000.

Bridgman, Mel

Born: April 28, 1955 in Trenton, Ontario
Drafted: By the Philadelphia Flyers from the Victoria Cougars in 1975, 1st round 1st overall. Also drafted by the Denver Spurs/Ottawa Civics (WHA), 1st round, 4th overall.

Career Junior, NHL and World Junior Statistics

	GP	G	A	PTS	PIM
WHL Regular Season 1971-75	136	93	131	224	324
WHL Playoffs	12	12	6	18	34
NHL Regular Season 1975-89	977	252	449	701	1625
NHL Playoffs	125	28	39	67	298
Canada 1975 World Juniors *in Manitoba*	5	4	1	5	9

Junior Highlights

Won Silver Medal at World Junior Championships in 1975
WHL First All-Star Team in 1975

Around the Rink

Reason for Bridgman being drafted by two WHA teams is because after 27 games in the 1975-76 WHA season the Denver franchised was moved to Ottawa where they played two games and then folded, that was the only season for Denver/Ottawa, Bridgman never played in the WHA. Traded to Calgary by Philadelphia for Brad Marsh, November 11, 1981. Traded to New Jersey by Calgary with Phil Russell for Steve Tambellini and Joel Quenneville, June 20, 1983. Traded to Detroit by New Jersey for Chris Cichocki and Detroit's 3rd round choice (later traded to Buffalo Buffalo selected Andrew MacVicar) in 1987 Entry Draft, March 9, 1987. Signed as a free agent by Vancouver, October 4, 1988. Retired in 1989.

Briere, Daniel

Born: October 6, 1977 in Gatineau, Quebec
Drafted: By the Phoenix Coyotes from the Drummondville Voltigeurs, 1st round, 24th overall.

Career Junior, NHL and World Junior Statistics

	GP	G	A	PTS	PIM
QMJHL Regular Season 1994-1997	198	170	246	416	224
QMJHL Playoffs	18	15	22	37	24
NHL Regular Season 1997-Present	272	77	81	158	158
NHL Playoffs	6	2	1	3	2
Canada 1997 World Juniors *in Switzerland*	7	2	4	6	4

Junior Highlights

QMJHL All-Rookie Team in 1995
QMJHL Offensive Rookie of the Year in 1995
QMJHL Second All-Star Team in 1996 and 1997
Won Gold Medal at World Junior Championships in 1997

Around the Rink

Briere was traded to Buffalo along with Phoenix's 3rd round pick in 2004, for Chris Gratton and Buffalo's 4th pick in 2003, on March 11, 2003.

Brind'Amour, Rod

Born: August 9, 1970 in Ottawa, Ontario - Raised in Campbell River, B.C.
Drafted: By the St. Louis Blues from Michigan State University in 1988, 1st round, 9th overall.

Career Junior, NHL and World Junior Statistics

	GP	G	A	PTS	PIM
NCAA 1988-89	42	27	32	59	63
NHL Regular Season 1989-Present	1031	339	534	873	848
NHL Playoffs	116	38	51	89	73
Canada 1989 World Juniors *in United States*	7	2	3	5	4

Brind'Amour, Rod Continued

Junior Highlights

Centennial Cup All-Star Team (High School) in 1988
Centennial Cup MVP (High School) in 1988
Central Collegiate Hockey Association (NCAA) Rookie of the Year in 1989

Around the Rink

Brind'Amour was drafted by the New Westminster Bruins (WHL) at the age of 13 but he chose to play high school hockey at Notre Dame in Saskatchewan where he won two Centennial Cup awards (see above), before moving onto Michigan State. Traded to Philadelphia by St. Louis with Dan Quinn for Ron Sutter and Murray Baron, September 22, 1991. Traded to Carolina by Philadelphia with Jean-Marc Pelletier and Philadelphia's 2nd round choice (later traded to Colorado - Colorado selected Agris Saviels) in 2000 Entry Draft for Keith Primeau and Carolina's 5th round choice (later traded to NY Islanders - NY Islanders selected Kristofer Ottosson) in 2000 Entry Draft, January 23, 2000.

Brisebois, Patrice

Born: January 27, 1971 in Montreal, Quebec
Drafted: By the Montreal Canadiens from the Laval Titan in 1989, 2nd round, 30th overall.

Career Junior, NHL and World Junior Statistics

	GP	G	A	PTS	PIM
QMJHL Regular Season 1987-91	208	65	193	258	370
QMJHL Playoffs	60	21	43	64	122
Memorial Cup 1989 and 1990	8	2	6	8	12
NHL Regular Season 1990-Present	720	75	236	311	479
NHL Playoffs	67	6	16	22	62
Canada 1990 World Juniors *in Finland*	7	2	2	4	6
Canada 1991 World Juniors *in Saskatchewan*	7	1	6	7	2
Canada Totals	**14**	**3**	**8**	**11**	**8**

Junior Highlights

Won Gold Medal at World Junior Championships in 1990 and 1991
QMJHL Second All-Star Team in 1990
QMJHL First All-Star Team in 1991
Canadian Major Junior Defenseman of the Year in 1991
Memorial Cup All-Star Team in 1991

Around the Rink

Brisebois was traded from Laval to the Drummondville Voltigeurs prior to the 1990-91 season. Laval moved to Bathurst New Brunswick in 1998. Played first NHL game on January 27, 1991 against Boston. Scored first NHL goal against Pittsburgh on February 22, 1992.

Brown, Curtis

Born: February 12, 1976 in Unity, Saskatchewan
Drafted: By the Buffalo Sabres from the Moose Jaw Warriors in 1994, 2nd round, 43rd overall.

Career Junior, NHL and World Junior Statistics

	GP	G	A	PTS	PIM
WHL Regular Season 1991-1996	257	123	146	269	213
WHL Playoffs	28	18	22	40	38
NHL Regular Season 1994-Present	474	100	131	231	258
NHL Playoffs	52	14	11	25	34
Canada 1996 World Juniors *in United States*	5	0	1	1	2

Junior Highlights

WHL East First All-Star Team in 1995
WHL East Second All-Star Team in 1996
Won Gold Medal at World Junior Championships in 1996

Around the Rink

Brown was traded from the Moose Jaw Warriors to the Prince Albert Raiders after 25 games in the 1995-96 WHL season. Made NHL debut on May 3, 1994 versus New Jersey, scoring a goal and adding an assist.

Brown, Keith

Born: May 6, 1960, in Cornerbrook, Newfoundland
Drafted: By the Chicago Blackhawks from the Portland Winter Hawks in 1979, 1st round, 7th overall.

Career Junior, NHL and World Junior Statistics

	GP	G	A	PTS	PIM
WHL Regular Season 1976-79	144	22	138	160	126
WHL Playoffs	33	3	33	36	23
NHL Regular Season 1979-95	876	68	274	342	916
NHL Playoffs	103	4	32	36	184
Canada 1979 World Juniors *in Sweden*	5	0	2	2	0

Junior Highlights

Alberta Junior Hockey League Rookie of the Year in 1977
AJHL Top Defenseman in 1977
WHL Co-Rookie of the Year with John Ogrodnick in 1978
WHL First All-Star Team in 1979

Around the Rink

Prior to joining the Portland Winter Hawks in 1976, Brown played for the Fort Saskatchewan Traders of the Alberta Junior Hockey League. Missed majority of 1981-82 season recovering from knee injury suffered in game vs. Philadelphia, December 23, 1981. Missed majority of 1987-88 season recovering from knee injury suffered in training camp, October 1987. Missed majority of 1992-93 season recovering from shoulder surgery, September 27, 1992. Traded to Florida by Chicago for Darin Kimble, September 30, 1993. Retired from playing in 1995.

Brown, Rob

Born: April 10, 1968 in Kingston, Ontario
Drafted: By the Pittsburgh Penguins from the Kamloops Blazers in 1986, 4th round, 67th overall.

Career Junior, NHL and World Junior Statistics

	GP	G	A	PTS	PIM
WHL Regular Season 1983-87	242	179	253	432	447
WHL Playoffs	51	33	43	76	65
Memorial Cup 1984 and 1986	9	6	9	15	22
NHL Regular Season 1987-2000	543	190	248	438	599
NHL Playoffs	54	12	14	26	45
Canada 1988 World Juniors *in Russia*	7	6	2	8	2

Junior Highlights

WHL West First All-Star Team in 1986 and 1987
WHL West MVP in 1986 and 1987
Canadian Major Junior Player of the Year in 1987
Won Gold Medal at World Junior Championships in 1988

Around the Rink

Brown played Junior hockey for Kamloops, in the spring of 1984 the Edmonton Oilers sold the righs to the Kamloops Junior Oilers to the citizens of Kamloops and the team became the Kamloops Blazers. Brown was traded to Hartford by Pittsburgh for Scott Young, December 21, 1990. Traded to Chicago by Hartford for Steve Konroyd, January 24, 1992. Signed as a free agent by Dallas, August 12, 1993. Signed as a free agent by LA Kings, June 14, 1994. Signed as a free agent by Pittsburgh, October 1, 1997. Signed as a free agent with the Chicago Wolves (IHL) in 2000. The team is now an AHL affiliate of the Atlanta Thrashers.

Burke, Sean

Born: January 29, 1967 in Windsor, Ontario
Drafted: By the New Jersey Devils from the Toronto Marlboros in 1985, 2nd round, 24th overall.

Career Junior, NHL and World Junior Statistics

	GP	W	L	T	SO	AVG
OHL Regular Season 1984-86	96	41	48	6	0	4.57
OHL Playoffs	9	1	7	0	0	5.83
NHL Regular Season 1987-Present	715	288	301	94	34	3.26
NHL Playoffs	34	12	22	0	1	3.33
Canada 1986 World Juniors *in Hamilton*	2	1	1	0	0	3.50

Junior Highlights

Recorded 5 assists with the Marlboros in 1985-86
Won Silver Medal at World Junior Championships in 1986

Around the Rink

Burke was traded to Hartford by New Jersey with Eric Weinrich for Bobby Holik and Hartford's 2nd round choice (Jay Pandolfo) in 1993 Entry Draft, August 28, 1992. Transferred to Carolina after Hartford franchise relocated, June 25, 1997. Traded to Vancouver by Carolina with Geoff Sanderson and Enrico Ciccone for Kirk McLean and Martin Gelinas, January 3, 1998. Traded to Philadelphia by Vancouver for Garth Snow, March 4, 1998. Signed as a free agent by Florida, September 12, 1998. Traded to Phoenix by Florida with Florida's 5th round choice (Nate Kiser) in 2000 Entry Draft for Mikhail Shtalenkov and Phoenix's 4th round choice (Chris Eade) in 2000 Entry Draft, November 18, 1999.

Butcher, Garth

Born: January 8, 1963 in Regina, Saskatchewan
Drafted: By the Vancouver Canucks from the Regina Pats in 1981, 1st round, 10th overall.

Career Junior, NHL and World Junior Statistics

	GP	G	A	PTS	PIM
WHL Regular Season 1979-1983	152	37	151	188	572
WHL Playoffs	45	12	42	54	216
Memorial Cup 1980	3	0	1	1	0
NHL Regular Season 1981-95	897	48	158	206	2302
NHL Playoffs	50	6	5	11	122
Canada 1982 World Juniors *in United States*	7	1	3	4	0

Junior Highlights

Won WHL Championship in 1979-80
WHL First All-Star Team in 1981 and 1982
Won Gold Medal at World Junior Championships in 1982

Around the Rink

Butcher played all but five games of his WHL career with the Regina Pats. He was dealt to the Kamloops Junior Oilers before the 1982-83 season. Traded to St. Louis by Vancouver with Dan Quinn for Geoff Courtnall, Robert Dirk, Sergio Momesso, Cliff Ronning and St. Louis' 5th round choice (Brian Loney) in 1992 Entry Draft, March 5, 1991. Traded to Quebec by St. Louis with Ron Sutter and Bob Bassen for Steve Duchesne and Denis Chase, January 23, 1994. Traded to Toronto by Quebec with Mats Sundin, Todd Warriner and Philadelphia's 1st round choice (previously acquired by Quebec later traded to Washington Washington selected Nolan Baumgartner) in 1994 Entry Draft for Wendel Clark, Sylvain Lefebvre, Landon Wilson and Toronto's 1st round choice (Jeffrey Kealty) in 1994 Entry Draft, June 28, 1994. Retired in 1995.

Byers, Lyndon

Born: February 29, 1964 in Nipawin, Saskatchewan
Drafted: By the Boston Bruins from the Regina Pats in 1982, 2nd round, 39th overall.

Career Junior, NHL and World Junior Statistics

	GP	G	A	PTS	PIM
WHL Regular Season 1981-84	185	82	120	202	476
WHL Playoffs	48	23	25	48	142
NHL Regular Season 1983-93	279	28	43	71	1081
NHL Playoffs	37	2	2	4	96
Canada 1984 World Juniors *in Sweden*	6	1	1	2	4

Junior Highlights

Saskatchewan Junior Hockey League Second Team All-Star with Notre Dame in 1981

Around the Rink

Byers missed majority of 1990-91 season recovering from foot injury suffered in game vs. Soviet Khimik, December 16, 1990. Signed as a free agent by San Jose, November 7, 1992. Signed as a free agent by San Diego (IHL) following release by San Jose, March 10, 1993. Retired from hockey in 1995 as a member of the Minnesota Moose (IHL).

Calder, Eric

Born: June 26, 1963 in Kitchener, Ontario
Drafted: By the Washington Capitals from the Cornwall Royals in 1981, 3rd round, 45th overall.

Career Junior, NHL and World Junior Statistics

	GP	G	A	PTS	PIM
QMJHL/OHL Regular Season 1980-83	197	26	100	126	206
QMJHL/OHL Playoffs	22	0	11	11	31
Memorial Cup 1981	5	3	1	4	8
NHL Regular Season 1982-83	2	0	0	0	0
NHL Playoffs	0	0	0	0	0
Canada 1981 World Juniors *in Germany*	5	1	0	1	4

Junior Highlights

Won Memorial Cup in 1981

Around the Rink

Cornwall moved from the QMJHL to the OHL after the 1980-81 season. Calder's NHL career was brief, just two games over two seasons, after playing the 1983-84 season in the minors, he took a year off and went to University and played three seasons with Wilfrid Laurier, where he was a three time Ontario All-Star and an All-Canadian in 1988. After University Calder headed to the European Leagues and retired from playing in 1997.

Calder, Kyle

Born: January 5, 1979 in Mannville, Alberta
Drafted: By the Chicago Black Hawks from the Regina Pats in 1997, 5th round, 130th overall.

Career Junior, NHL and World Junior Statistics

	GP	**G**	**A**	**PTS**	**PIM**
WHL Regular Season 1995-99	212	95	137	232	144
WHL Playoffs	33	9	11	20	12
NHL Regular Season 1999-Present	214	38	74	112	103
NHL Playoffs	5	2	0	2	2
Canada 1999 World Juniors *in Manitoba*	7	2	6	8	2

Junior Highlights

Won Gold Medal at World Junior Championships in 1999

Around the Rink

Regina traded Calder to Kamloops for Alan Manness, January 13, 1999. Calder spent his first two years of pro hockey between the NHL and the minors. He missed the 2000-01 training camp with a stomach injury. First NHL game was against Anaheim on October 21, 1999. First NHL goal and point was against San Jose on December 14, 1999. First NHL assist came on February 18, 2000 versus Washington.

Cammalleri, Mike

Born: June 8, 1982 in Toronto, Ontario
Drafted: By the Los Angeles Kings from the University of Michigan in 2001, 2nd round, 49th overall.

Career Junior, NHL and World Junior Statistics

	GP	G	A	PTS	PIM
NCAA 1999-2002	109	65	130	195	80
NHL Regular Season 2002-Present	28	5	3	8	22
NHL Playoffs	0	0	0	0	0
Canada 2001 World Juniors *in Russia*	7	4	2	6	2
Canada 2002 World Juniors *in Czech Republic*	7	7	4	11	10
Canada Totals	**14**	**11**	**6**	**17**	**12**

Junior Highlights

Won Bronze Medal at World Junior Championships in 2001
Central Collegiate Hockey Association (NCAA) First Team All-Star in 2000-01
Won Silver Medal at World Junior Championships in 2002

Around the Rink

Cammalleri played his first NHL game on November 8, 2002 versus Ottawa, he also recorded his first NHL point in that game with an assist. Scored his first NHL goal on November 16, 2002 against Edmonton.

Campbell, Brian

Born: May 23, 1979 in Strathroy, Ontario
Drafted: By the Buffalo Sabres from the Ottawa 67's in 1997, 6th round, 156th overall.

Career Junior, NHL and World Junior Statistics

	GP	G	A	PTS	PIM
OHL Regular Season 1995-99	260	38	172	210	93
OHL Playoffs	50	5	36	41	16
Memorial Cup 1999	5	1	3	4	2
NHL Regular Season 1999-Present	114	6	24	31	38
NHL Playoffs	0	0	0	0	0
Canada 1999 World Juniors *in Winnipeg*	7	1	1	2	4

Junior Highlights

Won Silver Medal at World Junior Championships in 1999
World Junior Championship All-Star Team in 1999
OHL First All-Star Team in 1999
OHL MVP in 1999
Canadian Major Junior First All-Star Team in 1999
Canadian Major Junior Player of the Year in 1999
Won George Parsons Trophy (Memorial Cup Most Sportsmanlike Player) in 1999

Around the Rink

Campbell spent his first three pro-seasons, traveling back and forth between Buffalo and their AHL affiliate Rochester. Made NHL debut on October 2, 1999 versus Detroit. Recorded first NHL points with a goal and an assist on October 8, 1999 against Washington. He made the Sabres full time at the start of the 2002-03 season.

Caprice, Frank

Born: April 2, 1962 in Hamilton, Ontario
Drafted: By the Vancouver Canucks from the London Knights in 1981, 9th round, 178th overall.

Career Junior, NHL and World Junior Statistics

	GP	W	L	T	SO	AVG
OHL Regular Season 1979-82	103	38	50	5	1	4.83
OHL Playoffs	7	2	4	0	0	5.03
NHL Regular Season 1982-88	102	31	46	11	1	4.19
NHL Playoffs	0	0	0	0	0	0.00
Canada 1982 World Juniors *in U.S.A.*	3	3	0	0	0	2.33

Junior Highlights

Won Gold Medal at World Junior Championships in 1982

Around the Rink

Caprice played all of his NHL games with Vancouver. Signed as a free agent with Milwaukee (IHL) in 1988. Did not play from 1990-92. Signed as a free agent with Gardena in the Italian league in 1992. Played in British league from 1996-99 with Cardiff and Ayr. Retired from playing in 1999. Also played professional roller hockey in 1994 with the Vancouver Voodoo.

Carkner, Terry

Born: March 7, 1966 in Smith Falls, Ontario
Drafted: By the New York Rangers from the Peterborough Petes in 1984, 1st round, 14th overall.

Career Junior, NHL and World Junior Statistics

	GP	G	A	PTS	PIM
OHL Regular Season 1983-86	184	30	100	130	322
OHL Playoffs	41	3	23	26	41
NHL Regular Season 1986-99	858	42	188	230	1588
NHL Playoffs	54	1	9	10	48
Canada 1986 World Juniors *in Hamilton*	7	0	4	4	0

Junior Highlights

OHL Second All-Star Team in 1985
Won Silver Medal at the World Junior Championships in 1986
OHL First All-Star Team in 1986

Around the Rink

Carkner was traded to Quebec by the NY Rangers with Jeff Jackson for John Ogrodnick and David Shaw, September 30, 1987. Traded to Philadelphia by Quebec for Greg Smyth and Philadelphia's 3rd round choice (John Tanner) in 1989 Entry Draft, July 25, 1988. Traded to Detroit by Philadelphia for Yves Racine and Detroit's 4th round choice (Sebastien Vallee) in 1994 Entry Draft, October 5, 1993. Signed as a free agent by Florida, August 8, 1995. Retired from playing in 1999.

Carter, Anson

Born: June 6, 1974 in Toronto, Ontario
Drafted: By the Quebec Nordiques from Michigan State University in 1992, 10th round, 220th overall.

Career Junior, NHL and World Junior Statistics

	GP	G	A	PTS	PIM
NCAA 1992-96	156	125	72	197	132
NHL Regular Season 1996-Present	452	143	167	310	150
NHL Playoffs	24	8	5	13	4
Canada 1994 World Juniors *in Czech Republic*	7	3	2	5	0

Junior Highlights

Won Gold Medal at World Junior Championships in 1994
Central Collegiate Hockey Association (NCAA) First All-Star Team in 1994 and 1995
NCAA West Second All-American Team in 1995
Central Collegiate Hockey Association (NCAA) Second All-Star Team in 1996

Around the Rink

Carter's rights transferred to Colorado after Quebec franchise relocated, June 21, 1995. Traded to Washington by Colorado for Washington's 4th round choice (Ben Storey) in 1996 Entry Draft, April 3, 1996. Traded to Boston by Washington with Jim Carey, Jason Allison and Washington's 3rd round choice (Lee Goren) in 1997 Entry Draft for Bill Ranford, Adam Oates and Rick Tocchet, March 1, 1997. Signed as a free agent by Utah (IHL) with Boston retaining NHL rights, October 20, 1998. Traded to Edmonton by Boston with Boston's 1st (Ales Hemsky) and 2nd (Doug Lynch) round choices in 2001 Entry Draft for Bill Guerin and future considerations, November 15, 2000. Traded to the New York Rangers with Ales Pisa by Edmonton for Radek Dvorak and Cory Cross, March 11, 2003.

Carter, Ron

Born: March 14, 1958 in Montreal, Quebec
Drafted: By the Montreal Canadiens from the Sherbrooke Beavers in 1978, 2nd round, 36th overall.

Career Junior, NHL and World Junior Statistics

	GP	**G**	**A**	**PTS**	**PIM**
QMJHL Regular Season 1975-78	208	199	172	371	58
QMJHL Playoffs	0	0	0	0	0
Memorial Cup 1977	4	1	1	2	0
NHL Regular Season 1979-80	2	0	0	0	0
NHL Playoffs	0	0	0	0	0
Canada 1976 World Juniors *in Finland*	4	0	0	0	0

Junior Highlights

Won Silver Medal at World Junior Championships in 1976
QMJHL First All-Star Team in 1978

Around the Rink

Carter signed as an underage free agent by Edmonton (WHA), July 1978. NHL rights retained by Edmonton prior to Expansion Draft, June 9, 1979. Claimed on waivers by Buffalo from Edmonton, July 1980. Both of his NHL games came with Edmonton. Signed with Nashville (ACHL) as a free agent in 1982. Retired from playing in 1986.

Cassels, Andrew

Born: July 23, 1969 in Bramalea, Ontario
Drafted: By the Montreal Canadiens from the Ottawa 67's in 1987, 1st round, 17th overall.

Career Junior, NHL and World Junior Statistics

	GP	G	A	PTS	PIM
OHL Regular Season 1986-89	183	111	266	377	133
OHL Playoffs	39	18	43	62	30
NHL Regular Season 1989-Present	926	194	500	694	370
NHL Playoffs	21	4	7	11	8
Canada 1989 World Juniors *in United States*	7	2	5	7	2

Junior Highlights

OHL Rookie of the Year in 1987
OHL First All-Star Team in 1988 and 1989
OHL MVP in 1988

Around the Rink

Cassels was traded to Hartford by Montreal for Hartford's 2nd round choice (Valeri Bure) in 1992 Entry Draft, September 17, 1991. Transferred to Carolina after Hartford franchise relocated, June 25, 1997. Traded to Calgary by Carolina with Jean-Sebastien Giguere for Gary Roberts and Trevor Kidd, August 25, 1997. Signed as a free agent by Vancouver, August 19, 1999. Signed as a free agent by Columbus, August 15, 2002.

Cassidy, Bruce

Born: May 20, 1965 in Ottawa, Ontario
Drafted: By the Chicago Black Hawks from the Ottawa 67's in 1983, 1st round, 18th overall.

Career Junior, NHL and World Junior Statistics

	GP	G	A	PTS	PIM
OHL Regular Season 1982-85	165	65	181	246	106
OHL Playoffs	22	9	25	34	16
Memorial Cup 1984	5	7	5	12	2
NHL Regular Season 1984-90	36	4	13	17	10
NHL Playoffs	1	0	0	0	0
Canada 1984 World Juniors *in Sweden*	7	0	0	0	6

Junior Highlights

OHL Rookie of the Year in 1983
OHL Second All-Star Team in 1984
Memorial Cup All-Star Team in 1984
Won Memorial Cup in 1984

Around the Rink

Cassidy missed majority of 1984-85 season recovering from knee injury suffered during summer training, June 1984. Released by Chicago after the 1990 season, he played in the IHL and Europe for four years. Signed as a free agent by Chicago, July 28, 1994, but he played in the minors and never re-surfaced in the NHL as a player. After five seasons as a minor league coach, Cassidy was named Head Coach of Washington, June 25, 2002.

Cassolato, Tony

Born: May 7, 1956 in Guelph, Ontario
Not Drafted: Signed as a Free Agent by San Diego (WHA) in 1976.

Career Junior, NHL and World Junior Statistics

	GP	G	A	PTS	PIM
OHL Regular Season 1973-76	198	80	112	192	158
OHL Playoffs	11	3	5	8	15
NHL Regular Season 1979-82	23	1	6	7	4
NHL Playoffs	0	0	0	0	0
Canada 1974 World Juniors *in Russia*	3	0	0	0	0

Junior Highlights

Won Bronze Medal at World Junior Championships in 1974

Around the Rink

Cassolato signed as a free agent with San Diego (WHA), October 1976. Signed as a free agent by Birmingham (WHA) after San Diego (WHA) franchise folded, September 1977. Signed as a free agent by Washington, August 12, 1979. Finished playing career with two seasons in Europe ending in 1985.

Chiasson, Steve

Born: April 14, 1967 in Barrie, Ontario - Passed Away: May 3, 1999
Drafted: By the Detroit Red Wings from the Guelph Platers in 1985, 3rd round, 50th overall.

Career Junior, NHL and World Junior Statistics

	GP	G	A	PTS	PIM
OHL Regular Season 1983-86	170	21	60	81	377
OHL Playoffs	18	10	10	20	37
Memorial Cup 1986	4	1	4	5	4
NHL Regular Season 1986-99	751	93	305	398	1107
NHL Playoffs	63	16	18	34	119
Canada 1987 World Juniors *in Czech Republic*	6	2	2	4	21

Junior Highlights

Won Stafford Smythe Memorial Trophy (Memorial Cup Tournament MVP) in 1986
Won Memorial Cup in 1986

Around the Rink

Chiasson was traded to Calgary by Detroit for Mike Vernon, June 29, 1994. Traded to Hartford by Calgary with Colorado's 3rd round choice (previously acquired, Hartford/Carolina selected Francis Lessard) in 1997 Entry Draft for Hnat Domenichelli, Glen Featherstone, New Jersey's 2nd round choice (previously acquired, Calgary selected Dimitri Kokorev) in 1997 Entry Draft and Vancouver's 3rd round choice (previously acquired, Calgary selected Paul Manning) in 1998 Entry Draft, March 5, 1997. Transferred to Carolina after Hartford franchise relocated, June 25, 1997.

Chicoine, Dan

Born: November 30, 1957 in Sherbrooke, Quebec
Drafted: By the Cleveland Barons from the Sherbrooke Beavers in 1977, 2nd round, 23rd overall. Also Drafted by the Quebec Nordiques (WHA) in 1977, 9th round, 81st overall.

Career Junior, NHL and World Junior Statistics

	GP	G	A	PTS	PIM
QMJHL Regular Season 1973-77	254	113	146	259	278
QMJHL Playoffs	Not Available				
Memorial Cup 1975 and 1977	7	1	0	1	8
NHL Regular Season 1977-80	31	1	2	3	12
NHL Playoffs	1	0	0	0	0
Canada 1976 World Juniors *in Finland*	4	2	0	2	2

Junior Highlights

Won Silver Medal at World Junior Championships in 1976

Around the Rink

Chicoine was placed on Minnesota Reserve List after Cleveland-Minnesota Dispersal Draft, June 15, 1978. Claimed by Minnesota as a fill-in during Expansion Draft, June 13, 1979. Traded to Quebec by Minnesota for Nelson Burton, June 9, 1981, he never played a game for Quebec. After spending 1980-81 in the minors with Oklahoma (AHL) he retired for one season and then made a comeback with Sherbrooke (AHL) before retiring for a final time in 1983.

Chimera, Jason

Born: May 2, 1979 in Edmonton, Alberta
Drafted: By the Edmonton Oilers from the Medicine Hat Tigers in 1997, 5th round, 121st overall.

Career Junior, NHL and World Junior Statistics

	GP	G	A	PTS	PIM
WHL Regular Season 1996-99	201	82	89	171	273
WHL Playoffs	9	4	2	6	12
NHL Regular Season 2000-Present	70	15	9	24	36
NHL Playoffs	2	0	2	2	0
Canada 1999 World Juniors *in Winnipeg*	7	2	2	4	2

Junior Highlights

Won Silver Medal at World Junior Championships in 1999

Around the Rink

Chimera was traded to Brandon (WHL) by Medicine Hat (WHL) for Justin Yeomans and future considerations, February 2, 1999. Made Edmonton full time in 2002-03 after spending three full seasons with the Oilers AHL affiliate in Hamilton.

Chouinard, Eric

Born: July 8, 1980 in Atlanta, Georgia - Raised in Montreal, Quebec
Drafted: By the Montreal Canadiens from the Quebec Remparts in 1998, 1st round, 16th overall.

Career Junior, NHL and World Junior Statistics

	GP	**G**	**A**	**PTS**	**PIM**
QMJHL Regular Season 1997-2000	180	148	148	296	179
QMJHL Playoffs	38	29	24	53	22
NHL Regular Season 2000-Present	41	5	7	12	8
NHL Playoffs	0	0	0	0	0
Canada 1999 World Juniors *in Winnipeg*	2	1	0	1	2
Canada 2000 World Juniors *in Sweden*	7	3	0	3	0
Canada Totals	**9**	**4**	**0**	**4**	**2**

Junior Highlights

Won Silver Medal at World Junior Championships in 1999
Won Bronze Medal at World Junior Championships in 2000

Around the Rink

Chouinard was born in the U.S. but he is a Canadian citizen. He is ineligible to represent the U.S. as he represented Canada after his 18th birthday and under IIHF rules you can only play for one country after your 18th birthday. Traded to Philadelphia for the Flyers 2nd round pick in 2003, January 29, 2003.

Chyzowski, Dave

Born: July 11, 1971 in Edmonton, Alberta
Drafted: By the New York Islanders from the Kamloops Blazers in 1989, 1st round, 2nd overall.

Career Junior, NHL and World Junior Statistics

	GP	G	A	PTS	PIM
WHL Regular Season 1987-90	138	76	67	143	273
WHL Playoffs	61	28	23	51	104
Memorial Cup 1990	3	4	3	7	13
NHL Regular Season 1989-1997	126	15	16	31	144
NHL Playoffs	2	0	0	0	0
Canada 1990 World Juniors *in Finland*	7	9	4	13	2

Junior Highlights

WHL West First All-Star Team in 1989
Won Gold Medal at World Junior Championships in 1990
World Junior Championship All-Star Team in 1990

Around the Rink

Chyzowski signed as a free agent by Detroit, August 29, 1995. Signed as a free agent by Chicago, September 26, 1996 but only played 8 games, spent most of the season with Indianapolis in the (IHL) after four more season in the (IHL) he went to play in Germany in 2000.

Ciccarelli, Dino

Born: February 8, 1960 in Sarnia, Ontario
Not Drafted: Signed as a Free Agent by the Minnesota North Stars in 1979

Career Junior, NHL and World Junior Statistics

	GP	G	A	PTS	PIM
OHL Regular Season 1976-80	226	169	177	346	191
OHL Playoffs	41	22	34	56	35
NHL Regular Season 1980-99	1232	608	592	1200	1429
NHL Playoffs	141	73	45	118	211
Canada 1980 World Juniors *in Finland*	5	5	1	6	2

Junior Highlights

OHL Second All-Star Team in 1978

Around the Rink

Ciccarelli played his entire junior career with the London Knights and he was never drafted by an NHL team he signed as a free agent by Minnesota, September 28, 1979. Traded to Washington by Minnesota with Bob Rouse for Mike Gartner and Larry Murphy, March 7, 1989. Traded to Detroit by Washington for Kevin Miller, June 20, 1992. Traded to Tampa Bay by Detroit for Tampa Bay's 4th round choice (later traded to Toronto Toronto selected Alexei Ponikarovsky) in 1998 Entry Draft, August 27, 1996. Traded to Florida by Tampa Bay with Jeff Norton for Mark Fitzpatrick and Jody Hull, January 15, 1998. Missed majority of 1998-99 season with back injury suffered in game vs. Chicago, November 4, 1998. Officially announced retirement, August 31, 1999.

Cimetta, Rob

Born: February 15, 1970 in Toronto, Ontario
Drafted: By the Boston Bruins from the Toronto Marlboros in 1988, 1st round, 18th overall.

Career Junior, NHL and World Junior Statistics

	GP	G	A	PTS	PIM
OHL Regular Season 1986-89	180	105	124	229	244
OHL Playoffs	10	5	5	10	22
NHL Regular Season 1988-92	103	16	16	32	66
NHL Playoffs	1	0	0	0	15
Canada 1989 World Juniors *in United States*	7	7	4	11	4

Junior Highlights

OHL First All-Star Team in 1989

Around the Rink

Cimetta was traded to Toronto by Boston for Steve Bancroft, November 9 1990. Signed as a free agent by Chicago, September 8, 1993 however he never played a game with the Black Hawks, he spent a season in the minors and then played in Germany from 1994 to 2000 when he retired from playing.

Cirella, Joe

Born: May 9, 1963 in Hamilton, Ontario
Drafted: By the Colorado Rockies from the Oshawa Generals in 1981, 1st round, 5th overall.

Career Junior, NHL and World Junior Statistics

	GP	G	A	PTS	PIM
OHL Regular Season 1980-83	115	18	87	105	340
OHL Playoffs	39	11	28	39	110
Memorial Cup 1983	5	3	8	11	10
NHL Regular Season 1981-95	828	64	211	275	1448
NHL Playoffs	38	0	13	13	98
Canada 1983 World Juniors *in Russia*	7	0	0	0	6

Junior Highlights

OHL First All-Star Team in 1983
Won Bronze Medal at World Junior Championships in 1983
Memorial Cup All-Star Team in 1983

Around the Rink

Cirella transferred to New Jersey after Colorado franchise relocated, June 30, 1982. Traded to Quebec by New Jersey with Claude Loiselle and New Jersey's 8th round choice (Alexander Karpovtsev) in 1990 Entry Draft for Walt Poddubny and Quebec's 4th round choice (Mike Bodnarchuk) in 1990 Entry Draft, June 17, 1989. Traded to NY Rangers by Quebec for Aaron Miller and NY Rangers' 5th round choice (Bill Lindsay) in 1991 Entry Draft, January 17, 1991. Claimed by Florida from NY Rangers in Expansion Draft, June 24, 1993. Signed as a free agent by Ottawa, October 10, 1995. Signed as a free agent by Milwaukee (IHL) following release from Ottawa, December 1, 1995. Assistant Coach with Florida in 1997-98, Assistant Coach with the Oshawa Generals since 1998.

Clark, Wendel

Born: October 25, 1966 in Kelvington, Saskatchewan
Drafted: By the Toronto Maple Leafs from the Saskatoon Blades in 1985, 1st round, 1st overall.

Career Junior, NHL and World Junior Statistics

	GP	G	A	PTS	PIM
WHL Regular Season 1983-85	136	55	100	155	478
WHL Playoffs	3	3	3	6	7
NHL Regular Season 1985-2000	793	330	234	564	1690
NHL Playoffs	95	37	32	69	201
Canada 1985 World Juniors *in Finland*	7	3	2	5	10

Junior Highlights

Won Gold Medal at World Junior Championships in 1985
WHL East First All-Star Team in 1985

Around the Rink

Clark was traded to Quebec by Toronto with Sylvain Lefebvre, Landon Wilson and Toronto's 1st round choice (Jeffrey Kealty) in 1994 Entry Draft for Mats Sundin, Garth Butcher, Todd Warriner and Philadelphia's 1st round choice (previously acquired by Quebec - later traded to Washington - Washington selected Nolan Baumgartner) in 1994 Entry Draft, June 28, 1994. Transferred to Colorado after Quebec franchise relocated, June 21, 1995. Traded to NY Islanders by Colorado for Claude Lemieux, October 3, 1995. Traded to Toronto by NY Islanders with Mathieu Schneider and D.J. Smith for Darby Hendrickson, Sean Haggerty, Kenny Jonsson and Toronto's 1st round choice (Roberto Luongo) in 1997 Entry Draft, March 13, 1996. Signed as a free agent by Tampa Bay, July 31, 1998. Traded to Detroit by Tampa Bay with Detroit's 6th round choice (previously acquired, Detroit selected Kent McDonell) in 1999 Entry Draft for Kevin Hodson and San Jose's 2nd round choice (previously acquired, Tampa Bay selected Sheldon Keefe) in 1999 Entry Draft, March 23, 1999. Signed as a free agent by Chicago, August 2, 1999. Signed as a free agent by Toronto following release by Chicago, January 14, 2000. Officially announced retirement, June 29, 2000.

Cloutier, Dan

Born: April 22, 1976 in Mont Laurier, Quebec
Drafted: By the New York Rangers from the Sault Ste. Marie Greyhounds in 1994, 1st round 26th overall.

Career Junior, NHL and World Junior Statistics

	GP	W	L	T	SO	AVG
OHL Regular Season 1992-96	142	68	51	10	5	3.76
OHL Playoffs	34	22	11	0	2	3.38
Memorial Cup 1996	3	0	3	0	0	4.00
NHL Regular Season 1997-Present	245	90	100	27	10	2.74
NHL Playoffs	15	6	8	0	0	3.33
Canada 1995 World Juniors *in Alberta*	3	3	0	0	0	2.67

Junior Highlights

Won Gold Medal at World Junior Championships in 1995
OHL Second All-Star Team in 1996

Around the Rink

Cloutier was traded from the Sault to Guelph after 13 games in 1995. Traded to Tampa Bay by NY Rangers with Niklas Sundstrom and NY Rangers' 1st (Nikita Alexeev) and 3rd (later traded to San Jose - later traded to Chicago - Chicago selected Igor Radulov) round choices in 2000 Entry Draft for Chicago's 1st round choice (previously acquired, NY Rangers selected Pavel Brendl) in 1999 Entry Draft, June 26, 1999. Traded to Vancouver by Tampa Bay for Adrian Aucoin and Vancouver's 2nd round choice (Alexander Polushin) in 2001 Entry Draft, February 7, 2001.

Colaiacovo, Carlo

Born: January 27, 1983 in Toronto, Ontario
Drafted: By the Toronto Maple Leafs from the Erie Otters in 2001, 1st round, 17th overall.

Career Junior, NHL and World Junior Statistics

	GP	G	A	PTS	PIM
OHL Regular Season 1999-2003	209	43	93	136	60
OHL Playoffs	48	13	21	34	45
NHL Regular Season 2002-Present	2	0	1	1	0
NHL Playoffs	0	0	0	0	0
Canada 2002 World Juniors *in Czech Republic*	7	0	3	3	2
Canada 2003 World Juniors *in Nova Scotia*	6	1	9	10	2
Canada Totals	**13**	**1**	**12**	**13**	**4**

Junior Highlights

Won Silver Medal at World Junior Championships in 2002 and 2003
World Junior Championship All-Star Team 2003
OHL Second Team All-Star in 2002

Around the Rink

Colaiacovo recorded his first NHL point in his first NHL game on October 23, 2002 against Florida, assisting on a second period goal by Nik Antropov. Returned to Erie (OHL) November 11, 2002.

Conroy, Al

Born: January 17, 1966 in Calgary, Alberta
Not Drafted: Signed as a Free Agent by the Detroit Red Wings in 1989.

Career Junior, NHL and World Junior Statistics

	GP	G	A	PTS	PIM
WHL Regular Season 1982-86	266	158	198	356	583
WHL Playoffs	54	26	45	71	129
NHL Regular Season 1991-94	114	9	14	23	156
NHL Playoffs	0	0	0	0	0
Canada 1986 World Juniors *in Hamilton*	7	4	4	8	6

Junior Highlights

Won Silver Medal at World Junior Championships in 1986
WHL East First All-Star Team in 1986

Around the Rink

Conroy signed as a free agent by Detroit August 16, 1989. Signed as a free agent by Philadelphia August 21, 1991. Officially announced retirement and named Assistant Coach of Charlotte (ECHL), August 15, 2001.

Contini, Joe

Born: January 29, 1957 in Galt, Ontario
Drafted: By the Colorado Rockies from the St. Catharines Fin Cups in 1977, 8th round, 126th overall.

Career Junior, NHL and World Junior Statistics

	GP	G	A	PTS	PIM
OHL Regular Season 1974-77	150	72	144	216	318
OHL Playoffs	37	13	39	52	77
Memorial Cup 1976	3	4	4	8	6
NHL Regular Season 1977-79	68	17	21	38	34
NHL Playoffs	2	0	0	0	0
Canada 1977 World Juniors *in Czech Republic*	7	4	5	9	32

Junior Highlights

Won Memorial Cup in 1976
Set a Memorial Cup Record for Most Points in One Game With 6 in 1976
Won Silver Medal at World Junior Championships in 1977

Around the Rink

Contini was re-claimed by Colorado as a fill-in during Expansion Draft, June 13, 1979. Signed as a free agent by Minnesota, February 1, 1980 but never played an NHL game for them. He retired from hockey in 1982 as a member of the Hershey Bears (AHL). Head coach of the Guelph Platers (OHL) from 1983-85.

Convery, Brandon

Born: February 4, 1974 in Kingston, Ontario
Drafted: By the Toronto Maple Leafs from the Sudbury Wolves in 1992, 1st round, 8th overall.

Career Junior, NHL and World Junior Statistics

	GP	G	A	PTS	PIM
OHL Regular Season 1990-94	210	151	145	296	144
OHL Playoffs	26	9	16	25	23
NHL Regular Season 1995-99	72	9	19	28	36
NHL Playoffs	5	0	0	0	2
Canada 1994 World Juniors *in Czech Republic*	7	1	0	1	2

Junior Highlights

Won Gold Medal at World Junior Championships in 1994

Around the Rink

Convery was traded by Sudbury after 7 games to Niagara Falls in 1992. Traded by Niagara Falls after 29 games in 1993 to Belleville. Traded to Vancouver by Toronto for Lonny Bohonos, March 7, 1998. Claimed on waivers by Los Angeles from Vancouver, November 21, 1998. Has played in Europe since 2000.

Cooke, Matt

Born: September 7, 1978 in Belleville, Ontario
Drafted: By the Vancouver Canucks from the Windsor Spitfires in 1997, 6th round, 144th overall.

Career Junior, NHL and World Junior Statistics

	GP	G	A	PTS	PIM
OHL Regular Season 1995-98	174	75	93	168	347
OHL Playoffs	24	14	16	30	36
NHL Regular Season 1998-Present	326	47	69	116	353
NHL Playoffs	16	3	3	6	8
Canada 1998 World Juniors *in Finland*	6	1	1	2	6

Junior Highlights

Recorded 95 points in only 65 games with Windsor in 1996-97

Around the Rink

Cooke was traded to Kingston (OHL) by Windsor (OHL) for Brent L'Hereux, December 17, 1997. Recorded his first NHL point, December 6, 1998, an assist versus Phoenix. Recorded his first NHL goal on January 25, 2000 versus Bill Ranford of Edmonton.

Corriveau, Yvon

Born: February 8, 1967 in Welland, Ontario
Drafted: By the Washington, Capitals from the Toronto Marlboros in 1985, 1st round, 19th overall.

Career Junior, NHL and World Junior Statistics

	GP	G	A	PTS	PIM
OHL Regular Season 1984-87	141	91	83	174	163
OHL Playoffs	7	1	1	2	5
NHL Regular Season 1985-94	280	48	40	88	310
NHL Playoffs	29	5	7	12	50
Canada 1987 World Juniors *in Czech Republic*	6	2	1	3	4

Junior Highlights

Scored 54 Goals in only 59 Games in 1985-86 With Toronto

Around the Rink

Corriveau was traded to Hartford by Washington for Mike Liut, March 6, 1990. Traded to Washington by Hartford to complete June 15, 1992 deal in which Mark Hunter and future considerations were traded to Washington for Nick Kypreos, August 20, 1992. Claimed by San Jose from Washington in Waiver Draft, October 4, 1992. Traded to Hartford by San Jose to complete October 9, 1992 trade in which Michel Picard was traded to San Jose for future considerations, January 21, 1993. Played in the minors from 1994-97. Has played in Europe since 1997.

Corso, Daniel

Born: April 3, 1978 in Montreal, Quebec
Drafted: By the St. Louis Blues from the Victoriaville Tigres in 1996, 7th round, 169th overall.

Career Junior, NHL and World Junior Statistics

	GP	G	A	PTS	PIM
QMJHL Regular Season 1994-98	219	151	210	361	153
QMJHL Playoffs	19	9	13	22	8
NHL Regular Season 2000-Present	70	14	10	24	20
NHL Playoffs	14	0	1	1	0
Canada 1998 World Juniors *in Finland*	7	0	3	3	4

Junior Highlights

QMJHL All-Rookie Team in 1995
QMJHL First All-Star Team in 1997
QMJHL MVP in 1997

Around the Rink

Corso scored his first NHL goal, in his first NHL game, and it was the only goal in a 1-0 win by St. Louis against the Mighty Ducks of Anaheim on Dec. 5, 2000. He has split his pro career between St. Louis and their AHL affiliate Worcester.

Corson, Shayne

Born: August 13, 1966 in Barrie, Ontario
Drafted: By the Montreal Canadiens from the Hamilton Steelhawks in 1984, 1st round, 8th overall.

Career Junior, NHL and World Junior Statistics

	GP	G	A	PTS	PIM
OHL Regular Season 1983-86	167	93	166	259	472
OHL Playoffs	17	7	8	15	45
NHL Regular Season 1986-Present	1139	268	415	683	2328
NHL Playoffs	135	38	48	86	279
Canada 1985 World Juniors *in Finland*	7	2	3	5	2
Canada 1986 World Juniors *in Hamilton*	7	7	7	14	6
Canada Totals	**14**	**9**	**10**	**19**	**8**

Junior Highlights

Won Gold Medal at World Junior Championships in 1985
Won Silver Medal at World Junior Championships in 1986
World Junior Championship All-Star Team in 1986

Around the Rink

Corson played his first year of Junior with the Brantford Alexanders in 1983-84, the team moved to Hamilton the following season. Traded to Edmonton by Montreal with Brent Gilchrist and Vladimir Vujtek for Vincent Damphousse and Edmonton's 4th round choice (Adam Wiesel) in 1993 Entry Draft, August 27, 1992. Signed as a free agent by St. Louis, July 28, 1995. Traded to Montreal by St. Louis with Murray Baron and St. Louis' 5th round choice (Gennady Razin) in 1997 Entry Draft for Pierre Turgeon, Rory Fitzpatrick and Craig Conroy, October 29, 1996. Signed as a free agent by Toronto, July 4, 2000. Resigned from the Toronto Maple Leafs, April 15, 2003.

Cote, Alain

Born: April 14, 1967 in Montmagny, Quebec
Drafted: By the Boston Bruins from the Quebec Remparts in 1985, 2nd round, 31st overall.

Career Junior, NHL and World Junior Statistics

	GP	G	A	PTS	PIM
QMJHL Regular Season 1983-87	193	23	78	101	446
QMJHL Playoffs	18	3	11	14	28
NHL Regular Season 1985-94	119	2	18	20	124
NHL Playoffs	11	0	2	2	26
Canada 1986 World Juniors *in Hamilton*	7	1	4	5	6

Junior Highlights

Won Silver Medal at World Junior Championships in 1986
World Junior Championships All-Star Team in 1986

Around the Rink

Cote played his first two seasons of junior with Quebec, at the end of 1984-85 the team folded and Cote ended up with the Granby Bisons. Traded to Washington by Boston for Bobby Gould, September 28, 1989. Traded to Montreal by Washington for Marc Deschamps, June 22, 1990. Traded to Tampa Bay by Montreal with Eric Charron and future considerations (Donald Dufresne, June 18, 1993) for Rob Ramage, March 20, 1993. Signed as a free agent by Quebec, July 2, 1993. From 1994-2002 Cote played in Slovenia, the IHL, Japan, Germany, Finland and the Quebec Senior league. He did not play in 2002-03.

Cote, Sylvain

Born: January 19, 1966 in Quebec City, Quebec
Drafted: By the Hartford Whalers from the Quebec Remparts in 1984, 1st round, 11th overall.

Career Junior, NHL and World Junior Statistics

	GP	G	A	PTS	PIM
QMJHL Regular Season 1982-86	158	35	107	142	153
QMJHL Playoffs	18	7	29	36	22
NHL Regular Season 1984-Present	1171	122	313	435	545
NHL Playoffs	102	11	22	33	62
Canada 1984 World Juniors *in Sweden*	7	0	2	2	13
Canada 1986 World Juniors *in Hamilton*	7	1	4	5	4
Canada Totals	**14**	**1**	**6**	**7**	**17**

Junior Highlights

QMJHL Second All-Star Team in 1984
Won Silver Medal at World Junior Championships in 1986
QMJHL First All-Star Team in 1986

Around the Rink

Cote played his first two years of junior from 1982-84 with Quebec, he spent the 1984-85 season with Hartford and after two games in 1985-86 Cote was returned to junior where the Hull Olympiques picked him up. He then returned to Hartford for the 186-87 season. Traded to Washington by Hartford for Washington's 2nd round choice (Andrei Nikolishin) in 1992 Entry Draft, September 8, 1991. Traded to Toronto by Washington for Jeff Brown, March 24, 1998. Traded to Chicago by Toronto for Chicago's 2nd round choice (Karel Pilar) in 2001 Entry Draft, October 8, 1999. Traded to Dallas by Chicago with Dave Manson for Kevin Dean, Derek Plante and Dallas' 2nd round choice (Matt Keith) in 2001 Entry Draft, February 8, 2000. Signed as a free agent by Washington, July 7, 2000. After one game of the 2002-2003 NHL season Cote was sent to Portland of the AHL, November 24, 2002.

Courteau, Yves

Born: April 25, 1964 in Montreal, Quebec
Drafted: By the Detroit Red Wings from the Laval Voisins in 1982, 2nd round, 23rd overall.

Career Junior, NHL and World Junior Statistics

	GP	G	A	PTS	PIM
QMJHL Regular Season 1980-84	264	143	230	373	199
QMJHL Playoffs	44	29	40	69	34
Memorial Cup 1984	3	2	3	5	0
NHL Regular Season 1984-87	22	2	5	7	4
NHL Playoffs	1	0	0	0	0
Canada 1984 World Juniors *in Sweden*	7	0	1	1	0

Junior Highlights

QMJHL Second All-Star Team in 1984
Recorded 120 Points in Just 62 Games in 1983-84

Around the Rink

Detroit traded Courteau's rights to Calgary for Bobby Francis, December 2, 1982. Traded to Hartford by Calgary for Mark Paterson, October 7, 1986. Suffered eventual career-ending stomach injury in training camp, October 1987.

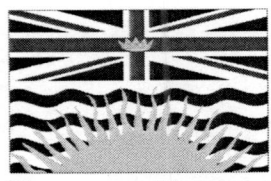

Courtnall, Russ

Born: June 2, 1965 in Duncan, B.C.
Drafted: By the Toronto Maple Leafs from the Victoria Cougars in 1983, 1st round, 7th overall.

Career Junior, NHL and World Junior Statistics

	GP	G	A	PTS	PIM
Canadian National Team 1983-84	23	5	10	15	12
WHL Regular Season 1982-84	92	65	98	163	96
WHL Playoffs	12	11	7	18	6
NHL Regular Season 1984-99	1029	297	447	744	557
NHL Playoffs	129	39	44	83	83
Canada 1984 World Juniors *in Sweden*	7	7	6	13	0

Junior Highlights

Played on Canadian Olympic Team in 1984

Around the Rink

Courtnall was dealt to Montreal by Toronto for John Kordic and Montreal's 6th round choice (Michael Doers) in 1989 Entry Draft, November 7, 1988. Traded to Minnesota by Montreal for Brian Bellows, August 31, 1992. Transferred to Dallas after Minnesota franchise relocated, June 9, 1993. Traded to Vancouver by Dallas for Greg Adams, Dan Kesa and Vancouver's 5th round choice (later traded to LA Kings LA Kings selected Jason Morgan) in 1995 Entry Draft, April 7, 1995. Traded to NY Rangers by Vancouver with Esa Tikkanen for Sergei Nemchinov and Brian Noonan, March 8, 1997. Signed as a free agent by LA Kings, November 7, 1997. Retired at the end of the 1999 season.

Courville, Larry

Born: April 2, 1975 in Timmins, Ontario
Drafted: By the Winnipeg Jets from the Newmarket Royals in 1993, 5th round, 119th overall. Re-Drafted by the Vancouver Canucks from the Oshawa Generals in 1995, 3rd round, 61st overall.

Career Junior, NHL and World Junior Statistics

	GP	G	A	PTS	PIM
OHL Regular Season 1991-95	207	83	88	171	525
OHL Playoffs	20	4	16	20	32
NHL Regular Season 1995-98	33	1	2	3	16
NHL Playoffs	0	0	0	0	0
Canada 1995 World Juniors *in Alberta*	7	2	3	5	6

Junior Highlights

Won Gold Medal at World Junior Championships in 1995
OHL Second All-Star Team in 1995

Around the Rink

Courville did not sign a contract with Winnipeg after being drafted by them, therefore he went back into the NHL draft and was selected by Vancouver. He played for four different OHL teams, Cornwall, Newmarket, Sarnia and Oshawa. Cornwall moved to Newmarket and Newmarket moved to Sarnia. He was traded to Oshawa from Sarnia after 16 games in 1984. Signed as a free agent by Kentucky (AHL), September 1, 1999. Signed as a free agent by San Jose, September 1, 2000 but never played a game, spending his time in the (AHL) with Hershey and Cincinnati.

Craig, Mike

Born: June 6, 1971 in London, Ontario
Drafted: By the Minnesota North Stars from the Oshawa Generals in 1989, 2nd round, 28th overall.

Career Junior, NHL and World Junior Statistics

	GP	G	A	PTS	PIM
OHL Regular Season 1987-90	167	78	86	164	164
OHL Playoffs	30	13	18	31	63
Memorial Cup 1990	3	5	4	9	10
NHL Regular Season 1990-2002	423	71	97	168	550
NHL Playoffs	26	2	2	4	49
Canada 1990 World Juniors *in Finland*	7	3	0	3	8
Canada 1991 World Juniors *in Saskatoon*	7	6	5	11	8
Canada Totals	**14**	**9**	**5**	**14**	**16**

Junior Highlights

Won Gold Medal at World Junior Championships in 1990 and 1991
Won Memorial Cup in 1990
World Junior Championships All-Star Team in 1991

Around the Rink

Craig transferred to Dallas after Minnesota franchise relocated, June 9, 1993. Signed as a free agent by Toronto, July 29, 1994. Signed as a free agent by San Jose, July 13, 1998. Signed as a free agent by Colorado, August 2, 2000. Signed as a free agent by San Jose, September 6, 2001. Signed as a free agent by SC Langnau (Swiss), May 1, 2002.

Craigwell, Dale

Born: April 24, 1971 in Toronto, Ontario
Drafted: By the San Jose Sharks from the Oshawa Generals in 1991, 10th round, 199th overall.

Career Junior, NHL and World Junior Statistics

	GP	G	A	PTS	PIM
OHL Regular Season 1988-91	175	58	123	181	88
OHL Playoffs	39	14	23	37	20
Memorial Cup 1990	4	1	5	6	0
NHL Regular Season 1991-94	98	11	18	29	28
NHL Playoffs	0	0	0	0	0
Canada 1991 World Juniors *in Saskatoon*	7	1	2	3	0

Junior Highlights

Won Memorial Cup in 1990
Won Gold Medal at World Junior Championships in 1991

Around the Rink

Craigwell missed the entire 1994-95 season recovering from ankle injury suffered during training camp, September 1994. Played in the IHL with San Francisco and Kansas City from 1995-99. Played in Europe from 1999-01. Retired in 2001.

Crawford, Marc

Born: February 13, 1961 in Belleville, Ontario
Drafted: By the Vancouver Canucks from the Cornwall Royals in 1980, 4th round, 70th overall.

Career Junior, NHL and World Junior Statistics

	GP	G	A	PTS	PIM
QMJHL Regular Season 1978-81	187	92	134	226	575
QMJHL Playoffs	37	28	35	63	75
Memorial Cup 1980 and 1981	10	3	7	10	6
NHL Regular Season 1981-87	176	19	31	50	229
NHL Playoffs	20	1	2	3	44
Canada 1981 World Juniors *in Germany*	5	1	3	4	4

Junior Highlights

Won Memorial Cup in 1980 and 1981
Memorial Cup All-Star Team in 1981

Around the Rink

Crawford never played a full NHL season, he travelled back and forth between the NHL and AHL for six years. Served as Player/Assistant Coach w/ Fredericton (AHL) in 1987-88 and w/ Milwaukee (IHL) in 1988-89. Since retiring from play in 1989, he has coached Cornwall, St. John's (AHL), Quebec/Colorado and currently Vancouver.

Creighton, Adam

Born: June 2, 1965 in Burlington, Ontario
Drafted: By the Buffalo Sabres from the Ottawa 67's in 1983, 1st round, 11th overall.

Career Junior, NHL and World Junior Statistics

	GP	G	A	PTS	PIM
OHL Regular Season 1981-85	194	105	136	241	263
OHL Playoffs	44	29	16	45	91
Memorial Cup 1984	5	5	7	12	15
NHL Regular Season 1983-97	708	187	216	403	1077
NHL Playoffs	61	11	14	25	137
Canada 1985 World Juniors *in Finland*	7	8	4	12	4

Junior Highlights

Memorial Cup All-Star Team in 1984
Won Stafford Smythe Memorial Trophy (Memorial Cup Tournament MVP) in 1984
Won Memorial Cup in 1984
Won Gold Medal at World Junior Championships in 1985

Around the Rink

Creighton was traded to Chicago by Buffalo for Rick Vaive, December 26, 1988. Traded to NY Islanders by Chicago with Steve Thomas for Brent Sutter and Brad Lauer, October 25, 1991. Claimed by Tampa Bay from NY Islanders in NHL Waiver Draft, October 4, 1992. Traded to St. Louis by Tampa Bay for Tom Tilley, October 6, 1994. Signed as a free agent by Chicago, October 9, 1996. Retired in 1999 after playing two seasons in Germany.

Crossman, Doug

Born: June 30, 1960 in Peterborough, Ontario
Drafted: By the Chicago Black Hawks from the Ottawa 67's in 1979, 6th round, 112th overall.

Career Junior, NHL and World Junior Statistics

	GP	G	A	PTS	PIM
OHL Regular Season 1976-80	199	36	164	200	128
OHL Playoffs	31	10	20	30	29
NHL Regular Season 1980-94	914	105	359	464	534
NHL Playoffs	97	12	39	51	105
Canada 1980 World Juniors *in Finland*	5	0	2	2	2

Junior Highlights

OHL First All-Star Team in 1980

Around the Rink

Crossman played one game for the London Knights in 1976-77, he was called up as an undrafted player from the Knights midget affiliate the Strathroy Blades of the Ontario Minor Hockey Association. In June of 1977 Crossman was drafted by the Ottawa 67's. Traded to Philadelphia by Chicago with Chicago's 2nd round choice (Scott Mellanby) in 1984 Entry Draft for Behn Wilson, June 8, 1983. Traded to LA Kings by Philadelphia for Jay Wells, September 29, 1988. Traded to NY Islanders by LA Kings to complete transaction that sent Mark Fitzpatrick and Wayne McBean to NY Islanders (February 22, 1989), May 23, 1989. Traded to Hartford by NY Islanders for Ray Ferraro, November 13, 1990. Traded to Detroit by Hartford for Doug Houda, February 20, 1991. Traded to Quebec by Detroit with Dennis Vial for cash, June 15, 1992. Claimed by Tampa Bay from Quebec in Expansion Draft, June 18, 1992. Traded to St. Louis by Tampa Bay with Basil McRae and Tampa Bay's 4th round choice (Andrei Petrakov) in 1996 Entry Draft for Jason Ruff, January 28, 1993. Retired in 1996 after playing two seasons in the minors with Peoria (IHL), Denver (IHL), Baltimore (AHL) and Chicago (IHL).

Cullimore, Jassen

Born: December 4, 1972 in Simcoe, Ontario
Drafted: By the Vancouver Canucks from the Peterborough Petes in 1991, 2nd round, 29th overall.

Career Junior, NHL and World Junior Statistics

	GP	G	A	PTS	PIM
OHL Regular Season 1988-92	195	21	60	81	210
OHL Playoffs	27	4	8	12	23
NHL Regular Season 1994-Present	445	17	42	59	446
NHL Playoffs	19	0	1	1	16
Canada 1992 World Juniors *in Germany*	7	1	0	1	2

Junior Highlights

OHL Second All-Star Team in 1992

Around the Rink

Cullimore was traded to Montreal by Vancouver for Donald Brashear, November 13, 1996. Claimed on waivers by Tampa Bay from Montreal, January 22, 1998. Loaned to Providence (AHL) by Tampa Bay, October 1, 1999.

Currie, Dan

Born: March 15, 1968 in Burlington, Ontario
Drafted: By the Edmonton Oilers from the Sault Ste. Marie Greyhounds in 1986, 4th round, 84th overall.

Career Junior, NHL and World Junior Statistics

	GP	G	A	PTS	PIM
OHL Regular Season 1985-88	189	102	133	235	143
OHL Playoffs	10	5	10	15	6
NHL Regular Season 1990-94	22	2	1	3	4
NHL Playoffs	0	0	0	0	0
Canada 1988 World Juniors *in Russia*	7	4	3	7	2

Junior Highlights

Won Gold Medal at World Junior Championships in 1988
OHL First All-Star Team in 1988

Around the Rink

Currie signed as a free agent by LA Kings, July 16, 1993. Played in the IHL from 1993 to 1998 and has played in Europe since 1998. Signed as a free agent by Hull Thunder (Britain), May 23, 2002.

Cyr, Denis

Born: February 4, 1961 in Verdun, Quebec
Drafted: By the Calgary Flames from the Montreal Juniors in 1980, 1st round, 13th overall.

Career Junior, NHL and World Junior Statistics

	GP	G	A	PTS	PIM
QMJHL Regular Season 1977-81	271	236	227	463	200
QMJHL Playoffs	28	23	24	47	69
NHL Regular Season 1980-86	193	41	43	84	36
NHL Playoffs	4	0	0	0	0
Canada 1981 World Juniors *in Germany*	5	2	1	3	0

Junior Highlights

QMJHL Second All-Star Team in 1979
QMJHL First All-Star Team in 1980

Around the Rink

Cyr was traded to Chicago by Calgary for the rights to Carey Wilson, November 8, 1982. Signed as a free agent by St. Louis, September 14, 1984. Retired from playing in 1987 after a full season in the minors with Peoria (IHL).

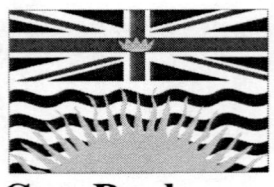

Cyr, Paul

Born: October 31, 1963 in Port Alberni, B.C.
Drafted: By the Buffalo Sabres from the Victoria Cougars in 1982, 1st round, 9th overall.

Career Junior, NHL and World Junior Statistics

	GP	G	A	PTS	PIM
WHL Regular Season 1979-83	142	109	100	209	313
WHL Playoffs	25	9	7	16	62
Memorial Cup 1981	4	2	3	5	6
NHL Regular Season 1982-92	470	101	140	241	623
NHL Playoffs	24	4	6	10	31
Canada 1982 World Juniors *in United States*	7	4	6	10	12
Canada 1983 World Juniors *in Russia*	7	1	3	4	19
Canada Totals	**14**	**5**	**9**	**14**	**31**

Junior Highlights

Won Gold Medal at World Junior Championships in 1982
WHL Second All-Star Team in 1982
Won Bronze Medal at World Junior Championships in 1983

Around the Rink

Cyr was traded to NY Rangers by Buffalo with Buffalo's 10th round choice (Eric Fenton) in 1988 Entry Draft for Mike Donnelly and NY Rangers' 5th round choice (Alexander Mogilny) in 1988 Entry Draft, December 31, 1987. Missed majority of 1988-89 season and entire 1989-90 season recovering from knee surgery. Signed as a free agent by Hartford, September 30, 1990. Retired in 1993 after a full season in the minors with Springfield (AHL).

Daigle, Alexandre

Born: February 7, 1975 in Montreal, Quebec
Drafted: By the Ottawa Senators from the Victoriaville Tigres in 1993, 1st round, 1st overall.

Career Junior, NHL and World Junior Statistics

	GP	G	A	PTS	PIM
QMJHL Regular Season 1991-95	134	94	187	281	164
QMJHL Playoffs	19	10	15	25	27
NHL Regular Season 1993-Present	492	104	144	248	160
NHL Playoffs	12	0	2	2	2
Canada 1993 World Juniors *in Sweden*	7	0	6	6	27
Canada 1995 World Juniors *in Alberta*	7	2	8	10	4
Canada Totals	**14**	**2**	**14**	**16**	**31**

Junior Highlights

QMJHL Second All-Star Team in 1992
QMJHL Offensive Rookie of the Year in 1992
Canadian Major Junior Rookie of the Year in 1992
Won Gold Medal at World Junior Championships in 1993
QMJHL First All-Star Team in 1993
Won Gold Medal at World Junior Championships in 1995

Around the Rink

Daigle played the entire 1993-94 season with Ottawa (NHL), he returned to Junior in 1994-95 during the NHL lockout. Traded to Philadelphia by Ottawa for Vaclav Prospal, Pat Falloon and Dallas' 2nd round choice (previously acquired, Ottawa selected Chris Bala) in 1998 Entry Draft, January 17, 1998. Traded to Edmonton by Philadelphia for Andrei Kovalenko, January 29, 1999. Traded to Tampa Bay by Edmonton for Alexander Selivanov, January 29, 1999. Traded to NY Rangers by Tampa Bay for cash, October 3, 1999. Retired and did not play from 2000-2002. Signed to a free agent tryout contract by Pittsburgh, August 13, 2002.

Daigneault, J.J.

Born: October 12, 1965 in Montreal, Quebec
Drafted: By the Vancouver Canucks from the Longeuil Chevaliers in 1984, 1st round, 10th overall.

Career Junior, NHL and World Junior Statistics

	GP	G	A	PTS	PIM
QMJHL Regular Season 1981-84	144	32	94	126	105
QMJHL Playoffs	47	8	27	35	67
NHL Regular Season 1984-2001	899	53	197	250	687
NHL Playoffs	99	5	26	31	100
Canada 1984 World Juniors *in Sweden*	7	0	2	2	2

Junior Highlights

QMJHL First All-Star Team 1983

Around the Rink

Daigneault played his first season of Junior with Laval in 1981-82, he was traded to Longeuil during the summer of 1982. Traded to Philadelphia by Vancouver with Vancouver's 2nd round choice (Kent Hawley) in 1986 Entry Draft and 5th round choice (later traded back to Vancouver - Vancouver selected Sean Fabian) in 1987 Entry Draft for Dave Richter, Rich Sutter and Vancouver's 3rd round choice (previously acquired, Vancouver selected Don Gibson) in 1986 Entry Draft, June 6, 1986. Traded to Montreal by Philadelphia for Scott Sandelin, November 7, 1988. Traded to St. Louis by Montreal for Pat Jablonski, November 7, 1995. Traded to Pittsburgh by St. Louis for Pittsburgh's 6th round choice (Stephen Wagner) in 1996 Entry Draft, March 20, 1996. Traded to Anaheim by Pittsburgh for Garry Valk, February 21, 1997. Traded to NY Islanders by Anaheim with Joe Sacco and Mark Janssens for Travis Green, Doug Houda and Tony Tuzzolino, February 6, 1998. Claimed by Nashville from NY Islanders in Expansion Draft, June 26, 1998. Traded to Phoenix by Nashville for future considerations, January 13, 1999. Signed as a free agent by Minnesota, July 24, 2000 but only played one game as he spent most of the season with Cleveland (IHL). Played 2001-02 in Switzerland and retired at the end of the season.

Daley, Pat

Born: March 27, 1959 In Maryville, France – Raised In Quebec
Drafted: By the Winnipeg Jets from the Laval Nationals in 1979, 4th round, 82nd overall.

Career Junior, NHL and World Junior Statistics

	GP	G	A	PTS	PIM
QMJHL Regular Season 1975-79	269	100	173	273	495
QMJHL Playoffs	0	0	0	0	0
NHL Regular Season 1979-81	12	1	0	1	13
NHL Playoffs	0	0	0	0	0
Canada 1978 World Juniors *in Montreal*	6	3	2	5	2

Junior Highlights

Won Bronze Medal at World Junior Championships in 1978
QMJHL First All-Star Team in 1978

Around the Rink

Daley was traded from Laval to Montreal after the 1977-78 season. Played all twelve NHL games with Winnipeg. Signed as a free agent by Quebec, July 1981 but never played game for the Nordiques as he spent the season in Fredericton (AHL). Played in France from 1982-94 and then retired from playing.

Daniels, Kimbi

Born: January 19, 1975 in Brandon, Manitoba
Drafted: By the Philadelphia Flyers from the Swift Current Broncos in 1990, 3rd round, 44th overall.

Career Junior, NHL and World Junior Statistics

	GP	G	A	PTS	PIM
WHL Regular Season 1988-93	234	143	172	315	345
WHL Playoffs	34	16	21	37	55
Memorial Cup 1989	5	5	1	6	8
NHL Regular Season 1990-92	27	1	2	3	4
NHL Playoffs	0	0	0	0	0
Canada 1992 World Juniors *in Germany*	7	3	4	7	16

Junior Highlights

Won Memorial Cup in 1989

Around the Rink

Daniels played his first three Junior seasons with Swift Current, he was traded to Seattle during the summer of 1992. Returned to Seattle (WHL) by Philadelphia, January 24, 1992. Traded to Tri-City (WHL) summer of 1993. Traded to Quebec (AHL) by Hamilton (AHL) for cash, December 12, 1999. Currently plays in the West Coast Hockey League with Anchorage.

Dawe, Jason

Born: May 29, 1973 in North York Ontario
Drafted: By the Buffalo Sabres from the Peterborough Petes in 1991, 2nd round, 35th overall.

Career Junior, NHL and World Junior Statistics

	GP	G	A	PTS	PIM
OHL Regular Season 1989-93	241	169	168	337	337
OHL Playoffs	39	30	41	71	22
Memorial Cup 1993	5	3	6	9	4
NHL Regular Season 1993-2002	366	86	90	176	162
NHL Playoffs	22	4	3	7	18
Canada 1993 World Juniors *in Sweden*	7	3	3	6	8

Junior Highlights

OHL First All-Star Team in 1993
Canadian Major Junior Second All-Star Team in 1993
Won Gold Medal at World Junior Championships in 1993
Won George Parsons Trophy (Memorial Cup Most Sportsmanlike Player) in 1993

Around the Rink

Traded to NY Islanders by Buffalo for Jason Holland and Paul Kruse, March 24, 1998. Claimed on waivers by Montreal from NY Islanders, December 15, 1998. Signed as a free agent by Nashville, October 2, 1999. Traded to NY Rangers by Nashville for John Namestnikov, February 3, 2000. Missed majority of 2000-01 season recovering from ankle injury originally suffered in game vs. Springfield (AHL), October 6, 2000. Signed as a free agent by St. Louis, July 23, 2002 but played the entire season with Worcester (AHL).

Daze, Eric

Born: July 2, 1975 in Montreal, Quebec
Drafted: By the Chicago Black Hawks from the Beauport Harfangs in 1993, 4th round, 90th overall.

Career Junior, NHL and World Junior Statistics

	GP	G	A	PTS	PIM
QMJHL Regular Season 1992-95	191	132	129	261	75
QMJHL Playoffs	31	25	20	45	25
NHL Regular Season 1995-Present	581	222	165	387	174
NHL Playoffs	37	5	7	12	8
Canada 1995 World Juniors *in Alberta*	7	8	2	10	0

Junior Highlights

QMJHL First All-Star Team in 1994 and 1995
Won Gold Medal at World Junior Championships in 1995
World Junior Championships All-Star Team in 1995
Canadian Major Junior Most Sportsmanlike Player of the Year in 1995

Around the Rink

Daze made his NHL debut April 27, 1995. Scored his first NHL goal on April 30, 1995 beating Detroit goalie Mike Vernon. Those games were in regular season as the season was extended due to the NHL lockout at the start of the 1994 season. Made Chicago full time in 1995-96, never played a game in the minors.

Delorme, Gilbert

Born: November 25, 1962 in Boucherville, Quebec
Drafted: By the Montreal Canadiens from the Chicoutimi Sagueneens in 1981, 1st round, 18th overall.

Career Junior, NHL and World Junior Statistics

	GP	G	A	PTS	PIM
QMJHL Regular Season 1978-81	213	65	212	277	198
QMJHL Playoffs	24	12	22	34	42
NHL Regular Season 1981-90	541	31	92	123	520
NHL Playoffs	56	1	9	10	56
Canada 1981 World Juniors *in Germany*	5	1	0	1	0

Junior Highlights

QMJHL Second All-Star Team in 1981

Around the Rink

Delorme was traded to St. Louis by Montreal with Greg Paslawski and Doug Wickenheiser for Perry Turnbull, December 21, 1983. Traded to Quebec by St. Louis for Bruce Bell, October 2, 1985. Traded to Detroit by Quebec with Brent Ashton and Mark Kumpel for Basil McRae, John Ogrodnick and Doug Shedden, January 17, 1987. Signed as a free agent by Pittsburgh, June 28, 1989. Missed entire 1990-91 season recovering from broken leg suffered during dryland training, July 1990. Played in the professional Roller Hockey League with the Montreal Roadrunners in 1996 (1-0-0-0-1). Assistant coach with Cleveland (IHL) 1992-94, Manitoba (IHL) 1998-99 and Montreal Rocket (QMJHL) 2000-02.

Denis, Marc

Born: August 1, 1977 in Montreal, Quebec
Drafted: By the Colorado Avalanche from the Chicoutimi Sagueneens in 1995, 1st round, 25th overall.

Career Junior, NHL and World Junior Statistics

	GP	W	L	T	SO	AVG
QMJHL Regular Season 1994-97	124	62	45	7	6	3.09
QMJHL Playoffs	43	23	20	0	2	3.70
Memorial Cup in 1997	3	0	3	0	0	5.02
NHL Regular Season 1996-Present	179	52	95	21	9	3.04
NHL Playoffs	0	0	0	0	0	0.00
Canada 1996 World Juniors *in U.S.A.*	2	2	0	0	0	1.00
Canada 1997 World Juniors *in Switzerland*	7	5	0	2	1	1.86
Canada Totals	**9**	**7**	**0**	**2**	**1**	**1.67**

Junior Highlights

Won Gold Medal at World Junior Championships in 1996 and 1997
Named Best Goaltender at World Junior Championships in 1997
QMJHL First All-Star Team in 1997
Canadian Major Junior First All-Star Team in 1997
Canadian Major Junior Goaltender of the Year in 1997

Around the Rink

Denis made his NHL debut on December 7, 1996 for Colorado. Traded to Columbus by Colorado for Columbus' 2nd round choice (later traded to Carolina - Carolina selected Tomas Kurka) in 2000 Entry Draft, June 7, 2000.

DeRouville, Philippe

Born: August 7, 1974 in Victoriaville, Quebec
Drafted: By the Pittsburgh Penguins from Verdun College-Francais in 1992, 5th round, 115th overall.

Career Junior, NHL and World Junior Statistics

	GP	W	L	T	SO	AVG
QMJHL Regular Season 1990-94	166	91	61	5	4	3.27
QMJHL Playoffs	19	7	10	0	1	3.39
NHL Regular Season 1994-97	3	1	2	0	0	3.15
NHL Playoffs	0	0	0	0	0	0.00
Canada 1993 World Juniors *in Sweden*	1	0	1	0	0	7.00

Junior Highlights

QMJHL Defensive Rookie of the Year in 1992
Won Gold Medal at World Junior Championships in 1993
QMJHL Second All-Star Team in 1993 and 1994

Around the Rink

DeRouville played all three of his NHL games with Pittsburgh. He played over 160 games in the minor leagues from 1994-99. Played in Europe from 1999-2001 and finished the 2002 season in the Quebec Senior Pro Hockey League.

Desjardins, Eric

Born: June 14, 1969 in Rouyn-Noranda, Quebec
Drafted: By the Montreal Canadiens from the Granby Bisons in 1987, 2nd round, 38th overall.

Career Junior, NHL and World Junior Statistics

	GP	G	A	PTS	PIM
QMJHL Regular Season 1986-88	128	32	73	105	316
QMJHL Playoffs	13	3	5	8	20
NHL Regular Season 1988-Present	1050	131	408	539	673
NHL Playoffs	162	22	54	76	87
Canada 1988 World Juniors *in Russia*	7	0	0	0	6
Canada 1989 World Juniors *in United States*	7	1	4	5	6
Canada Totals	**14**	**1**	**4**	**5**	**12**

Junior Highlights

QMJHL Second All-Star Team in 1987
Won Gold Medal at World Junior Championships in 1988
QMJHL First All-Star Team in 1988

Around the Rink

Desjardins only played three games in the minors, 1987-88 Sherbrooke (AHL). Traded to Philadelphia by Montreal with Gilbert Dionne and John LeClair for Mark Recchi and Philadelphia's 3rd round choice (Martin Hohenberger) in 1995 Entry Draft, February 9, 1995.

Devereaux, Boyd

Born: April 16, 1978 in Seaforth, Ontario
Drafted: By the Edmonton Oilers from the Kitchener Rangers in 1996, 1st round, 6th overall.

Career Junior, NHL and World Junior Statistics

	GP	G	A	PTS	PIM
OHL Regular Season 1995-97	120	48	79	127	70
OHL Playoffs	25	7	18	28	12
NHL Regular Season 1997-Present	370	32	62	94	103
NHL Playoffs	24	2	4	6	4
Canada 1997 World Juniors *in Switzerland*	7	4	0	4	0

Junior Highlights

Canadian Major Junior Scholastic Player of the Year in 1996
Won Gold Medal at World Junior Championships in 1997

Around the Rink

Devereaux played his first NHL game on October 5, 1997 against Colorado. Scored his first NHL goal January 20, 1998 against Phoenix. Signed as a free agent by Detroit, August 23, 2000. Scored first goal as a Red Wing October 31, 2000 against Washington.

Diduck, Gerald

Born: April 6, 1965 in Edmonton, Alberta
Drafted: By the New York Islanders from the Lethbridge Broncos in 1983, 1st round, 16th overall.

Career Junior, NHL and World Junior Statistics

	GP	G	A	PTS	PIM
WHL Regular Season 1981-84	203	19	55	74	365
WHL Playoffs	37	4	19	23	106
Memorial Cup 1983	3	0	1	1	2
NHL Regular Season 1985-2001	932	56	156	212	1612
NHL Playoffs	114	8	16	24	212
Canada 1984 World Juniors *in Sweden*	7	0	0	0	4

Junior Highlights

Won Western Hockey League Championship in 1983

Around the Rink

Diduck was traded to Montreal by NY Islanders for Craig Ludwig, September 4, 1990. Traded to Vancouver by Montreal for Vancouver's 4th round choice (Vladimir Vujtek) in 1991 Entry Draft, January 12, 1991. Traded to Chicago by Vancouver for Bogdan Savenko and Hartford's 3rd round choice (previously acquired, Vancouver selected Larry Courville) in 1995 Entry Draft, April 7, 1995. Signed as a free agent by Hartford, August 24, 1995. Traded to Phoenix by Hartford for Chris Murray, March 18, 1997. Signed as a free agent by Toronto, February 3, 2000. Traded to Dallas by Toronto for future considerations, October 29, 2000. Missed majority of 2000-01 season recovering from ankle injury suffered in game vs. San Jose, December 6, 2000. Retired at the end of the 2000-2001 season.

DiMaio, Rob

Born: February 19, 1968 in Calgary, Alberta
Drafted: By the New York Islanders from the Medicine Hat Tigers in 1987, 6th round, 118th overall.

Career Junior, NHL and World Junior Statistics

	GP	G	A	PTS	PIM
WHL Regular Season 1984-88	240	104	135	239	361
WHL Playoffs	63	26	39	65	146
Memorial Cup 1987 and 1988	10	8	6	14	38
NHL Regular Season 1988-Present	764	93	143	236	758
NHL Playoffs	50	6	5	11	32
Canada 1988 World Juniors *in Russia*	7	1	0	1	10

Junior Highlights

Won Memorial Cup in 1987 and 1988
Won Gold Medal at World Junior Championships in 1988
Won Stafford Smythe Memorial Trophy (Memorial Cup Tournament MVP) in 1988

Around the Rink

DiMaio was traded after six games in 1985 from Kamloops to Medicine Hat. Claimed by Tampa Bay from NY Islanders in Expansion Draft, June 18, 1992. Traded to Philadelphia by Tampa Bay for Jim Cummins and Philadelphia's 4th round choice (later traded back to Philadelphia - Philadelphia selected Radovan Somik) in 1995 Entry Draft, March 18, 1994. Claimed by San Jose from Philadelphia in NHL Waiver Draft, September 30, 1996. Traded to Boston by San Jose for Boston's 5th round choice (Adam Nittel) in 1997 Entry Draft, September 30, 1996. Traded to NY Rangers by Boston for Mike Knuble, March 10, 2000. Traded to Carolina by NY Rangers with Darren Langdon for Sandy McCarthy and Carolina's 4th round choice (Bryce Lampman) in 2001 Entry Draft, August 4, 2000. Signed as a free agent by Dallas, July 1, 2001.

Doig, Jason

Born: January 29, 1977 in Montreal, Quebec
Drafted: By the Winnipeg Jets from the Laval Titans in 1995, 2nd round, 34th overall.

Career Junior, NHL and World Junior Statistics

	GP	G	A	PTS	PIM
QMJHL Regular Season 1993-97	186	42	128	160	646
QMJHL Playoffs	50	19	42	61	167
Memorial Cup 1996	4	3	2	5	10
NHL Regular Season 1995-Present	93	4	9	13	180
NHL Playoffs	6	0	1	1	6
Canada 1997 World Juniors *in Switzerland*	7	0	2	2	37

Junior Highlights

QMJHL All-Rookie Team in 1994
Won Memorial Cup in 1996
Memorial Cup All-Star Team in 1996
Won Gold Medal at World Junior Championships in 1997

Around the Rink

Doig was traded to Granby after five games in 1995-96. Transferred to Phoenix after Winnipeg franchise relocated July 1, 1996. Traded to NY Rangers by Phoenix with Phoenix's 6th round choice (Jay Dardis) in 1999 Entry Draft for Stan Neckar, March 23, 1999. Traded to Ottawa by NY Rangers with Jeff Ulmer for Sean Gagnon, June 29, 2001 but never played a game for the Senators as he spent the entire 2001-02 with Grand Rapids (AHL). Signed as a free agent with Washington September 13, 2002.

Dollas, Bobby

Born: January 31, 1965 in Montreal, Quebec
Drafted: By the Winnipeg Jets from the Laval Voisins in 1983, 1st round, 14th overall.

Career Junior, NHL and World Junior Statistics

	GP	G	A	PTS	PIM
QMJHL Regular Season 1982-84	117	28	78	106	224
QMJHL Playoffs	25	6	13	19	46
Memorial Cup 1984	3	0	1	1	7
NHL Regular Season 1983-2001	646	42	96	138	467
NHL Playoffs	47	2	1	3	41
Canada 1985 World Juniors *in Finland*	7	0	2	2	12

Junior Highlights

QMJHL Second All-Star Team in 1983
QMJHL Defensive Rookie of the Year in 1983
Won Gold Medal at World Junior Championships in 1985
World Junior Championships All-Star Team in 1985

Around the Rink

Dollas was traded to Quebec by Winnipeg for Stu Kulak, December 17, 1987. Signed as a free agent by Detroit, October 18, 1990. Claimed by Anaheim from Detroit in Expansion Draft, June 24, 1993. Traded to Edmonton by Anaheim for Drew Bannister, January 9, 1998. Traded to Pittsburgh by Edmonton with Tony Hrkac for Josef Beranek, June 16, 1998. Signed as a free agent by Long Beach, October 12, 1999. Signed as a free agent by Ottawa, November 9, 1999. Claimed on waivers by Calgary from Ottawa, November 11, 1999. Signed as a free agent by San Jose, November 4, 2000. Traded to Pittsburgh by San Jose with Johan Hedberg for Jeff Norton, March 12, 2001. Signed as a free agent by Laval (QSPHL), January 22, 2002.

Domenichelli, Hnat

Born: February 16, 1976 in Edmonton, Alberta
Drafted: By the Hartford Whalers from the Kamloops Blazers in 1994, 4th round, 83rd overall.

Career Junior, NHL and World Junior Statistics

	GP	G	A	PTS	PIM
WHL Regular Season 1992-96	248	150	199	349	117
WHL Playoffs	65	27	31	58	40
Memorial Cup 1994 and 1995	8	4	3	7	6
NHL Regular Season 1996-Present	267	52	61	113	104
NHL Playoffs	0	0	0	0	0
Canada 1996 World Juniors *in United States*	6	2	3	5	6

Junior Highlights

Won Memorial Cup in 1994 and 1995
WHL West Second All-Star Team in 1995
WHL West First All-Star Team in 1996
Canadian Major Junior First All-Star Team in 1996
Canadian Major Junior Most Sportsmanlike Player of the Year in 1996
Won Gold Medal at World Junior Championships in 1996

Around the Rink

Domenichelli was traded to Calgary by Hartford with Glen Featherstone, New Jersey's 2nd round choice (previously acquired, Calgary selected Dimitri Kokorev) in 1997 Entry Draft and Vancouver's 3rd round choice (previously acquired, Calgary selected Paul Manning) in 1998 Entry Draft for Steve Chiasson and Colorado's 3rd round choice (previously acquired, Carolina selected Francis Lessard) in 1997 Entry Draft, March 5, 1997. Traded to Atlanta by Calgary with Dmitri Vlasenkov for Darryl Shannon and Jason Botterill, February 11, 2000. Traded to Minnesota by Atlanta for Andy Sutton, January 22, 2002.

Donovan, Shean

Born: January 22, 1975 in Timmins, Ontario
Drafted: By the San Jose Sharks from the Ottawa 67's in 1993, 2nd round, 28th overall.

Career Junior, NHL and World Junior Statistics

	GP	G	A	PTS	PIM
OHL Regular Season 1991-95	215	97	99	196	151
OHL Playoffs	28	11	11	22	19
NHL Regular Season 1996-Present	536	67	68	135	348
NHL Playoffs	12	0	1	1	8
Canada 1995 World Juniors *in Alberta*	7	0	0	0	6

Junior Highlights

Won Gold Medal at World Junior Championships in 1995

Around the Rink

Donovan was traded to Colorado by San Jose with San Jose's 1st round choice (Alex Tanguay) in 1998 Entry Draft for Mike Ricci and Colorado's 2nd round choice (later traded to Buffalo - Buffalo selected Jaroslav Kristek), in 1998 Entry Draft, November 21, 1997. Traded to Atlanta by Colorado for Rick Tabaracci, December 8, 1999. Claimed on waivers by Pittsburgh from Atlanta, March 15, 2002. Traded to Calgary by Pittsburgh for Micki Dupont and Mathias Johansson, March 11, 2003.

Douris, Peter

Born: February 19, 1966 in Toronto, Ontario
Drafted: By the Winnipeg Jets from the University of New Hampshire in 1984, 2nd overall, 30th overall.

Career Junior, NHL and World Junior Statistics

	GP	G	A	PTS	PIM
NCAA 1983-85	80	46	39	85	48
NHL Regular Season 1985-98	321	54	67	121	80
NHL Playoffs	27	3	5	8	11
Canada 1986 World Juniors *in Hamilton*	7	4	2	6	6

Junior Highlights

Won Silver Medal at World Junior Championships in 1986

Around the Rink

Douris was traded to St. Louis by Winnipeg for Kent Carlson, St. Louis' 12th round choice (Sergei Kharin) in 1989 Entry Draft and 4th round choice (Scott Levins) in 1990 Entry Draft, September 29, 1988. Signed as a free agent by Boston, June 27, 1989. Signed as a free agent by Anaheim, July 22, 1993. Signed as a free agent by Dallas, July 16, 1997 but only played one game. Has played in Europe since 1998-99.

Draper, Kris

Born: May 24, 1971 in Toronto, Ontario
Drafted: By the Winnipeg Jets from the Canadian National Team in 1989, 3rd round, 62nd overall.

Career Junior, NHL and World Junior Statistics

	GP	G	A	PTS	PIM
Canadian National Team 1988-90	122	23	37	60	60
OHL Regular Season 1990-91	39	19	42	61	35
OHL Playoffs	17	8	11	19	20
NHL Regular Season 1990-Present	657	84	112	196	495
NHL Playoffs	136	17	17	34	96
Canada 1990 World Juniors *in Finland*	7	0	2	2	4
Canada 1991 World Juniors *in Saskatoon*	7	1	3	4	0
Canada Totals	**14**	**1**	**5**	**6**	**4**

Junior Highlights

Won Gold Medal at World Junior Championships in 1990 and 1991

Around the Rink

Draper left bantam hockey in 1988 to join the Canadian National Team instead of playing major junior hockey. After two seasons and a World Junior Championship appearance Draper played a season with the Ottawa 67`s. Traded to Detroit by Winnipeg for future considerations, June 30, 1993.

Druken, Harold

Born: January 26, 1979 in St. John`s, Newfoundland
Drafted: By the Vancouver Canucks from the Plymouth Whalers in 1997, 2nd round, 36th overall.

Career Junior, NHL and World Junior Statistics

	GP	G	A	PTS	PIM
OHL Regular Season 1996-99	187	123	120	243	60
OHL Playoffs	31	21	25	46	78
NHL Regular Season 1999-Present	131	27	31	58	32
NHL Playoffs	4	0	1	1	0
Canada 1999 World Juniors *in Winnipeg*	7	1	1	2	2

Junior Highlights

OHL All-Rookie Team in 1997
Won Silver Medal at World Junior Championships in 1999
OHL Second All-Star Team in 1999

Around the Rink

Druken played his first year of junior in 1996-97 with the Detroit Whalers, the team moved to Plymouth for the 1997-98 season. Missed majority of 2001-02 season recovering from ankle injury suffered in game vs. Dallas, December 2, 2001. Traded by Vancouver to Carolina with Jan Hlavac for Marik Malik and Darren Langdon, November 1, 2002. Claimed off waivers by Toronto from Carolina December 11, 2002. Claimed off waivers by Carolina from Toronto January 17, 2003.

Dube, Christian

Born: April 25, 1977 in Sherbrooke, Quebec
Drafted: By the New York Rangers from the Sherbrooke Faucons in 1995, 2nd round, 39th overall.

Career Junior, NHL and World Junior Statistics

	GP	G	A	PTS	PIM
QMJHL Regular Season 1993-97	224	134	221	355	197
QMJHL Playoffs	39	16	30	46	36
Memorial Cup 1997	4	6	7	13	2
NHL Regular Season 1996-1999	33	1	1	2	4
NHL Playoffs	3	0	0	0	0
Canada 1996 World Juniors *in United States*	6	4	2	6	0
Canada 1997 World Juniors *in Switzerland*	7	4	3	7	0
Canada Totals	**13**	**8**	**5**	**13**	**0**

Junior Highlights

QMJHL All-Rookie Team in 1994
QMJHL Offensive Rookie of the Year in 1994
Won Gold Medal at World Junior Championships in 1996 and 1997
QMJHL First All-Star Team in 1996
QMJHL MVP in 1996
Canadian Major Junior First All-Star Team in 1996
Canadian Major Junior Player of the Year in 1996
World Junior Championships All-Star Team in 1997
Won Memorial Cup in 1997
Won Stafford Smythe Memorial Trophy (Memorial Cup MVP) in 1997

Around the Rink

Dube was traded by Sherbrooke to Hull in the summer of 1996. Played all NHL games with the New York Rangers and spent considerable time with their farm team in Hartford. Signed as a free agent with Lugano in the Swiss league in 1999.

Duguay, Ron

Born: July 6, 1957 in Sudbury, Ontario
Drafted: By the New York Rangers from the Sudbury Wolves in 1977, 1st round, 13th overall. Also Drafted by the Winnipeg Jets (WHA), 1st round, 3rd overall.

Career Junior, NHL and World Junior Statistics

	GP	G	A	PTS	PIM
OHL Regular Season 1973-77	245	131	230	361	326
OHL Playoffs	42	26	21	47	65
NHL Regular Season 1977-89	864	274	346	620	582
NHL Playoffs	89	31	22	53	118
Canada 1977 World Juniors *in Czech Republic*	5	1	4	5	11

Junior Highlights

Won Silver Medal at World Junior Championships in 1977

Around the Rink

Duguay was traded to Detroit by NY Rangers with Eddie Mio and Eddie Johnstone for Willie Huber, Mark Osborne and Mike Blaisdell, June 13, 1983. Traded to Pittsburgh by Detroit for Doug Shedden, March 11, 1986. Traded to NY Rangers by Pittsburgh for Chris Kontos, January 21, 1987. Traded to LA Kings by NY Rangers for Mark Hardy, February 23, 1988. Signed with Manheim of the German league in 1989. Played from 1990-92 with San Diego of the (IHL), retired at the end of the season. Made a comeback with San Diego from 1995-98. Played one game for Jacksonville (ECHL) in 1998-99 and retired again. Came out of retirement once more in 2002-03 and played six games with Jacksonville (ACHL) and recorded four points, but retired for a third time to become the Head Coach of Jacksonville.

Dumont, J.P.

Born: April 1, 1978 in Montreal, Quebec
Drafted: By the New York Islanders from the Val d`Or Foreurs in 1996, 1st round, 3rd overall.

Career Junior, NHL and World Junior Statistics

	GP	G	A	PTS	PIM
QMJHL Regular Season 1994-98	231	154	177	321	284
QMJHL Playoffs	45	52	30	82	52
Memorial Cup 1998	3	3	2	5	4
NHL Regular Season 1998-Present	303	79	84	163	168
NHL Playoffs	13	4	3	7	8
Canada 1998 World Juniors *in Finland*	7	0	0	0	0

Junior Highlights

QMJHL Second All-Star Team in 1997
Scored a Total of 91 Goals in 77 Games in 1997-98

Around the Rink

Dumont`s rights traded to Chicago by NY Islanders with Chicago's 5th round choice (later traded to Philadelphia - Philadelphia selected Francis Belanger) in 1998 Entry Draft for Dmitri Nabokov, May 30, 1998. Traded to Buffalo by Chicago with Doug Gilmour for Michal Grosek, March 10, 2000.

Dykhuis, Karl

Born: July 8, 1972 in Sept-Iles, Quebec
Drafted: By the Chicago Black Hawks from the Hull Olympiques in 1990, 1st round, 16th overall.

Career Junior, NHL and World Junior Statistics

	GP	G	A	PTS	PIM
Canada National Team 1990-92	56	3	11	14	32
QMJHL Regular Season 1988-92	164	18	93	111	233
QMJHL Playoffs	45	5	31	36	28
Memorial Cup 1992	3	0	0	0	0
NHL Regular Season 1991-Present	635	42	91	133	493
NHL Playoffs	62	8	10	18	50
Canada 1991 World Juniors *in Saskatoon*	7	0	3	3	2
Canada 1992 World Juniors *in Germany*	7	0	0	0	8
Canada Totals	**14**	**0**	**3**	**3**	**10**

Junior Highlights

QMJHL All-Rookie Team in 1989
QMJHL Defensive Rookie of the Year in 1989
QMJHL First All-Star Team in 1990
Won Gold Medal at World Junior Championships in 1991

Around the Rink

Dykhuis had quite the junior tour, he played from 1988-90 with the Hull. Spent the majority of 1990-91 with the Canadian National team but played three games for Longeuil. Played nineteen games with the Canadian National team in 1991-92 and finished off the season with Verdun. Traded to Philadelphia by Chicago for Bob Wilkie and Philadelphia's 5th round choice (Kyle Calder) in 1997 Entry Draft, February 16, 1995. Traded to Tampa Bay by Philadelphia with Mikael Renberg for Philadelphia's 1st round choices (previously acquired by Tampa Bay) in 1998 (Simon Gagne), 1999 (Maxime Ouellet), 2000 (Justin Williams) and 2001 (later traded to Ottawa - Ottawa selected Tim Gleason) Entry Drafts, August 20, 1997. Traded to Philadelphia by Tampa Bay for Petr Svoboda, December 28, 1998. Traded to Montreal by Philadelphia for cash, October 20, 1999.

Eagles, Mike

Born: March 7, 1963 in Sussex, New Brunswick
Drafted: By the Quebec Nordiques from the Kitchener Rangers in 1981, 6th round, 116th overall.

Career Junior, NHL and World Junior Statistics

	GP	G	A	PTS	PIM
WHL Regular Season 1979-80	5	0	1	1	0
WHL Playoffs	4	0	0	0	4
OHL Regular Season 1980-83	176	63	103	166	345
OHL Playoffs	45	12	20	32	90
Memorial Cup 1981 and 1982	10	4	4	8	4
NHL Regular Season 1982-2000	853	74	122	196	928
NHL Playoffs	44	2	6	8	34
Canada 1983 World Juniors *in Russia*	7	2	4	6	2

Junior Highlights

Won Memorial Cup in 1982
Won Bronze Medal at World Junior Championships in 1983

Around the Rink

Eagles played his first year of junior with Billings of the WHL before transferring to Kitchener of the OHL. Missed majority of 1984-85 season recovering from hand injury suffered in practice, October 1984. Traded to Chicago by Quebec for Bob Mason, July 5, 1988. Traded to Winnipeg by Chicago for Winnipeg's 4th round choice (Igor Kravchuk) in 1991 Entry Draft, December 14, 1990. Traded to Washington by Winnipeg with Igor Ulanov for Washington's 3rd (later traded to Dallas - Dallas selected Sergey Gusev) and 5th (Brian Elder) round choices in 1995 Entry Draft, April 7, 1995. Retired from playing in 2000.

Eakin, Bruce

Born: September 28, 1962 in Winnipeg, Manitoba
Drafted: By the Calgary Flames from the Saskatoon Blades in 1981, 10th round, 204th overall.

Career Junior, NHL and World Junior Statistics

	GP	G	A	PTS	PIM
WHL Regular Season 1980-82	118	60	171	231	174
WHL Playoffs	5	4	6	10	0
NHL Regular Season 1981-86	13	2	2	4	4
NHL Playoffs	0	0	0	0	0
Canada 1982 World Juniors *in United States*	7	4	7	11	4

Junior Highlights

Won Gold Medal at World Junior Championships in 1982
WHL First All-Star Team in 1982
CHL Second All-Star Team in 1984

Around the Rink

Eakin signed as a free agent by Detroit, July 18, 1985. Traded to Edmonton by Detroit for Billy Carroll, December 28, 1985. Signed as a free agent by Springfield (AHL), March 10, 1987. Retired at the end of the 1987-88 season. Made a comeback in 1992 in the German league, played in Europe until 1999 when he retired again.

Eatough, Jeff

Born: June 2, 1963 in Toronto, Ontario
Drafted: By the Buffalo Sabres from the Cornwall Royals in 1981, 4th round, 80th overall.

Career Junior, NHL and World Junior Statistics

	GP	G	A	PTS	PIM
QMJHL/OHL Regular Season 1980-83	199	113	107	220	417
QMJHL/OHL Playoffs	31	7	17	24	85
Memorial Cup 1981	5	0	3	3	12
NHL Regular Season 1981-82	1	0	0	0	0
NHL Playoffs	0	0	0	0	0
Canada 1981 World Juniors *in Germany*	5	1	2	3	4

Junior Highlights

Won Memorial Cup in 1981

Around the Rink

Eatough played six games with Niagara Falls in 1979-80 he was called up from N.F.'s bantam affiliate Aurora. Drafted in the summer of 1980 by Cornwall of the QMJHL. Cornwall moved to the OHL for the 1981-82 season. Traded to North Bay after nine games in 1982-83. Played his only NHL game with Buffalo. Retired in 1988 after playing four seasons in the minor leagues.

Elynuik, Pat

Born: October 30, 1967 in Foam Lake, Saskatchewan
Drafted: By the Winnipeg Jets from the Prince Albert Raiders in 1986, 1st round, 8th overall.

Career Junior, NHL and World Junior Statistics

	GP	G	A	PTS	PIM
WHL Regular Season 1982-87	204	128	135	263	156
WHL Playoffs	41	21	17	38	36
Memorial Cup 1985	5	1	0	1	12
NHL Regular Season 1987-96	506	154	188	342	459
NHL Playoffs	20	6	9	15	25
Canada 1987 World Juniors *in Czech Republic*	6	6	5	11	2

Junior Highlights

Won Memorial Cup in 1985
WHL East First All-Star Team in 1986 and 1987

Around the Rink

Elynuk was traded to Washington by Winnipeg for John Druce and Toronto's 4th round choice (previously acquired by Washington later traded to Detroit Detroit selected John Jakopin) in 1993 Entry Draft, October 1, 1992. Traded to Tampa Bay by Washington for future considerations, October 22, 1993. Signed as a free agent by Ottawa, June 21, 1994. Signed as a free agent by Dallas, September 6, 1996 but played the entire 1996-97 season in the minors with Michigan (IHL), retired at the end of year.

Eminger, Steve

Born: October 31, 1983 in Woodbridge, Ontario
Drafted: By the Washington Capitals from the Kitchener Rangers in 2002, 1st round, 12th overall.

Career Junior, NHL and World Junior Statistics

	GP	G	A	PTS	PIM
OHL Regular Season 1999-2003	191	29	106	135	273
OHL Playoffs	14	0	4	4	14
NHL Regular Season 2002-Present	17	0	2	2	24
NHL Playoffs	0	0	0	0	0
Canada 2003 World Juniors *in Nova Scotia*	6	0	2	2	16

Junior Highlights

OHL Second Team All-Star in 2002
Won Silver Medal at World Junior Championships in 2003

Around the Rink

Eminger made the Capitals out of training camp in 2002-03. First NHL game October 11, 2002 vs. Nashville. Recorded first NHL point an assist vs. Toronto on November 26, 2002. Assigned to Team Canada for WJC, December 9, 2002. Returned to Kitchener (OHL) January 7, 2003.

Evans, Paul

Born: February 24, 1955 in Peterborough, Ontario
Drafted: By the Toronto Maple Leafs from the Peterborough Petes in 1975, 9th round, 149th overall. Also Drafted by the Indianapolis Racers (WHA) in 1975, 13th round, 162nd overall.

Career Junior, NHL and World Junior Statistics

	GP	G	A	PTS	PIM
OHL Regular Season 1973-75	137	40	100	140	373
OHL Playoffs	10	5	7	12	39
NHL Regular Season 1976-78	11	1	1	2	21
NHL Playoffs	2	0	0	0	0
Canada 1974 World Juniors *in Russia*	5	1	0	1	8

Junior Highlights

Won Bronze Medal at World Junior Championships in 1974

Around the Rink

Evans played all eleven of his NHL games with Toronto. Signed as a free agent with Saginaw (IHL) in 1978, traded to Flint after eleven games and retired at the end of the season.

Evason, Dean

Born: August 22, 1960 in Flin Flon, Manitoba
Drafted: By the Washington Capitals from the Kamloops Jr. Oilers in 1982, 5th round, 89th overall.

Career Junior, NHL and World Junior Statistics

	GP	G	A	PTS	PIM
WHL Regular Season 1980-84	200	150	251	401	303
WHL Playoffs	28	27	28	55	41
Memorial Cup 1984	4	2	2	4	0
NHL Regular Season 1983-96	803	139	233	372	1002
NHL Playoffs	55	9	20	29	132
Canada 1984 World Juniors *in Sweden*	7	6	3	9	0

Junior Highlights

WHL West First All-Star Team in 1984
Scored 71 goals in 70 Games in 1982-83

Around the Rink

Evason was traded from the Spokane Flyers (WHL) to the Kamloops Jr. Oilers after twenty-six games in 1981-82. Traded to Hartford by Washington with Peter Sidorkiewicz for David Jensen, March 12, 1985. Traded to San Jose by Hartford for Dan Keczmer, October 2, 1991. Traded to Dallas by San Jose for San Jose's 6th round choice (previously acquired, San Jose selected Petri Varis) in 1993 Entry Draft, June 26, 1993. Signed as a free agent by Calgary, August 1, 1995. Signed as a free agent with Zug in the Swiss league in 1996 nut only played three games, spent the majority of the season with Canada's National team. Signed as a free agent with Landshut of the German league in 1997. Retired from playing in 1999. Head coach of the Kamloops Blazers (WHL) 1999-2002. Head coach of the Vancouver Giants (WHL) 2002-Present.

Falloon, Pat

Born: September 22, 1972 in Foxwarren, Manitoba
Drafted: By the San Jose Sharks from the Spokane Chiefs in 1991, 1st round, 2nd overall.

Career Junior, NHL and World Junior Statistics

	GP	G	A	PTS	PIM
WHL Regular Season 1988-91	204	146	194	340	122
WHL Playoffs	21	15	22	37	14
Memorial Cup 1991	4	8	4	12	2
NHL Regular Season 1991-2000	575	143	179	322	141
NHL Playoffs	66	11	7	18	16
Canada 1991 World Juniors *in Saskatoon*	7	3	3	6	2

Junior Highlights

WHL West Second All-Star Team in 1989
WHL West First All-Star Team in 1991
Won Gold Medal at World Junior Championships in 1991
Won Memorial Cup in 1991
Canadian Major Junior Most Sportsmanlike Player of the Year in 1991
Memorial Cup All-Star Team in 1991
Won Stafford Smythe Memorial Trophy (Memorial Cup Tournament MVP) in 1991

Around the Rink

Falloon was San Jose's first ever draft pick. Traded to Philadelphia by San Jose for Martin Spanhel, Philadelphia's 1st round choice (later traded to Buffalo - later traded to Phoenix - Phoenix selected Daniel Briere) in 1996 Entry Draft and Philadelphia's 4th round choice (later traded to Buffalo - Buffalo selected Mike Martone), in 1996 Entry Draft, November 16, 1995. Traded to Ottawa by Philadelphia with Vaclav Prospal and Dallas' 2nd round choice (previously acquired, Ottawa selected Chris Bala) in 1998 Entry Draft for Alexandre Daigle, January 17, 1998. Signed as a free agent by Edmonton, August 21, 1998. Claimed on waivers by Pittsburgh from Edmonton, February 4, 2000. Signed as a free agent by HC Davos (Swiss), August 25, 2000. Played in his hometown of Foxwarren (NCHL) in 2001-2002, retired from playing at the end of the season.

Fata, Rico

Born: February 12, 1980 in Sault Ste. Marie, Ontario
Drafted: By the Calgary Flames from the London Knights in 1998, 1st round, 6th overall.

Career Junior, NHL and World Junior Statistics

	GP	G	A	PTS	PIM
OHL Regular Season 1995-99	208	88	100	188	279
OHL Playoffs	45	19	17	36	91
NHL Regular Season 1998-Present	100	7	13	20	26
NHL Playoffs	0	0	0	0	0
Canada 1999 World Juniors *in Winnipeg*	7	1	3	4	8

Junior Highlights

Won Silver Medal at World Junior Championships in 1999

Around the Rink

Fata played the 1995-96 season with the Sault Ste. Marie Greyhounds as an undrafted call up from the Greyhounds bantam affiliate the Sault Ste. Marie Legion. Drafted in the summer of 1996 by the London Knights. Claimed on waivers by the New York Rangers from Calgary October 3, 2001. Traded to Pittsburgh with Richard Lintner, Joel Bouchard and Mikael Samuelsson for Alexei Kovalev, Dan LaCouture, Janne Laukkanen, Mike Wilson and future considerations on February 10, 2003.

Fenyves, David

Born: April 29, 1960 in Dunnville, Ontario
Not Drafted: Signed as a Free Agent with the Buffalo Sabres in 1979

Career Junior, NHL and World Junior Statistics

	GP	G	A	PTS	PIM
OHL Regular Season 1977-80	191	14	71	85	250
OHL Playoffs	54	1	9	10	51
Memorial Cup 1978 and 1979	10	0	1	1	0
NHL Regular Season 1982-91	203	3	32	35	119
NHL Playoffs	11	0	0	0	9
Canada 1980 World Juniors *in Finland*	5	0	0	0	8

Junior Highlights

Won Memorial Cup in 1979
OHL Second All-Star Team in 1980

Around the Rink

Fenyves was signed as a free agent by Buffalo on October 31, 1979. Claimed by Philadelphia from Buffalo in waiver draft, October 5, 1987. Spent 1991-93 in the minors with Hershey (AHL) and retired at the end of the 1992-93 season.

Ference, Andrew

Born: March 17, 1979 in Edmonton, Alberta
Drafted: By the Pittsburgh Penguins from the Portland Winter Hawks in 1997, 8th round, 208th overall.

Career Junior, NHL and World Junior Statistics

	GP	G	A	PTS	PIM
WHL Regular Season 1994-99	258	41	141	182	568
WHL Playoffs	33	5	27	32	62
NHL Regular Season 1999-Present	179	11	29	40	163
NHL Playoffs	18	3	7	10	16
Canada 1999 World Juniors *in Winnipeg*	7	1	2	3	6

Junior Highlights

WHL West First All-Star Team in 1998
Won Silver Medal at World Junior Championships in 1999
WHL West Second All-Star Team in 1999

Around the Rink

Ference played his first NHL game October 1, 1999 vs. Dallas. Recorded first point October 16, 1999 an assist vs. Chicago. Scored first goal November 13, 1999 vs. Nashville. Traded to Calgary by Pittsburgh for a conditional draft pick, February 10, 2003.

Ference, Brad

Born: April 2, 1979 in Calgary, Alberta
Drafted: By the Vancouver Canucks from the Spokane Chiefs in 1997, 1st round, 10th overall.

Career Junior, NHL and World Junior Statistics

	GP	G	A	PTS	PIM
WHL Regular Season 1995-99	177	24	88	112	796
WHL Playoffs	39	1	20	21	153
Memorial Cup 1998	4	1	2	3	12
NHL Regular Season 1999-Present	182	4	25	29	460
NHL Playoffs	0	0	0	0	0
Canada 1998 World Juniors *in Finland*	7	0	1	1	6
Canada 1999 World Juniors *in Winnipeg*	7	0	2	2	25
Canada Totals	**14**	**0**	**3**	**3**	**31**

Junior Highlights

Memorial Cup All-Star Team in 1998
Won Silver Medal at World Junior Championships in 1999

Around the Rink

Ference was traded to Tri-City (WHL) by Spokane (WHL) for David Boychuk, February 2, 1999. Traded to Florida by Vancouver with Pavel Bure, Bret Hedican and Vancouver's 3rd round choice (Robert Fried) in 2000 Entry Draft for Ed Jovanovski, Dave Gagner, Mike Brown, Kevin Weekes and Florida's 1st round choice (Nathan Smith) in 2000 Entry Draft, January 17, 1999. Traded to Phoenix by Florida for Darcy Hordichuk and Phoenix's 2nd round draft choice in 2003 Entry Draft, March 8, 2003.

Finley, Brian

Born: July 13, 1981 in Sault Ste. Marie, Ontario
Drafted: By the Nashville Predators from the Barrie Colts in 1999, 1st round, 6th overall.

Career Junior, NHL and World Junior Statistics

	GP	W	L	T	SO	AVG
OHL Regular Season 1997-01	167	95	47	12	8	2.89
OHL Playoffs	42	24	16	0	2	2.75
Memorial Cup 2000	4	3	1	Not Available		0.00
NHL Regular Season 2003-Present	1	0	0	0	0	3.83
NHL Playoffs	0	0	0	0	0	0.00
Canada 1999 World Juniors *in Winnipeg*	1	0	0	0	0	6.00
Canada 2000 World Juniors *in Sweden*	1	1	0	0	0	3.00
Canada Totals	**2**	**1**	**0**	**0**	**0**	**3.75**

Junior Highlights

OHL All-Rookie Team in 1998
Won Silver Medal at World Junior Championships in 1999
OHL First Team All-Star in 1999
OHL Goaltender of the Year in 1999
Won Bronze Medal at World Junior Championships in 2000
Won the Wayne Gretzky Award as the OHL Playoff Most Valuable Player in 2000
OHL First Team All-Star in 2000

Around the Rink

Finley was traded by Barrie to Brampton after sixteen games in 2000. Made his NHL debut January 1, 2003 against Colorado, entering the game at the 13 minute mark of the first period.

Fiset, Stephane

Born: June 17, 1970 in Montreal, Quebec
Drafted: By the Quebec Nordiques from the Victoriavlle Tigres in 1988, 2nd round, 24th overall.

Career Junior, NHL and World Junior Statistics

	GP	W	L	T	SO	AVG
QMJHL Regular Season 1987-90	107	54	37	7	3	3.46
QMJHL Playoffs	28	16	10	0	0	3.31
NHL Regular Season 1990-2002	390	164	153	44	16	3.06
NHL Playoffs	14	1	7	0	0	3.94
Canada 1989 World Juniors *in U.S.A.*	6	3	2	1	0	3.28
Canada 1990 World Juniors *in Finland*	7	5	1	1	1	2.57
Canada Totals	**13**	**8**	**3**	**2**	**1**	**2.88**

Junior Highlights

QMJHL First All-Star Team in 1989
Canadian Major Junior Goaltender of the Year in 1989
Won Gold Medal at World Junior Championships in 1990
World Junior Championship All-Star Team in 1990
Named Best Goaltender at World Junior Championship in 1990

Around the Rink

Fiset's rights were transferred to Colorado after Quebec franchise relocated, June 21, 1995. Traded to LA Kings by Colorado with Colorado's 1st round choice (Mathieu Biron) in 1998 Entry Draft for Eric Lacroix and LA Kings' 1st round choice (Martin Skoula) in 1998 Entry Draft, June 20, 1996. Missed majority of 2000-01 season recovering from knee injury suffered in exhibition game vs. Anaheim, September 22, 2000. Played 12 seconds of playoff game vs. Colorado, April 28, 2001. Traded to Montreal by LA Kings for future considerations, March 19, 2002. Retired at the end of the 2001-02 season.

Flatley, Patrick

Born: October 3, 1963 in Toronto, Ontario
Drafted: By the New York Islanders from the University of Wisconsin in 1982, 1st round, 21st overall.

Career Junior, NHL and World Junior Statistics

	GP	G	A	PTS	PIM
NCAA 1981-1983	76	42	64	106	141
NHL Regular Season 1983-97	780	170	340	510	686
NHL Playoffs	70	18	15	33	75
Canada 1983 World Juniors *in Russia*	7	4	0	4	6

Junior Highlights

Won NCAA Championship in 1983
NCAA West First All-American Team in 1983
NCAA Championship All-Tournament Team in 1983
Won Bronze Medal at World Junior Championships in 1983

Around the Rink

Flatley joined Canada's National Team in early 1983 winning bronze at the World Championships. Played for Canada at the 1984 Olympics. Played his first NHL game in February 1984 with the New York Islanders. Signed as a free agent by the New York Rangers, September 26, 1996. Retired from playing at the end of the 1996-97 season.

Fleury, Theoren

Born: June 29, 1968 in Oxbow, Saskatchewan
Drafted: By the Calgary Flames from the Moose Jaw Warriors in 1987, 8th round, 166th overall.

Career Junior, NHL and World Junior Statistics

	GP	G	A	PTS	PIM
WHL Regular Season 1984-88	274	201	271	472	551
WHL Playoffs	22	14	22	36	50
NHL Regular Season 1988-Present	1084	455	633	1088	1840
NHL Playoffs	77	34	45	79	116
Canada 1987 World Juniors *in Czech Republic*	6	2	3	5	2
Canada 1988 World Juniors *in Russia*	7	6	2	8	4
Canada Totals	**13**	**8**	**5**	**13**	**6**

Junior Highlights

WHL East First All-Star Team in 1987
Won Gold Medal at World Junior Championships in 1988
World Junior Championships All-Star Team in 1988
WHL East Second All-Star Team in 1988

Around the Rink

Fleury was traded to Colorado by Calgary with Chris Dingman for Rene Corbet, Wade Belak, Robyn Regehr and Colorado's 2nd round compensatory choice (Jarret Stoll) in 2000 Entry Draft, February 28, 1999. Signed as a free agent by NY Rangers, July 8, 1999. Traded to San Jose by NY Rangers to complete transaction that sent San Jose's 6th round choice (Kim Hirschovits) in 2002 Entry Draft for NY Rangers' 6th round choice in 2003 Entry Draft (June 23, 2002), June 26, 2002. Signed as a free agent by Chicago, August 15, 2002.

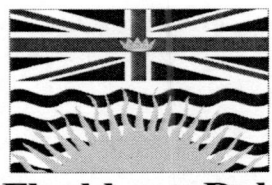

Flockhart, Rob

Born: February 6, 1956 in Sicamous, B.C.
Drafted: By the Vancouver Canucks from the Kamloops Blazers in 1976, 3rd round, 44th overall. Also Drafted by the Cleveland Crusaders (WHA) in 1976, 6th round, 63rd overall.

Career Junior, NHL and World Junior Statistics

	GP	G	A	PTS	PIM
WHL Regular Season 1973-76	175	83	83	166	192
WHL Playoffs	11	3	9	12	32
NHL Regular Season 1976-81	55	2	5	7	14
NHL Playoffs	1	1	0	1	2
Canada 1975 World Juniors *in Manitoba*	4	1	0	1	6

Junior Highlights

Won Silver Medal at World Junior Championships in 1975

Around the Rink

Signed as a free agent by Minnesota, October 12, 1979. Signed as a free agent by Chicago, December 1, 1982 but never played a game with the Black Hawks. Played five seasons in the minors with Nashville (CHL), Springfield (AHL), Toledo (IHL) and New Haven (AHL) before retiring in 1985.

Forbes, Mike

Born: September 20, 1957 in Brampton, Ontario
Drafted: By the Boston Bruins from the St. Catharines Fincups in 1977, 3rd round, 52nd overall.

Career Junior, NHL and World Junior Statistics

	GP	G	A	PTS	PIM
OHL Regular Season 1974-77	173	16	64	80	349
OHL Playoffs	27	2	6	8	60
NHL Regular Season 1977-82	50	1	11	12	41
NHL Playoffs	0	0	0	0	0
Canada 1977 World Juniors *in Czech Republic*	7	0	1	1	22

Junior Highlights

Won Silver Medal at World Junior Championships in 1977

Around the Rink

Forbes was traded by the Kingston Canadiens to the St. Catharines Fincups after the 1975-76 season. Claimed by Edmonton from Boston in Expansion Draft, June 13, 1979. Retired from playing in 1987 after playing five years in the minors in the CHL and IHL.

Foster, Corey

Born: October 27, 1969 in Ottawa, Ontario
Drafted: By the New Jersey Devils from the Peterborough Petes in 1988, 1st round, 12th overall.

Career Junior, NHL and World Junior Statistics

	GP	G	A	PTS	PIM
OHL Regular Season 1986-89	121	30	77	107	104
OHL Playoffs	29	6	26	32	25
Memorial Cup 1989	5	0	4	4	0
NHL Regular Season 1988-97	45	5	6	11	24
NHL Playoffs	3	0	0	0	4
Canada 1989 World Juniors *in United States*	7	1	3	4	4

Junior Highlights

Recorded 56 Points in 55 Games in 1988-89

Around the Rink

Foster was traded to Edmonton by New Jersey for Edmonton's 1st round choice (Jason Miller) in 1989 Entry Draft, June 17, 1989. Traded to Philadelphia by Edmonton with Dave Brown and Jari Kurri for Craig Fisher, Scott Mellanby and Craig Berube, May 30, 1991. Signed as a free agent by Ottawa, June 20, 1994. Signed as a free agent by Pittsburgh, August 7, 1995. Claimed by NY Islanders from Pittsburgh in Waiver Draft, September 30, 1996. Signed as a free agent with Kokudo of the Japanese league in 1997. Signed as a free agent with Berlin of the German league in 2001. Signed as a free agent with Springfield (AHL) in 2002.

Foster, Dwight

Born: April 2, 1957 in Toronto, Ontario
Drafted: By the Boston Bruins from the Kitchener Rangers in 1977, 1st round, 16th overall. Also Drafted by the Houston Aeros (WHA) in 1977, 2nd round, 10th overall.

Career Junior, NHL and World Junior Statistics

	GP	G	A	PTS	PIM
OHL Regular Season 1973-77	323	194	282	476	457
OHL Playoffs	19	10	16	26	58
NHL Regular Season 1977-87	541	111	163	274	420
NHL Playoffs	35	5	12	17	4
Canada 1977 World Juniors *in Czech Republic*	7	2	5	7	4

Junior Highlights

Won Silver Medal at World Junior Championships in 1977
Recorded 143 Points in 64 Games in 1976-77

Around the Rink

Foster signed as a Free Agent by Colorado, July 21, 1981. Transferred to New Jersey when Colorado franchise relocated, June 30, 1982. Rights traded to Detroit by New Jersey for cash, October 29, 1982. Traded to Boston by Detroit for Dave Donnelly, March 11, 1986. Retired in 1987.

Foster, Norm

Born: February 10, 1965 in Vancouver, B.C.
Drafted: By the Boston Bruins from the Michigan State Spartans in 1983, 11th round, 222nd overall.

Career Junior, NHL and World Junior Statistics

	GP	**W**	**L**	**T**	**SO**	**AVG**
NCAA 1983-87	106	76	24	2	2	3.19
NHL Regular Season 1990-92	13	623	7	4	0	3.27
NHL Playoffs	0	0	0	0	0	0.00
Canada 1985 World Juniors *in Finland*	2	2	0	0	1	0.50

Junior Highlights

NCAA (Central Collegiate Hockey Association) Second All-Star Team in 1984
Won Gold Medal at World Junior Championships in 1985
NCAA Championship All-Tournament Team in 1985
Won NCAA Championship in 1986

Around the Rink

Foster was traded to Edmonton by Boston for Edmonton's 6th round choice (Jiri Dopita) in 1992 Entry Draft, September 11, 1991. Signed as a free agent by Philadelphia, August 4, 1993 but never played a game for the Flyers. Played in the minors from 1992-95 with Cape Breton (AHL), Kansas City (IHL), Hershey (AHL), Detroit (IHL), Las Vegas (IHL) and Detroit (CHL), retired in 1995.

Fountain, Mike

Born: January 26, 1972 in North York, Ontario
Drafted: By the Vancouver Canucks from the Oshawa Generals in 1992, 2nd round, 45th overall.

Career Junior, NHL and World Junior Statistics

	GP	W	L	T	SO	AVG
OHL Regular Season 1990-92	77	40	20	7	1	3.66
OHL Playoffs	15	4	8	0	0	4.32
NHL Regular Season 1996-2001	11	2	6	0	1	3.47
NHL Playoffs	0	0	0	0	0	0.00
Canada 1992 World Juniors *in Germany*	0	0	0	0	0	0.00

Junior Highlights

OHL First All-Star Team in 1992

Around the Rink

Fountain was traded by Sault Ste. Marie to Oshawa after seven games in 1990. Recorded shutout (3-0) in NHL debut vs. New Jersey, November 14, 1996. Signed as a free agent by Carolina, August 19, 1997. Signed as a free agent by Ottawa, July 30, 1999 but only played two games over two seasons. Signed as a free agent with Lada in the Russian League in 2001, retired at the end of the season.

Fox, Jim

Born: May 18, 1960 in Coniston, Ontario
Drafted: By the Los Angeles Kings from the Ottawa 67's in 1980, 1st round, 10th overall.

Career Junior, NHL and World Junior Statistics

	GP	G	A	PTS	PIM
OHL Regular Season 1976-80	164	146	250	396	46
OHL Playoffs	32	18	32	50	4
NHL Regular Season 1980-90	578	186	293	479	143
NHL Playoffs	22	4	8	12	0
Canada 1980 World Juniors *in Finland*	5	3	2	5	0

Junior Highlights

OHL First All-Star Team in 1980
OHL MVP in 1980

Around the Rink

Fox played four playoff games with Sudbury in 1976, he was called up as an undrafted player from Sudbury`s bantam affiliate North Bay (NOJHA). Drafted by Ottawa in the summer of 1977 Missed entire 1988-89 season recovering from knee injury originally suffered in game vs. Boston, March 10, 1988. Retired from playing in 1990.

Fraser, Curt

Born: January 12, 1958 in Cincinnati, Ohio-Raised in British Columbia
Drafted: By the Vancouver Canucks from the Victoria Cougars in 1978, 2nd round, 22nd overall.

Career Junior, NHL and World Junior Statistics

	GP	G	A	PTS	PIM
WHL Regular Season 1974-78	265	142	181	323	610
WHL Playoffs	47	19	20	39	92
NHL Regular Season 1978-90	704	193	240	433	1304
NHL Playoffs	65	15	18	33	198
Canada 1978 World Juniors *in Montreal*	5	0	2	2	0

Junior Highlights

Won Bronze Medal at World Junior Championships in 1978

Around the Rink

Fraser was traded to Chicago by Vancouver for Tony Tanti, January 6, 1983. Missed majority of 1983-84 season recovering from knee injury suffered in game vs. Minnesota, November 5, 1983. Traded to Minnesota by Chicago for Dirk Graham, January 4, 1988. Retired from playing in 1990. Assistant/Head Coach, Milwaukee Admirals (IHL) 1990-94. Assistant Coach, Syracuse Crunch (AHL) 1994-95. Head Coach, Orlando Solar Bears (IHL) 1995-99. Head Coach, Atlanta Thrashers 1999-2002.

Friesen, Jeff

Born: August 5, 1976 in Meadow Lake, Saskatchewan
Drafted: By the San Jose Sharks from the Regina Pats in 1994, 1st round, 11th overall.

Career Junior, NHL and World Junior Statistics

	GP	G	A	PTS	PIM
WHL Regular Season 1991-95	165	120	128	248	95
WHL Playoffs	17	10	12	22	10
NHL Regular Season 1994-Present	689	191	265	455	399
NHL Playoffs	34	5	10	15	30
Canada 1994 World Juniors *in Czech Republic*	5	0	2	2	0
Canada 1995 World Juniors *in Alberta*	7	5	2	7	4
Canada Totals	**12**	**5**	**4**	**9**	**4**

Junior Highlights

WHL Rookie of the Year in 1993
Canadian Major Junior Rookie of the Year in 1993
Won Gold Medal at World Junior Championships in 1994 and 1995

Around the Rink

Friesen was traded to Anaheim by San Jose with Steve Shields and future considerations for Teemu Selanne, March 5, 2001. Traded to New Jersey by Anaheim with Oleg Tverdovsky and Maxim Balmochnykh for Petr Sykora, Mike Commodore, Jean-Francois Damphousse and Igor Pohanka, July 6, 2002.

Gagne, Simon

Born: February 29, 1980 in Ste. Foy, Quebec
Drafted: By the Philadelphia Flyers from the Quebec Remparts in 1998, 1st round, 22nd overall.

Career Junior, NHL and World Junior Statistics

	GP	G	A	PTS	PIM
QMJHL Regular Season 1996-99	165	89	131	220	107
QMJHL Playoffs	25	20	13	33	27
NHL Regular Season 1999-Present	274	89	111	200	16
NHL Playoffs	28	8	5	13	4
Canada 1999 World Juniors *in Winnipeg*	7	7	1	8	2

Junior Highlights

Won Silver Medal at World Junior Championships in 1999
QMJHL Second All-Star Team in 1999
Had His #12 Retired by the Quebec Remparts September 14, 2001

Around the Rink

Gagne played his first junior season with Beauport in 1996-97, the team moved to Quebec for the following season. Has never played a game in the minors. Played first NHL game October 2, 1999 vs. Ottawa. Scored his first two NHL goals October 12, 1999 vs. Washington.

Gagner, Dave

Born: December 11, 1964 in Chatham, Ontario
Drafted: By the New York Rangers from the Brantford Alexanders in 1983, 1st round, 12th overall.

Career Junior, NHL and World Junior Statistics

	GP	G	A	PTS	PIM
OHL Regular Season 1981-84	150	92	125	217	92
OHL Playoffs	25	8	11	19	16
NHL Regular Season 1984-99	946	318	401	719	1016
NHL Playoffs	57	22	26	48	64
Canada 1984 World Juniors *in Sweden*	7	4	2	6	4

Junior Highlights

OHL Second All-Star Team in 1983
Played on Canadian Olympic Team in 1984

Around the Rink

Gagner was traded to Minnesota by NY Rangers with Jay Caufield for Jari Gronstrand and Paul Boutilier, October 8, 1987. Transferred to Dallas after Minnesota franchise relocated, June 9, 1993. Played four games in Italy for Courmaosta during the NHL lockout of 1994. Traded to Toronto by Dallas with Dallas' 6th round choice (Dmitri Yakushin) in 1996 Entry Draft for Benoit Hogue and Randy Wood, January 29, 1996. Traded to Calgary by Toronto for Calgary's 3rd round choice (Mike Lankshear) in 1996 Entry Draft, June 22, 1996. Signed as a free agent by Florida, July 12, 1997. Traded to Vancouver by Florida with Ed Jovanovski, Mike Brown, Kevin Weekes and Florida's 1st round choice (Nathan Smith) in 2000 Entry Draft for Pavel Bure, Bret Hedican, Brad Ference and Vancouver's 3rd round choice (Robert Fried) in 2000 Entry Draft, January 17, 1999. Officially announced retirement, September 9, 1999.

Gardner, Bill

Born: March 19, 1960 in Toronto, Ontario
Drafted: By the Chicago Black Hawks from the Peterborough Petes in 1979, 3rd round, 49th overall.

Career Junior, NHL and World Junior Statistics

	GP	G	A	PTS	PIM
OHL Regular Season 1976-1980	193	98	166	264	264
OHL Playoffs	53	24	44	68	18
Memorial Cup 1978, 1979 and 1980	15	7	12	19	0
NHL Regular Season 1980-89	380	73	115	188	68
NHL Playoffs	45	3	8	11	17
Canada 1980 World Juniors *in Finland*	5	0	4	4	14

Junior Highlights

Won Memorial Cup in 1979
Memorial Cup All-Star Team in 1980

Around the Highlights

Gardner was traded to Hartford by Chicago for Hartford's 3rd round choice (Mike Dagenais) in 1987 Entry Draft, February 3, 1986. Signed as a free agent by Chicago, September 25, 1987. Signed as a free agent with Kapfenberg of the Austrian league in 1989. Retired in 1993 after his fourth season playing in Europe.

Garon, Mathieu

Born: January 9, 1978 in Chandler, Quebec
Drafted: By the Montreal Canadiens from the Victoriaville Tigres in 1996, 2nd round, 44th overall.

Career Junior, NHL and World Junior Statistics

	GP	W	L	T	SO	AVG
QMJHL Regular Season 1995-98	151	74	63	5	12	3.25
QMJHL Playoffs	24	11	12	0	1	3.68
NHL Regular Season 2000-Present	24	8	14	1	4	2.66
NHL Playoffs	0	0	0	0	0	0.00
Canada 1998 World Juniors *in Finland*	5	2	3	0	2	1.91

Junior Highlights

QMJHL All-Rookie Team in 1996
QMJHL Defensive Rookie of the Year in 1996
QMJHL First All-Star Team in 1998
Canadian Major Junior First All-Star Team in 1998
Canadian Major Junior Goaltender of the Year in 1998

Around the Rink

Garon has spent his brief career transferring back and forth from Montreal to their AHL affiliates, Fredericton, Quebec and Hamilton.

Gartner, Mike

Hockey Hall of Famer, Inducted 2001
Born: October 29, 1959 in Ottawa, Ontario
Drafted: By the Washington Capitals from the Niagara Falls Flyers in 1979, 1st round, 4th overall.

Career Junior, NHL and World Junior Statistics

	GP	G	A	PTS	PIM
OHL Regular Season 1975-78	129	75	94	169	181
OHL Playoffs	4	1	0	1	2
NHL Regular Season 1979-98	1432	708	627	1335	1159
NHL Playoffs	122	43	50	93	125
Canada 1978 World Juniors *in Montreal*	6	3	3	6	4

Junior Highlights

Won Bronze Medal at World Junior Championships in 1978
OHL All-Star Team in 1978

Around the Rink

Gartner signed a four year contract as an underage free agent by Cincinnati (WHA), May 1978, the WHA merged with the NHL in 1979. Traded to Minnesota by Washington with Larry Murphy for Dino Ciccarelli and Bob Rouse, March 7, 1989. Traded to NY Rangers by Minnesota for Ulf Dahlen, LA Kings' 4th round choice (previously acquired, Minnesota selected Cal McGowan) in 1990 Entry Draft, March 6, 1990. Traded to Toronto by NY Rangers for Glenn Anderson, the rights to Scott Malone and Toronto's 4th round choice (Alexander Korobolin) in 1994 Entry Draft, March 21, 1994. Traded to Phoenix by Toronto for Chicago's 4th round choice (previously acquired, Toronto selected Vladimir Antipov) in 1996 Entry Draft, June 22, 1996. Retired in 1998.

Gaulin, Jean-Marc

Born: March 3, 1962 in Balve, Germany-Raised in Quebec
Drafted: By the Quebec Nordiques from the Sorel Black Hawks in 1981, 3rd round, 53rd overall.

Career Junior, NHL and World Junior Statistics

	GP	G	A	PTS	PIM
QMJHL Regular Season 1978-82	256	147	171	318	458
QMJHL Playoffs	18	2	18	20	15
NHL Regular Season 1983-86	26	4	3	7	8
NHL Playoffs	1	0	0	0	0
Canada 1981 World Juniors *in Germany*	5	2	0	2	4

Junior Highlights

QMJHL Second All-Star Team in 1981
Scored 50 goals in 56 Games in 1981-82

Around the Rink

Gaulin played his first season of junior with Sherbrooke and was dealt to Verdun after 16 games in the 1979-80 season. Verdun merged with Sorel during the 1979-80 season. Traded to Hull by Sorel in the summer of 1981. Spent most of his career in the minors with Quebecs AHL affiliate in Fredericton. Signed as a free agent with Mont-Blanc in the French league in 1987. Spent nine seasons in France before retiring in 1996.

Gauthier, Denis

Born: October 1, 1976 in Montreal, Quebec
Drafted: By the Calgary Flames from the Drummondville Voltigeurs in 1995, 1st round, 20th overall.

Career Junior, NHL and World Junior Statistics

	GP	G	A	PTS	PIM
QMJHL Regular Season 1992-96	238	35	94	129	642
QMJHL Playoffs	29	6	14	20	125
NHL Regular Season 1997-Present	304	12	30	42	402
NHL Playoffs	0	0	0	0	0
Canada 1996 World Juniors *in United States*	6	1	1	2	6

Junior Highlights

Won Gold Medal at World Junior Championships in 1996
QMJHL First All-Star Team in 1996
Canadian Major Junior First All-Star Team in 1996

Around the Rink

Gauthier played his first NHL game on October 9, 1997. Scored first goal February 12, 1999 vs. Boston. Missed majority of 1999-2000 season recovering from hip injury suffered in game vs. St. Louis, February 1, 2000.

Gavey, Aaron

Born: February 22, 1974 in Sudbury, Ontario
Drafted: By the Tampa Bay Lightning from the Sault Ste. Marie Greyhounds in 1992, 4th round, 74th overall.

Career Junior, NHL and World Junior Statistics

	GP	G	A	PTS	PIM
OHL Regular Season 1991-94	170	94	110	204	259
OHL Playoffs	51	21	20	41	68
Memorial Cup 1992 and 1993	8	1	6	7	12
NHL Regular Season 1995-Present	355	41	50	91	270
NHL Playoffs	19	1	2	3	14
Canada 1994 World Juniors *in Switzerland*	7	4	2	6	26

Junior Highlights

Won Memorial Cup in 1993
Won Gold Medal at World Junior Championships in 1994

Around the Rink

Gavey was traded to Calgary by Tampa Bay for Rick Tabaracci, November 19, 1996. Traded to Dallas by Calgary for Bob Bassen, July 14, 1998. Traded to Minnesota by Dallas with Pavel Patera, Dallas' 8th round choice (Eric Johansson) in 2000 Entry Draft and Minnesota's 4th round choice (previously acquired) in 2002 Entry Draft for Brad Lukowich and Minnesota's 3rd (Yared Hagos) and 9th (Dale Sullivan) round choices in 2001 Entry Draft, June 25, 2000. Signed as a free agent by Toronto, July 24, 2002. Sent to St. John`s (AHL) October 5, 2002. Called up by Toronto from St. John`s, January 3, 2003. Returned to St. John`s, January 15, 2003.

Gelinas, Martin

Born: June 5, 1970 in Shawinigan, Quebec
Drafted: By the Los Angeles Kings from the Hull Olympiques in 1988, 1st round, 7th overall.

Career Junior, NHL and World Junior Statistics

	GP	G	A	PTS	PIM
QMJHL Regular Season 1987-89	106	101	107	208	105
QMJHL Playoffs	26	20	22	42	46
Memorial Cup 1988	4	2	2	4	8
NHL Regular Season 1988-Present	976	252	268	520	614
NHL Playoffs	121	15	26	41	85
Canada 1989 World Juniors *in United States*	7	0	2	2	8

Junior Highlights

QMJHL First All-Star Team in 1988
QMJHL Offensive Rookie of the Year in 1988
Canadian Major Junior Rookie of the Year in 1988
Won George Parsons Trophy (Memorial Cup Most Sportsmanlike Player) in 1988

Around the Rink

Gelinas was traded to Edmonton by LA Kings with Jimmy Carson and LA Kings' 1st round choices in 1989 (later traded to New Jersey - New Jersey selected Jason Miller), 1991 (Martin Rucinsky) and 1993 (Nick Stajduhar) Entry Drafts and cash for Wayne Gretzky, Mike Krushelnyski and Marty McSorley, August 9, 1988. Traded to Quebec by Edmonton with Edmonton's 6th round choice (Nicholas Checco) in 1993 Entry Draft for Scott Pearson, June 20, 1993. Claimed on waivers by Vancouver from Quebec, January 15, 1994. Traded to Carolina by Vancouver with Kirk McLean for Sean Burke, Geoff Sanderson and Enrico Ciccone, January 3, 1998. Signed as a free agent by Calgary, July 2, 2002.

Gendron, Martin

Born: February 15, 1974 in Valleyfield, Quebec
Drafted: By the Washington Capitals from the St. Hyacinthe Lasers in 1992, 3rd round, 71st overall.

Career Junior, NHL and World Junior Statistics

	GP	G	A	PTS	PIM
Canadian National Team 1993-94	19	4	5	9	2
QMJHL Regular Season 1990-94	224	217	186	403	140
QMJHL Playoffs	30	29	23	52	22
NHL Regular Season 1995-98	30	4	2	6	10
NHL Playoffs	0	0	0	0	0
Canada 1993 World Juniors *in Sweden*	7	5	2	7	2
Canada 1994 World Juniors *in Czech Republic*	7	6	4	10	6
Canada Totals	**14**	**11**	**6**	**17**	**8**

Junior Highlights

QMJHL All-Rookie Team in 1991
QMJHL First All-Star Team in 1992
Canadian Major Junior Most Sportsmanlike Player of the Year in 1992
Won Gold Medal at World Junior Championships in 1993 and 1994
QMJHL Second All-Star Team in 1993
Canadian Major Junior First All-Star Team in 1993

Around the Rink

Gendron was traded to Chicago by Washington with Washington's 6th round choice (Jonathan Pelletier) in 1998 Entry Draft for Chicago's 5th round choice (Erik Wendell) in 1998 Entry Draft, October 10, 1997. Traded to Montreal by Chicago for David Ling, March 14, 1998. Signed as a free agent Vancouver, August 25, 1999. Loaned to Springfield (AHL) by Syracuse (AHL) for loan of Sean McCann, March 15, 2000. Signed as a free agent by Frankfurt of the German league in the summer of 2000. Signed as a free agent with Asiago of the Italian league in 2001, retired at the end of the season.

Gillis, Jere

Born: January 18, 1957 in Bend, Oregon – Raised in Quebec
Drafted: By the Vancouver Canucks from the Sherbrooke Beavers in 1977, 1st round, 4th overall. Also Drafted by the Cincinnati Stingers (WHA) in 1977, 1st round, 7th overall.

Career Junior, NHL and World Junior Statistics

	GP	G	A	PTS	PIM
QMJHL Regular Season 1973-77	255	161	216	377	303
QMJHL Playoffs	35	19	26	45	67
Memorial Cup 1977	4	4	1	5	0
NHL Regular Season 1977-87	386	78	95	173	230
NHL Playoffs	19	4	7	11	9
Canada 1976 World Juniors *in Finland*	4	1	2	3	2

Junior Highlights

Won Silver Medal at World Junior Championships in 1976
QMJHL First All-Star Team in 1977
Memorial Cup All-Star Team in 1977

Around the Rink

Gillis was traded to NY Rangers by Vancouver with Jeff Bandura for Mario Marois and Jim Mayer, November 11, 1980. Traded to Quebec by NY Rangers with Dean Talafous (later changed to Pat Hickey (March 8, 1982) when Talafous decided to retire) for Robbie Ftorek and Quebec's 8th round choice (Brian Glynn) in 1982 Entry Draft, December 30, 1981. Signed as a free agent by Buffalo, September 11, 1982. Signed as a free agent by Vancouver, September 26, 1983. Signed as a free agent by Philadelphia, October 1986. Played in Europe from 1987 to 1991 and retired from playing to coach in Britain for one season in 1991-92. Came out of retirement in 1996 to play in the Quebec Senior Pro League and retired after five games.

Gilmour, Doug

Born: June 25, 1963 in Kingston, Ontario
Drafted: By the St. Louis Blues from the Cornwall Royals in 1982, 7th round, 134th overall.

Career Junior, NHL and World Junior Statistics

	GP	G	A	PTS	PIM
QMJHL/OHL Regular Season 1980-83	186	128	203	331	139
QMJHL/OHL Playoffs	32	22	32	54	24
Memorial Cup 1981	5	2	5	7	8
NHL Regular Season 1983-Present	1474	450	964	1414	1299
NHL Playoffs	182	60	128	188	235
Canada 1981 World Juniors *in Germany*	5	0	0	0	0

Junior Highlights

Won Memorial Cup in 1981
OHL First All-Star Team in 1983
OHL MVP in 1983

Around the Rink

Cornwall moved to the OHL from the QMJHL after the 1980-81 season. Gilmour was traded to Calgary by St. Louis with Mark Hunter, Steve Bozek and Michael Dark for Mike Bullard, Craig Coxe and Tim Corkery, September 6, 1988. Traded to Toronto by Calgary with Jamie Macoun, Ric Nattress, Kent Manderville and Rick Wamsley for Gary Leeman, Alexander Godynyuk, Jeff Reese, Michel Petit and Craig Berube, January 2, 1992. Traded to New Jersey by Toronto with Dave Ellett and New Jersey's 3rd round choice (previously acquired, New Jersey selected Andre Lakos) in 1999 Entry Draft for Jason Smith, Steve Sullivan and the rights to Alyn McCauley, February 25, 1997. Signed as a free agent by Chicago, July 28, 1998. Traded to Buffalo by Chicago with J-P Dumont for Michal Grosek, March 10, 2000. Signed as a free agent by Montreal, October 5, 2001. Traded to Toronto by Montreal for the Leafs 6th round choice in 2003 Entry Draft.

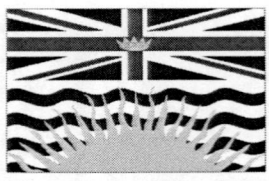

Gordon, Robb

Born: January 13, 1976 in Murrayville, B.C.
Drafted: By the Vancouver Canucks from the Powell River Paper Kings (BCJHL) in 1994, 2nd round, 39th overall.

Career Junior, NHL and World Junior Statistics

	GP	G	A	PTS	PIM
BCJHL Regular Season 1992-94	120	124	127	251	217
BCJHL Playoffs	28	19	24	43	29
NCAA 1994-95	39	15	26	41	72
WHL Regular Season 1995-96	58	51	63	114	84
WHL Playoffs	6	3	6	9	19
NHL Regular Season 1998-99	4	0	0	0	2
NHL Playoffs	0	0	0	0	0
Canada 1996 World Juniors *in United States*	6	0	4	4	0

Junior Highlights

BCJHL Rookie of the Year in 1993
BCJHL First All-Star Team in 1994
BCJHL MVP in 1994
Won Gold Medal at World Junior Championships in 1996
WHL West First All-Star Team in 1996

Around the Rink

Gordon played for the University of Michigan (NCAA) and for Kamloops (WHL) after his two seasons in the British Columbia Junior Hockey League. Spent most of his career with Syracuse of the AHL, Vancouver`s farm team. Signed as a free agent by Long Beach (IHL), August 23, 1999. Signed as a free agent with Manchester of the British league in 2000. Retired from playing in 2001.

Gosselin, Mario

Born: June 15, 1963 in Thetford Mines, Quebec
Drafted: By the Quebec Nordiques from the Shawinigan Cataractes in 1982, 3rd round, 55th overall.

Career Junior, NHL and World Junior Statistics

	GP	W	L	T	SO	AVG
QMJHL Regular Season 1980-83	126	59	43	3	3	3.82
QMJHL Playoffs	23	12	10	0	0	4.22
NHL Regular Season 1983-94	241	91	107	14	6	3.74
NHL Playoffs	32	16	15	0	0	3.27
Canada 1983 World Juniors *in Russia*	0	0	0	0	0	0.00

Junior Highlights

QMJHL Second All-Star Team in 1982
Won Bronze Medal at World Junior Championships in 1983
QMJHL First All-Star Team in 1983

Around the Rink

Gosselin recorded a shutout (5-0) in NHL debut vs. St. Louis, February 26, 1984. Signed as a free agent by LA Kings, June 14, 1989. Signed as a free agent by Hartford, September 4, 1991. Suffered eventual career-ending knee injury in game vs. Florida, November 27, 1993.

Gratton, Chris

Born: July 5, 1975 in Brantford, Ontario
Drafted: By the Tampa Bay Lightning from the Kingston Frontenacs in 1993, 1st round, 3rd overall.

Career Junior, NHL and World Junior Statistics

	GP	G	A	PTS	PIM
OHL Regular Season 1991-93	120	82	93	175	160
OHL Playoffs	16	11	18	29	42
NHL Regular Season 1993-Present	770	161	277	438	1240
NHL Playoffs	29	8	7	15	55
Canada 1993 World Juniors *in Sweden*	7	2	2	4	6

Junior Highlights

OHL All-Rookie Team in 1992
OHL Rookie of the Year in 1992
Won Gold Medal at World Junior Championships in 1993

Around the Rink

Gratton signed as a free agent by Philadelphia, August 14, 1997. Traded to Tampa Bay by Philadelphia with Mike Sillinger for Mikael Renberg and Daymond Langkow, December 12, 1998. Traded to Buffalo by Tampa Bay with Tampa Bay's 2nd round choice (Derek Roy) in 2001 Entry Draft for Cory Sarich, Wayne Primeau, Brian Holzinger and Buffalo's 3rd round choice (Alexander Kharitonov) in 2000 Entry Draft, March 9, 2000. Traded to Phoenix with Buffalo's 4th round choice in 2004 Entry Draft for Daniel Briere, and Phoenix's 3rd round choice in 2004 Entry Draft.

Gratton, Dan

Born: December 7, 1966 in Brantford, Ontario
Drafted: By the Los Angeles Kings from the Oshawa Generals in 1985, 1st round, 10th overall.

Career Junior, NHL and World Junior Statistics

	GP	G	A	PTS	PIM
OHL Regular Season 1982-86	240	112	147	259	222
OHL Playoffs	53	31	27	58	42
Memorial Cup 1983	5	2	0	2	0
NHL Regular Season 1987-88	7	1	0	1	5
NHL Playoffs	0	0	0	0	0
Canada 1985 World Juniors *in Finland*	7	2	3	5	16

Junior Highlights

Won Gold Medal at World Junior Championships in 1985

Around the Rink

Gratton was traded to Ottawa by Oshawa after ten games in 1985-86, after twenty-five games with Ottawa he was traded to Belleville. All seven NHL games came with L.A. Signed as a free agent by Minnesota, August 22, 1990 but never played a regular season game. Played most of his career in Europe including stops in Austria, Denmark, Italy, Switzerland and England. Retired from playing in 1998 from the Muskegon Fury of the UHL and became their Assistant Coach for one season.

Graves, Adam

Born: April 12, 1968 in Tecumseh, Ontario
Drafted: By the Detroit Red Wings from the Windsor Spitfires in 1986, 2nd round, 22nd overall.

Career Junior, NHL and World Junior Statistics

	GP	G	A	PTS	PIM
OHL Regular Season 1985-88	165	100	124	224	212
OHL Playoffs	42	28	37	65	58
Memorial Cup 1988	4	2	3	5	8
NHL Regular Season 1987-Present	1152	329	287	616	1224
NHL Playoffs	125	38	27	65	119
Canada 1988 World Juniors *in Russia*	7	5	0	5	4

Junior Highlights

Won Gold Medal at World Junior Championships in 1988

Around the Rink

Graves was traded to Edmonton by Detroit with Petr Klima, Joe Murphy and Jeff Sharples for Jimmy Carson, Kevin McClelland and Edmonton's 5th round choice (later traded to Montreal - Montreal selected Brad Layzell) in 1991 Entry Draft, November 2, 1989. Signed as a free agent by NY Rangers, September 3, 1991. Traded to San Jose by NY Rangers with future considerations for Mikael Samuelsson and Christian Gosselin, June 24, 2001.

Greenlaw, Jeff

Born: February 28, 1968 in Alymer, Ontario
Drafted: By the Washington Capitals from the Canadian National Team in 1986, 1st round, 19th overall.

Career Junior, NHL and World Junior Statistics

	GP	G	A	PTS	PIM
Canadian National Team 1985-86	57	3	16	19	81
NHL Regular Season 1986-94	57	3	6	9	108
NHL Playoffs	2	0	0	0	21
Canada 1986 World Juniors *in Hamilton*	7	3	1	4	4

Junior Highlights

Won Silver Medal at World Junior Championships in 1986

Around the Rink

Greenlaw played for St. Catharines Junior B (OJHL) for two seasons before joining the Canadian National Team. Signed as a free agent by Florida, July 14, 1993. Signed as a free agent by Cincinnati (IHL), August 29, 1995. Signed as a free agent by Austin (WPHL), October 1, 1998. Player-Assistant Coach with Austin in 2002-03.

Gretzky, Wayne

Hockey Hall of Famer, Inducted 1999
IIHF Hall of Famer, Inducted 2000
Born: January 26, 1961 in Brantford, Ontario
Not Drafted: Signed as a Free Agent by the Indianapolis Racers (WHA) in 1978

Career Junior, NHL and World Junior Statistics

	GP	G	A	PTS	PIM
OHL Regular Season 1977-78	66	70	115	185	14
OHL Playoffs	13	6	20	26	0
NHL Regular Season 1979-99	1487	894	1963	2857	577
NHL Playoffs	208	122	260	382	66
Canada 1978 World Juniors *in Montreal*	6	8	9	17	2

Junior Highlights

Won bronze medal at World Junior Championships in 1978
Won OHL Scoring Title in 1977-78
OHL Seasonal Rookie Records for Points and Assists in 1977-78

Around the Rink

Gretzky played three games for the Peterborough Petes (OHL) in 1976-77 he was called up from Peterborough's bantam affiliate the Seneca Eagles as an undrafted player. He was then drafted by the Sault Ste. Marie Greyhounds (OHL) in the summer of 1977 and played one season for the Greyhounds in 1977-78. Signed as an underage free agent by Indianapolis (WHA), June 12, 1978. Traded to Edmonton (WHA) by Indianapolis (WHA) with Eddie Mio and Peter Driscoll for $700,000 and future considerations, November 2, 1978. Reclaimed by Edmonton as an under-age junior prior to Expansion Draft, June 9, 1979. Claimed as priority selection by Edmonton, June 9, 1979. Traded to LA Kings by Edmonton with Mike Krushelnyski and Marty McSorley for Jimmy Carson, Martin Gelinas, LA Kings' 1st round choices in 1989 (later traded to New Jersey New Jersey selected Jason Miller), 1991 (Martin Rucinsky) and 1993 (Nick Stajduhar) Entry Drafts and cash, August 9, 1988. Traded to St. Louis by LA Kings for Craig Johnson, Patrice Tardif, Roman Vopat, St.Louis 5th round choice (Peter Hogan) in 1996 Entry Draft and 1st round choice (Matt Zultek) in 1997 Entry Draft, February 27, 1996. Signed as a free agent by NY Rangers, July 21, 1996. Officially announced retirement, April 16, 1999.

Habscheid, Marc

Born: March 1, 1963 in Swift Current, Ontario
Drafted: By the Edmonton Oilers from the Saskatoon Blades in 1981, 6th round, 113th overall.

Career Junior, NHL and World Junior Statistics

	GP	G	A	PTS	PIM
WHL Regular Season 1979-83	148	107	169	276	134
WHL Playoffs	5	3	4	7	4
NHL Regular Season 1981-92	345	72	91	163	171
NHL Playoffs	12	1	3	4	13
Canada 1982 World Juniors *in United States*	7	6	6	12	2

Junior Highlights

Won Gold Medal at World Junior Championships in 1982
WHL Second All-Star Team 1982

Around the Rink

Habscheid was traded by Saskatoon to Kamloops after the 1981-82 season. Suspended by Edmonton for refusing to report to Nova Scotia (AHL), October 1985. Traded to Minnesota by Edmonton with Don Barber and Emanuel Viveiros for Gord Sherven and Don Biggs, December 20, 1985. Signed as a free agent by Detroit, June 9, 1989. Traded to Calgary by Detroit for Brian MacLellan, June 11, 1991. Signed as a free agent with Bern of the Swiss league in 1992. Signed as a free agent with Las Vegas (IHL) in 1993, finished the season in the Swiss league. Signed with Augsburger of the German league in 1995 and retired from playing and the end of the season. Head Coach of the Kamloops Blazers (WHL) from 1997-99. Head Coach of the Kelowna Rockets (WHL) 1999-Present.

Hackett, Jeff

Born: June 1, 1968 in London, Ontario
Drafted: By the New York Islanders from the Oshawa Generals in 1987, 2nd round, 34th overall.

Career Junior, NHL and World Junior Statistics

	GP	W	L	T	SO	AVG
OHL Regular Season 1986-88	84	48	30	4	2	3.59
OHL Playoffs	22	11	11	0	0	3.19
Memorial Cup 1987	3	2	1	0	0	4.00
NHL Regular Season 1988-Present	473	156	234	50	23	2.93
NHL Playoffs	9	2	5	0	0	4.32
Canada 1988 World Juniors *in Russia*	0	0	0	0	0	0.00

Junior Highlights

Won Gold Medal at World Junior Championships in 1988

Around the Rink

Hackett was claimed by San Jose from NY Islanders in Expansion Draft, May 30, 1991. Traded to Chicago by San Jose for Chicago's 3rd round choice (Alexei Yegorov) in 1994 Entry Draft, July 13, 1993. Traded to Montreal by Chicago with Eric Weinrich, Alain Nasreddine and Tampa Bay's 4th round choice (previously acquired, Montreal selected Chris Dyment) in 1999 Entry Draft for Jocelyn Thibault, Dave Manson and Brad Brown, November 16, 1998. Missed majority of 2000-01 season recovering from hand injury originally suffered in game vs. Minnesota, October 24, 2000. Missed majority of 2001-02 season recovering from shoulder injury originally suffered in game vs. Buffalo, October 20, 2001. Traded to Boston in three team deal, January 23, 2003.

Haller, Kevin

Born: December 5, 1970 in Trochu, Alberta
Drafted: By the Buffalo Sabres from the Regina Pats in 1989, 1st round, 14th overall.

Career Junior, NHL and World Junior Statistics

	GP	G	A	PTS	PIM
WHL Regular Season 1987-90	125	26	69	95	194
WHL Playoffs	15	3	10	13	18
NHL Regular Season 1989-2002	642	41	96	137	907
NHL Playoffs	64	7	16	23	71
Canada 1990 World Juniors *in Finland*	7	2	2	4	8

Junior Highlights

Won Gold Medal at World Junior Championships in 1990
WHL East First All-Star Team in 1990

Around the Rink

Traded to Montreal by Buffalo for Petr Svoboda, March 10, 1992. Traded to Philadelphia by Montreal for Yves Racine, June 29, 1994. Traded to Hartford by Philadelphia with Philadelphia's 1st round choice (later traded to San Jose - San Jose selected Scott Hannan) in 1997 Entry Draft and Hartford/Carolina's 7th round choice (previously acquired, Carolina selected Andrew Merrick) in 1997 Entry Draft for Paul Coffey and Hartford/Carolina's 3rd round choice (Kris Mallette) in 1997 Entry Draft, December 15, 1996. Transferred to Carolina after Hartford franchise relocated, June 25, 1997. Traded to Anaheim by Carolina with Stu Grimson for Dave Karpa and Anaheim's 4th round choice (later traded to Atlanta - Atlanta selected Blake Robson) in 2000 Entry Draft, August 11, 1998. Signed as a free agent by NY Islanders, July 3, 2000. Missed majority of 2000-01 season recovering from hernia injury suffered in game vs. Ottawa, December 16, 2000. Missed majority of 2001-02 season recovering from groin injury suffered in game vs. LA Kings, October 19, 2001. Did not play in 2002-03.

Halward, Doug

Born: November 1, 1955 in Toronto, Ontario
Drafted: By the Boston Bruins from the Peterborough Petes in 1975, 1st round, 14th overall. Also Drafted by the Quebec Nordiques (WHA) in 1975, 2nd round, 29th overall.

Career Junior, NHL and World Junior Statistics

	GP	G	A	PTS	PIM
OHL Regular Season 1973-1975	137	12	67	79	200
OHL Playoffs	3	1	2	3	5
NHL Regular Season 1975-89	663	69	224	293	774
NHL Playoffs	47	7	10	17	113
Canada 1974 World Juniors *in Russia*	5	0	0	0	2

Junior Highlights

Won Bronze Medal at World Junior Championships in 1974

Around the Rink

Halward was traded to LA Kings by Boston for future considerations, September 18, 1978. Claimed by LA Kings as a fill-in during Expansion Draft, June 13, 1979. Traded to Vancouver by LA Kings for Vancouver's 5th round choice (Ulf Isaksson) in 1982 Entry Draft and future considerations (Gary Bromley, May 12, 1981), March 8, 1981. Traded to Detroit by Vancouver for Detroit's 6th round choice (Phil Von Stefenelli) in 1988 Entry Draft, November 21, 1986. Traded to Edmonton by Detroit for Edmonton's 12th round choice (Jason Glickman) in 1989 Entry Draft, January 23, 1989. Retired from playing in 1989.

Harlock, David

Born: March 16, 1971 in Toronto, Ontario
Drafted: By the New Jersey Devils from the University of Michigan in 1990, 2nd round, 24th overall.

Career Junior, NHL and World Junior Statistics

	GP	G	A	PTS	PIM
NCAA 1989-93	163	8	36	44	252
NHL Regular Season 1993-2002	212	2	14	16	188
NHL Playoffs	0	0	0	0	0
Canada 1991 World Juniors *in Saskatchewan*	7	0	2	2	2

Junior Highlights

Won Gold Medal at World Junior Championships in 1990

Around the Rink

Harlock did not play a game for New Jersey. Signed as a free agent by Toronto, August 20, 1993. Signed as a free agent by Washington August 20, 1997. Signed as a free agent by NY Islanders, August 24, 1998. Claimed by Atlanta from NY Islanders in Expansion Draft, June 25, 1999. Traded to Philadelphia by Atlanta with Atlanta's 3rd and 7th round choices in 2003 Entry Draft for Francis Lessard, March 15, 2002. Has yet to play a game for the Flyers.

Hartsburg, Craig

Born: June 29, 1959 in Stratford, Ontario
Drafted: By the Minnesota North Stars from the Sault Ste. Marie Greyhounds in 1979, 1st round, 6th overall.

Career Junior, NHL and World Junior Statistics

	GP	G	A	PTS	PIM
OHL Regular Season 1975-78	161	53	125	178	308
OHL Playoffs	34	5	19	24	70
NHL Regular Season 1979-89	570	98	315	413	818
NHL Playoffs	61	15	27	42	70
Canada 1978 World Juniors *in Montreal*	6	1	4	5	8

Junior Highlights

OHL Second All-Star Team in 1977
Won Bronze Medal at World Junior Championships in 1978

Around the Rink

Hartsburg signed as an underage free agent by Birmingham (WHA), June 1978 and played one season. Retired from playing in 1989. Assistant Coach with Minnesota 1989-90, Philadelphia 1990-94. Head Coach with Guelph (OHL) 1994-95, Chicago 1995-98, Anaheim 1998-2001. Assistant Coach with Philadelphia 2002-Present.

Harvey, Todd

Born: February 17, 1975 in Hamilton, Ontario
Drafted: By the Dallas Stars from the Detroit Jr. Red Wings in 1993, 1st round, 9th overall.

Career Junior, NHL and World Junior Statistics

	GP	G	A	PTS	PIM
OHL Regular Season 1991-95	172	113	158	271	311
OHL Playoffs	39	22	29	51	95
NHL Regular Season 1994-Present	561	82	125	207	880
NHL Playoffs	42	1	3	4	46
Canada 1994 World Juniors *in Czech Republic*	7	4	3	7	6
Canada 1995 World Juniors *in Alberta*	7	6	0	6	4
Canada Totals	**14**	**10**	**3**	**13**	**10**

Junior Highlights

OHL All-Rookie Team in 1992
Won Gold Medal at World Junior Championships in 1994 and 1995

Around the Rink

Harvey played his first season of junior in 1991-92 with the Detroit Compuware Ambassadors. The team was sold at the end of the season and changed their name to the Jr. Red Wings. Traded to NY Rangers by Dallas with Bob Errey and Dallas' 4th round choice (Boyd Kane) in 1998 Entry Draft for Brian Skrudland, Mike Keane and NY Rangers' 6th round choice (Pavel Patera) in 1998 Entry Draft, March 24, 1998. Traded to San Jose by NY Rangers with NY Rangers' 4th round choice (Dimitri Patzold) in 2001 Entry Draft for Radek Dvorak, December 30, 1999.

Hawerchuk, Dale

Hockey Hall of Famer, Inducted 2001
Born: April 4, 1963 in Toronto, Ontario
Drafted: By the Winnipeg Jets from the Cornwall Royals in 1981, 1st round, 1st overall.

Career Junior, NHL and World Junior Statistics

	GP	G	A	PTS	PIM
QMJHL Regular Season 1979-81	144	114	168	286	90
QMJHL Playoffs	37	35	45	80	8
Memorial Cup 1980 and 1981	10	9	9	18	4
NHL Regular Season 1981-97	1188	518	891	1409	742
NHL Playoffs	97	30	69	99	67
Canada 1981 World Juniors *in Germany*	5	5	4	9	2

Junior Highlights

Won Memorial Cup in 1980 and 1981

Around the Rink

Hawerchuk was traded to Buffalo by Winnipeg with Winnipeg's 1st round choice (Brad May) in 1990 Entry Draft for Phil Housley, Scott Arniel, Jeff Parker and Buffalo's 1st round choice (Keith Tkachuk) in 1990 Entry Draft, June 16, 1990. Signed as a free agent by St. Louis, September 8, 1995. Traded to Philadelphia by St. Louis for Craig MacTavish, March 15, 1996. Retired from playing in 1997.

Hawgood, Greg

Born: August 10, 1968 in St. Albert, Alberta
Drafted: By the Boston Bruins from the Kamloops Blazers in 1986, 10th round, 202nd overall.

Career Junior, NHL and World Junior Statistics

	GP	G	A	PTS	PIM
WHL Regular Season 1983-88	310	147	326	473	478
WHL Playoffs	66	29	71	100	84
Memorial Cup 1984 and 1986	8	3	7	10	6
NHL Regular Season 1987-2002	474	60	164	224	426
NHL Playoffs	42	2	8	10	37
Canada 1987 World Juniors *in Czech Republic*	6	2	2	4	6
Canada 1988 World Juniors *in Russia*	7	1	8	9	6
Canada Totals	**13**	**3**	**10**	**13**	**12**

Junior Highlights

WHL West First All-Star Team in 1986, 1987 and 1988
Won Gold Medal at World Junior Championships in 1988
World Junior Championships All-Star Team in 1988
Canadian Major Junior Defenseman of the Year in 1988

Around the Rink

Hawgood played his first year of junior in 1983-84 for the Kamloops Jr. Oilers, the team was owned by the Edmonton Oilers and was sold to a local group in Kamloops after the 1983-84 season and the team became the Blazers. Traded to Edmonton by Boston for Vladimir Ruzicka, October 22, 1990. Traded to Philadelphia by Edmonton with Josef Beranek for Brian Benning, January 16, 1993. Traded to Florida by Philadelphia for cash, November 30, 1993. Traded to Pittsburgh by Florida for Jeff Daniels, March 19, 1994. Signed as a free agent by San Jose, September 25, 1996. Signed as a free agent by Vancouver, September 30, 1999. Signed as a free agent by Dallas, July 17, 2001. Played the entire 2002-03 season in the minors with Utah (AHL).

Hay, Dwayne

Born: February 17, 1977 in London, Ontario
Drafted: By the Washington Capitals from the Guelph Storm in 1995, 2nd round, 43rd overall.

Career Junior, NHL and World Junior Statistics

	GP	G	A	PTS	PIM
OHL Regular Season 1994-97	167	71	75	146	107
OHL Playoffs	41	13	22	35	24
Memorial Cup 1996	3	0	0	0	2
NHL Regular Season 1997-2001	79	2	4	6	22
NHL Playoffs	0	0	0	0	0
Canada 1997 World Juniors *in Switzerland*	7	0	0	0	2

Junior Highlights

Won Silver Medal at World Junior Championships in 1997

Around the Rink

Hay was traded to Florida by Washington with future considerations for Esa Tikkanen, March 9, 1998. Traded to Tampa Bay by Florida with Ryan Johnson for Mike Sillinger, March 14, 2000. Claimed on waivers by Calgary from Tampa Bay, October 3, 2000. Played 2002-03 season with the St. John's Maple Leafs.

Hazlett, Steve

Born: December 12, 1957 in Sarnia, Ontario
Drafted: By the Vancouver Canucks from the St. Catharines Fincups in 1977, 5th round, 76th overall.

Career Junior, NHL and World Junior Statistics

	GP	G	A	PTS	PIM
OHL Regular Season 1975-78	98	64	87	151	72
OHL Playoffs	48	20	17	37	28
Memorial Cup 1976	3	5	1	6	2
NHL Regular Season 1979-80	1	0	0	0	0
NHL Playoffs	0	0	0	0	0
Canada 1977 World Juniors *in Czech Republic*	7	6	0	6	6

Junior Highlights

Won Silver Medal at World Junior Championships in 1977

Around the Rink

Hazlett played three years of junior. In 1975-76 with the Hamilton Fincups, the team then moved to St. Catharines for the 1976-77 season and then moved back to Hamilton for the 1977-78 season. His lone NHL game came with Vancouver. Spent six seasons in the minors with three different teams, four seasons with Dallas (CHL) 1978-82, two different stints with Fort Wayne (IHL) 1977-78 and 1982-83. Played part of a season with Tulsa (CHL) 1977-78. Retired from playing in 1983.

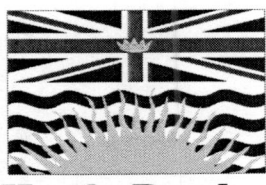

Heath, Randy

Born: November 11, 1964 in Vancouver, B.C.
Drafted: By the New York Rangers from the Portland Winter Hawks in 1983, 2nd round, 33rd overall.

Career Junior, NHL and World Junior Statistics

	GP	G	A	PTS	PIM
WHL Regular Season 1980-84	199	179	162	341	224
WHL Playoffs	43	28	43	71	26
Memorial Cup 1982 and 1983	8	7	9	16	4
NHL Regular Season 1984-86	13	2	4	6	15
NHL Playoffs	0	0	0	0	0
Canada 1984 World Juniors *in Sweden*	7	3	6	9	12

Junior Highlights

WHL First All-Star Team in 1983
Won Memorial Cup in 1983
Memorial Cup All-Star Team in 1983
WHL West First All-Star Team in 1984

Around the Rink

Heath played all 13 of his NHL games with the New York Rangers over two seasons. Spent most of his time with New Haven the Rangers AHL affiliate. Played in Sweden from 1986-89. Retired from playing in 1989.

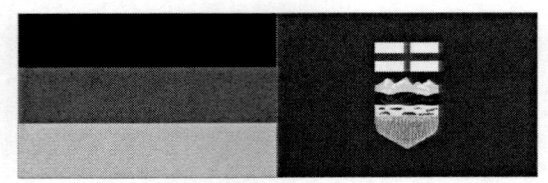

Heatley, Dany

Born: January 21, 1981 in Freibourg, Germany – Raised in Calgary, Alberta
Drafted: By the Atlanta Thrashers from the University of Wisconsin in 2000, 1st round, 2nd overall.

Career Junior, NHL and World Junior Statistics

	GP	G	A	PTS	PIM
NCAA 1999-2001	77	52	61	113	106
NHL Regular Season 2001-Present	159	67	89	156	114
NHL Playoffs	0	0	0	0	0
Canada 2000 World Juniors *in Sweden*	7	2	2	4	4
Canada 2001 World Juniors *in Russia*	7	3	2	5	10
Canada Totals	**14**	**5**	**4**	**9**	**14**

Junior Highlights

Alberta Junior Hockey League Player of the Year in 1999
Canadian Junior "A" Player of the Year With the Calgary Canucks in 1999
Won Bronze Medal at World Junior Championships in 2000 and 2001
Western Collegiate Hockey Association (NCAA) First All-Star Team in 2000
WCHA Rookie of the Year in 2000
NCAA West Second All-American Team in 2000
WCHA Second All-Star Team in 2001
NCAA West First All-American Team in 2001

Around the Rink

Heatley has never played a game in the minors. Played his first NHL game on October 4, 2001 against Buffalo and earned an assist. Scored his first NHL goal October 19, 2001 against Dan Blackburn of the New York Rangers.

Herter, Jason

Born: October 2, 1970 in Hafford, Saskatchewan
Drafted: By the Vancouver Canucks from the University of North Dakota in 1989, 1st round, 8th overall.

Career Junior, NHL and World Junior Statistics

	GP	G	A	PTS	PIM
NCAA 1988-91	118	30	89	119	154
NHL Regular Season 1995-96	1	0	1	1	0
NHL Playoffs	0	0	0	0	0
Canada 1990 World Juniors *in Finland*	7	0	1	1	2

Junior Highlights

Won Gold Medal at World Junior Championships in 1990
Western Collegiate Hockey Association (NCAA) Second All-Star Team in 1990 and 1991

Around the Rink

Hafford played his only NHL game with the New York Islanders. Signed as a free agent by Dallas, August 6, 1993. Traded to NY Islanders by Dallas for cash, September 21, 1995. Played in the IHL with Kansas City and Orlando from 1996-98. Played in Germany from 1998-2002 with Landshut and Munich. Did not play in 2002-03.

Hidi, Andre

Born: June 5, 1960 in Toronto, Ontario
Drafted: By the Colorado Rockies from the Peterborough Petes in 1980, 8th round, 148th overall.

Career Junior, NHL and World Junior Statistics

	GP	G	A	PTS	PIM
OHL Regular Season 1979-81	71	31	36	67	51
OHL Playoffs	19	6	11	17	42
Memorial Cup 1980	5	2	3	5	2
NHL Regular Season 1983-85	7	2	1	3	9
NHL Playoffs	2	0	0	0	0
Canada 1980 World Juniors *in Finland*	5	2	0	2	2

Junior Highlights

Won OHL Championship in 1980

Around the Rink

Hidi played at the Unioversity of Toronto from 1980-84, where he was a two time all-star and a playoff MVP. All of his NHL games came with Washington. Signed as a free agent by Washington, March 29, 1984. He retired from playing in 1986 after two seasons in the minors with Binghamton.

Hodgson, Dan

Born: August 29, 1965 in Fort Vermillion, Alberta
Drafted: By the Toronto Maple Leafs from the Prince Albert Raiders in 1983, 5th round, 83rd overall.

Career Junior, NHL and World Junior Statistics

	GP	G	A	PTS	PIM
WHL Regular Season 1980-85	209	188	305	493	217
WHL Playoffs	18	15	29	44	39
Memorial Cup 1985	5	1	13	14	6
NHL Regular Season 1985-89	114	29	45	74	64
NHL Playoffs	0	0	0	0	0
Canada 1984 World Juniors *in Sweden*	7	1	4	5	4
Canada 1985 World Juniors *in Finland*	7	5	2	7	0
Canada Totals	**14**	**6**	**6**	**12**	**7**

Junior Highlights

WHL Rookie of the Year in 1983
Won Gold Medal at World Junior Championships in 1985
Won Memorial Cup in 1985
WHL East First All-Star Team in 1985
Memorial Cup All-Star Team in 1985
Canadian Major Junior Player of the Year in 1985
Won Stafford Smythe Memorial Trophy (Memorial Cup MVP) in 1985

Around the Rink

Hodgson played two games with Spokane in 1980 as an undrafted call up. Drafted in the summer of 1981 by Prince Albert. Traded to Vancouver by Toronto with Jim Benning for Rick Lanz, December 2, 1986. Has played in Europe since 1989, two seasons in Germany and twelve in Switzerlad.

Hodgson, Rick

Born: May 23, 1956 in Medicine Hat, Alberta
Drafted: By the Atlanta Flames from the Calgary Centennials in 1976, 3rd round, 46th overall. Also Drafted by the San Diego Mariners (WHA) in 1976, 6th round, 65th overall.

Career Junior, NHL and World Junior Statistics

	GP	G	A	PTS	PIM
WHL Regular Season 1973-76	171	22	128	150	563
WHL Playoffs	14	1	9	10	34
NHL Regular Season 1979-80	6	0	0	0	6
NHL Playoffs	1	0	0	0	0
Canada 1975 World Juniors *in Manitoba*	3	0	1	1	0

Junior Highlights

Won Silver Medal at World Junior Championships in 1975

Around the Rink

Hodgson played all six of his NHL games with Hartford. Claimed by Hartford from Atlanta in Expansion Draft, June 13, 1979. Retired from playing in 1980.

Holden, Josh

Born: January 18, 1978 in Calgary, Alberta
Drafted: By the Vancouver Canucks from the Regina Pats in 1996, 1st round, 12th overall.

Career Junior, NHL and World Junior Statistics

	GP	G	A	PTS	PIM
WHL Regular Season 1994-98	246	167	185	352	432
WHL Playoffs	22	12	10	22	43
NHL Regular Season 1998-Present	59	5	9	14	16
NHL Playoffs	0	0	0	0	0
Canada 1998 World Juniors *in Finland*	7	4	0	4	14

Junior Highlights

WHL East Second All-Star Team in 1998

Around the Rink

Holden was claimed by Carolina from Vancouver in Waiver Draft, September 28, 2001. Claimed on waivers by Vancouver from Carolina, October 25, 2001. Traded to Toronto by Vancouver for Jeff Farkas, June 23, 2002.

Holland, Jason

Born: April 30, 1976 in Morinville, Alberta
Drafted: By the New York Islanders from the Kamloops Blazers in 1994, 2nd round, 38th overall.

Career Junior, NHL and World Junior Statistics

	GP	G	A	PTS	PIM
WHL Regular Season 1992-96	197	47	80	127	127
WHL Playoffs	55	8	19	27	35
Memorial Cup 1994 and 1995	8	0	6	6	4
NHL Regular Season 1996-Present	29	1	2	3	12
NHL Playoffs	1	0	0	0	0
Canada 1996 World Juniors *in United States*	6	2	1	3	4

Junior Highlights

Won Memorial Cup in 1994 and 1995
WHL West First All-Star Team in 1996
Won Gold Medal at World Junior Championships in 1996

Around the Rink

Holden was traded to Buffalo by the New York Islanders with Paul Kruse for Jason Dawe, March 24, 1998. Signed as a free agent by LA Kings, August 23, 2001.

Huber, Willie

Born: January 15, 1958 in Strasskirchen, Germany – Raised in Hamilton, Ontario
Drafted: By the Detroit Red Wings from the Hamilton Fincups in 1978, 1st round, 9th overall.

Career Junior, NHL and World Junior Statistics

	GP	G	A	PTS	PIM
OHL Regular Season 1975-78	155	24	77	101	343
OHL Playoffs	44	10	27	37	102
Memorial Cup 1976	3	0	0	0	8
NHL Regular Season 1978-88	655	104	217	321	950
NHL Playoffs	33	5	5	10	35
Canada 1977 World Juniors *in Czech Republic*	7	1	2	3	13
Canada 1978 World Juniors *in Montreal*	6	0	2	2	2
Canada Totals	**13**	**1**	**4**	**5**	**15**

Junior Highlights

Won Memorial Cup in 1976
Won Silver Medal at World Junior Championships in 1977
Won Bronze Medal at World Junior Championships in 1978
OHL Second All-Star Team in 1978

Around the Rink

Huber played all three years of junior with the Fincups. Hamilton 1975-76, 1977-78 and St. Catharines 1976-77. Traded to NY Rangers by Detroit with Mike Blaisdell and Mark Osborne for Ron Duguay, Eddie Mio and Eddie Johnstone, June 13, 1983. Traded to Vancouver by NY Rangers with Larry Melynk for Michel Petit, November 4, 1987. Traded to Philadelphia by Vancouver for Paul Lawless and Vancouver's 5th round choice (previously acquired, later traded to Edmonton Edmonton selected Peter White) in 1989 Entry Draft, March 1, 1988.

Huffman, Kerry

Born: January 3, 1968 in Peterborough, Ontario
Drafted: By the Philadelphia Flyers from the Guelph Platers in 1986, 1st round, 20th overall.

Career Junior, NHL and World Junior Statistics

	GP	G	A	PTS	PIM
OHL Regular Season 1985-87	100	7	55	62	55
OHL Playoffs	25	1	12	13	18
Memorial Cup 1986	4	0	3	3	2
NHL Regular Season 1986-96	401	37	108	145	361
NHL Playoffs	11	0	0	0	2
Canada 1987 World Juniors *in Czech Republic*	6	0	1	1	2

Junior Highlights

Won Memorial Cup in 1986
Won George Parsons Trophy (Memorial Cup Most Sportsmanlike Player) in 1986
OHL First All-Star Team in 1987

Around the Rink

Huffman was traded to Quebec by Philadelphia with Steve Duchesne, Peter Forsberg, Mike Ricci, Ron Hextall, Philadelphia's 1st round choice (Jocelyn Thibault) in 1993 Entry Draft, $15,000,000 and future considerations (Chris Simon and Philadelphia's 1st round choice (later traded to Toronto later traded to Washington Washington selected Nolan Baumgartner) in 1994 Entry Draft, July 21, 1992) for Eric Lindros, June 30, 1992. Claimed on waivers by Ottawa from Quebec, January 15, 1994. Traded to Philadelphia by Ottawa for future considerations, March 19, 1996. Signed as a free agent by Las Vegas (IHL), October 12, 1996. Signed as a free agent by Grand Rapids (IHL), October 16, 1997. Retired from playing in 1999.

Hughes, Ryan

Born: January 17, 1972 in Montreal, Quebec
Drafted: By the Quebec Nordiques from Cornell University in 1990, 2nd round, 22nd overall.

Career Junior, NHL and World Junior Statistics

	GP	G	A	PTS	PIM
NCAA 1989-93	113	43	77	120	129
NHL Regular Season 1995-96	3	0	0	0	0
NHL Playoffs	0	0	0	0	0
Canada 1992 World Juniors *in Germany*	7	0	1	1	0

Junior Highlights

Had a Career Junior High in Points With 52 in 32 Games in 1990-91
Played in NCAA Frozen Four Tournament in 1992

Around the Rink

Hughes played all three of his NHL games with Boston. Signed as a free agent by Boston, October 6, 1995. Retired from playing in 1997 after splitting the season in the IHL with Chicago and Quebec.

Hull, Jody

Born: February 2, 1969 in Petrolia, Ontario
Drafted: By the Hartford Whalers from the Peterborough Petes in 1987, 1st round, 18th overall.

Career Junior, NHL and World Juniors Statistics

	GP	G	A	PTS	PIM
OHL Regular Season 1985-88	170	88	100	188	84
OHL Playoffs	40	15	22	37	26
NHL Regular Season 1988-Present	830	124	137	261	156
NHL Playoffs	67	4	5	9	14
Canada 1988 World Juniors *in Russia*	7	2	1	3	2

Junior Highlights

Won Gold Medal at World Junior Championships in 1988
OHL Second All-Star Team in 1988

Around the Rink

Hull was traded to the New York Rangers by Hartford for Carey Wilson and NY Rangers' 3rd round choice (Michael Nylander) in the 1991 Entry Draft, July 9, 1990. Traded to Ottawa by NY Rangers for future considerations, July 28, 1992. Signed as a free agent by Florida, August 10, 1993. Traded to Tampa Bay by Florida with Mark Fitzpatrick for Dino Ciccarelli and Jeff Norton, January 15, 1998. Signed as a free agent by Philadelphia, October 7, 1998. Claimed by Atlanta from Philadelphia in Expansion Draft, June 25, 1999. Traded to Philadelphia by Atlanta for cash, October 15, 1999. Signed as a free agent by Ottawa, January 24, 2002.

Hunter, Dave

Born: January 1, 1958 in Petrolia, Ontario
Drafted: By the Montreal Canadiens from the Sudbury Wolves in 1978, 1st round, 17th overall.

Career Junior, NHL and World Junior Statistics

	GP	G	A	PTS	PIM
OHL Regular Season 1975-78	183	81	121	202	413
OHL Playoffs	23	1	12	13	62
NHL Regular Season 1979-89	746	133	190	323	914
NHL Playoffs	105	16	24	40	211
Canada 1977 World Juniors *in Czech Republic*	7	6	2	8	2

Junior Highlights

Won Silver Medal at World Junior Championships in 1977

Around the Rink

Hunter signed as an underage free agent by Edmonton (WHA), June 1978. Claimed by Edmonton from Montreal in Expansion Draft, June 13, 1979. Traded to Pittsburgh by Edmonton with Paul Coffey and Wayne Van Dorp for Craig Simpson, Dave Hannan, Moe Mantha and Chris Joseph, November 24, 1987. Transferred to Edmonton by Pittsburgh as compensation for Pittsburgh's claiming Dave Hannan in Waiver Draft, October 3, 1988. Claimed by Winnipeg from Edmonton in Waiver Draft, October 3, 1988. Claimed on waivers by Edmonton from Winnipeg, January 14, 1989. Retired from playing in 1989.

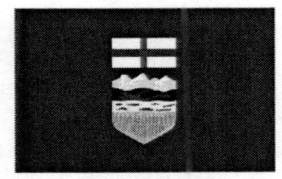

Iginla, Jarome

Born: July 1, 1977 in Edmonton, Alberta
Drafted: By the Dallas Stars from the Kamloops Blazers in 1995, 1st round, 11th overall.

Career Junior, NHL and World Junior Statistics

	GP	G	A	PTS	PIM
WHL Regular Season 1993-96	183	102	134	236	264
WHL Playoffs	56	26	30	56	88
Memorial Cup 1994 and 1995	8	4	4	8	11
NHL Regular Season 1996-Present	545	209	221	430	338
NHL Playoffs	2	1	1	2	0
Canada 1996 World Juniors *in United States*	6	5	7	12	4

Junior Highlights

Won Memorial Cup in 1994 and 1995
Won George Parsons Trophy (Memorial Cup Most Sportsmanlike Player) in 1995
Won Gold Medal at World Junior Championships in 1996
World Junior Championships All-Star Team in 1996
Named Best Forward at World Junior Championships in 1996
WHL West First All-Star Team in 1996
Canadian Major Junior First All-Star Team in 1996

Around the Rink

Iginla was traded to Calgary by Dallas with Corey Millen for Joe Nieuwendyk, December 19, 1995.

Intranuovo, Ralph

Born: December 11, 1973 in Toronto, Ontario
Drafted: By the Edmonton Oilers from the Sault Ste. Marie Greyhounds in 1992, 4th round, 96th overall.

Career Junior, NHL and World Junior Statistics

	GP	G	A	PTS	PIM
OHL Regular Season 1990-93	182	106	152	258	127
OHL Playoffs	50	27	43	70	59
Memorial Cup 1991, 1992 and 1993	11	4	7	11	12
NHL Regular Season 1994-97	22	2	4	6	4
NHL Playoffs	0	0	0	0	0
Canada 1993 World Juniors *in Sweden*	7	3	2	5	4

Junior Highlights

Won Gold Medal at World Junior Championships in 1993
Won Memorial Cup in 1993
Memorial Cup All-Star Team in 1993
Won Stafford Smythe Memorial Trophy (Memorial Cup MVP) in 1993

Around the Rink

Intranuovo was claimed by Toronto from Edmonton in waiver draft, September 30, 1996. Claimed on waivers by Edmonton from Toronto, October 25, 1996. Signed as a free agent with Manitoba (IHL) in 1997. Played in Germany from 1999-2002. Did not play in 2002-03.

Isbister, Brad

Born: May 7, 1977 in Edmonton, Alberta
Drafted: By the Winnipeg Jets from the Portland Winter Hawks in 1995, 3rd round, 67th overall.

Career Junior, NHL and World Junior Statistics

	GP	G	A	PTS	PIM
WHL Regular Season 1993-97	226	83	92	175	397
WHL Playoffs	23	4	7	11	36
NHL Regular Season 1997-Present	358	83	82	165	463
NHL Playoffs	14	1	2	3	31
Canada 1997 World Juniors *in Switzerland*	7	4	3	7	8

Junior Highlights

Won Gold Medal at World Junior Championships in 1997
WHL West Second All-Star Team in 1997

Around the Rink

Isbister's rights were transferred to Phoenix after Winnipeg franchise relocated July 1, 1996. Traded to NY Islanders by Phoenix with Phoenix's 3rd round choice (Brian Collins) in 1999 Entry Draft for Robert Reichel, NY Islanders' 3rd round choice (Jason Jaspers) in 1999 Entry Draft and Ottawa's 4th round choice (previously acquired, Phoenix selected Preston Mizzi) in 1999 Entry Draft, March 20, 1999. Traded with Raffi Torres to Edmonton for Janne Niinimaa and Edmonton's 2nd round pick in the 2003 entry draft on March 11, 2003.

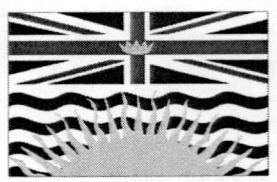

Jackman, Barret

Born: March 5, 1981 in Trail, B.C.
Drafted: By the St. Louis Blues from the Regina Pats in 1999, 1st round, 17th overall.

Career Junior, NHL and World Junior Statistics

	GP	G	A	PTS	PIM
WHL Regular Season 1997-2001	234	28	111	129	796
WHL Playoffs	21	1	7	8	59
Memorial Cup 2001	5	1	1	2	12
NHL Regular Season 2001-Present	83	3	16	19	190
NHL Playoffs	6	0	0	0	16
Canada 2000 World Juniors in Sweden	7	0	1	1	8
Canada 2001 World Juniors in Russia	7	0	3	3	10
Canada Totals	**14**	**0**	**4**	**4**	**18**

Junior Highlights

Won Bronze Medal at World Junior Championships in 2000 and 2001
WHL East Second All-Star Team in 2000

Around the Rink

Jackman made St. Louis full time in 2002-03 after playing just one game in 2001-02. First NHL game April 14 2002 against Detroit. First NHL point, an assist against Colorado, October 17, 2002. First NHL goal, against Detroit, December 8, 2002.

Jackman, Richard

Born: June 28, 1978 in Toronto, Ontario
Drafted: By the Dallas Stars from the Sault Ste. Marie Greyhounds in 1996, 1st round, 5th overall.

Career Junior, NHL and World Junior Statistics

	GP	G	A	PTS	PIM
OHL Regular Season 1995-98	179	59	103	162	324
OHL Playoffs	14	3	6	9	39
NHL Regular Season 1999-Present	82	1	4	5	67
NHL Playoffs	0	0	0	0	0
Canada 1997 World Juniors *in Switzerland*	7	2	0	2	0

Junior Highlights

OHL All-Rookie Team in 1996
Won Gold Medal at World Junior Championships in 1997
OHL Second All-Star Team in 1998

Around the Rink

Jackman was traded to Boston by Dallas for Cameron Mann, June 23, 2001. Missed majority of 2001-02 season recovering from shoulder injury suffered in game vs. St. Louis, October 21, 2001. Traded to Toronto by Boston for the rights to Kris Vernarsky, May 13, 2002.

Jackson, Jeff

Born: April 24, 1965 in Chatham, Ontario
Drafted: By the Toronto Maple Leafs from the Brantford Alexanders in 1983, 2nd round, 28th overall.

Career Junior, NHL and World Junior Statistics

	GP	G	A	PTS	PIM
OHL Regular Season 1982-85	142	58	81	139	192
OHL Playoffs	27	9	13	22	53
NHL Regular Season 1984-92	263	38	48	86	313
NHL Playoffs	6	1	1	2	16
Canada 1985 World Juniors *in Finland*	7	1	7	8	10

Junior Highlights

Won Gold Medal at World Junior Championships in 1985

Around the Rink

Jackson played his first two seasons of junior with Brantford, the team moved to Hamilton and became the Steelhawks at the start of the 1984-85 season. Traded to NY Rangers by Toronto with Toronto's 3rd round choice (Rob Zamuner) in 1989 Entry Draft for Mark Osborne, March 5, 1987. Traded to Quebec by NY Rangers with Terry Carkner for John Ogrodnick and David Shaw, September 30, 1987. Signed as a free agent by Chicago, February 19, 1992 but only played one game. Retired at the end of the 1991-92 season as a member of the Indianapolis Ice (IHL).

Jarvis, Doug

Born: March 24, 1955 in Brantford, Ontario
Drafted: By the Toronto Maple Leafs from the Peterborough Petes in 1975, 2nd round, 24th overall. Also Drafted by the Houston Aeros (WHA) in 1975, 2nd round, 30th overall.

Career Junior, NHL and World Junior Statistics

	GP	G	A	PTS	PIM
OHL Regular Season 1972-75	139	96	190	286	80
OHL Playoffs	11	4	11	15	8
NHL Regular Season 1975-88	964	139	264	403	263
NHL Playoffs	105	14	27	41	42
Canada 1974 World Juniors *in Russia*	5	4	1	5	2

Junior Highlights

Won Gold Medal at World Junior Championships in 1974
OHL Second All-Star Team in 1975

Around the Rink

Jarvis was traded to Montreal by Toronto for Greg Hubick, June 26, 1975. Traded to Washington by Montreal with Rod Langway, Craig Laughlin and Brian Engblom for Ryan Walter and Rick Green, September 9, 1982. Traded to Hartford by Washington for Jorgen Pettersson, December 6, 1985. Retired from playing in 1988 after twenty-four games with Binghamton (AHL) to become their Head Coach. Assistant Coach Minnesota/Dallas 1988-Present.

Jaspers, Jason

Born: April 8, 1981 in Thunder Bay, Ontario
Drafted: By the Phoenix Coyotes from the Sudbury Wolves in 1999, 3rd round, 71st overall.

Career Junior, NHL and World Junior Statistics

	GP	G	A	PTS	PIM
OHL Regular Season 1998-2001	199	116	136	252	265
OHL Playoffs	28	9	23	32	58
NHL Regular Season 2001-Present	6	0	1	1	4
NHL Playoffs	0	0	0	0	0
Canada 2001 World Juniors *in Russia*	7	1	0	1	6

Junior Highlights

OHL Second All-Star Team in 2000
Won Bronze Medal at World Junior Championships in 2001

Around the Rink

Jaspers has spent most of his pro-career with Springfield (AHL), Phoenix's farm team. Played first NHL game January 21, 2002 against Nashville. Recorded first NHL point, an assist versus Detroit, January 25, 2002.

Jensen, Al

Born: November 27, 1958 in Hamilton, Ontario
Drafted: By the Detroit Red Wings from the Hamilton Fincups in 1978, 2nd round, 31st overall.

Career Junior, NHL and World Junior Statistics

	GP	W	L	T	SO	AVG
OHL Regular Season 1975-78	119	NOT AVAILABLE			5	3.63
OHL Playoffs	33	17	10	5	3	2.81
Memorial Cup 1976	0	0	0	0	0	0.00
NHL Regular Season 1980-87	179	95	53	18	8	3.35
NHL Playoffs	12	5	5	0	0	3.21
Canada 1977 World Juniors *in Czech Rep*.	7	5	1	1	0	2.85
Canada 1978 World Juniors *in Montreal*	3	NOT AVAILABLE				4.00
Canada Totals	**10**	**5**	**1**	**1**	**0**	**3.20**

Junior Highlights

Won Memorial Cup in 1976
Won Silver Medal at World Junior Championships in 1977
OHL Second All-Star Team in 1977
Won Bronze Medal at World Junior Championships in 1978
OHL First All-Star Team in 1978

Around the Rink

Jensen played three years of junior for the same franchise, the Hamilton Fincups in 1975-76 and 1977-78 and the St. Catharines Fincups 1976-77. Traded to Washington by Detroit for Mark Lofthouse, July 23, 1981. Traded to LA Kings by Washington for Garry Galley, February 14, 1987. Retired from playing in 1988 after spending the season in the minors with New Haven (AHL).

Johansen, Trevor

Born: March 30, 1957 in Thunder Bay, Ontario
Drafted: By the Toronto Maple Leafs from the Toronto Marlboros in 1977, 1st round, 12th overall.

Career Junior, NHL and World Junior Statistics

	GP	G	A	PTS	PIM
OHL Regular Season 1974-77	177	16	89	105	493
OHL Playoffs	23	2	8	10	48
Memorial Cup 1975	4	0	2	2	4
NHL Regular Season 1977-82	286	11	46	57	282
NHL Playoffs	13	0	3	3	21
Canada 1977 World Juniors *in Czech Republic*	5	0	0	0	5

Junior Highlights

Won Memorial Cup in 1975
Won Silver Medal at World Junior Championships in 1977
OHL First All-Star Team in 1977

Around the Rink

Johansen was traded to Colorado by Toronto with Don Ashby for Paul Gardner, March 13, 1979. Claimed by LA Kings from Colorado in Waiver Draft, October 5, 1981. Claimed on waivers by Toronto from LA Kings, February 19, 1982. Retired in 1983 after spending a season in the AHL with Springfield.

Johnson, Greg

Born: March 16, 1971 in Thunder Bay, Ontario
Drafted: By the Philadelphia Flyers from the University of North Dakota in 1989, 2nd round, 33rd overall.

Career Junior, NHL and World Junior Statistics

	GP	G	A	PTS	PIM
NCAA 1989-93	155	74	198	272	43
NHL Regular Season 1993-Present	635	120	198	318	302
NHL Playoffs	26	6	3	9	12
Canada 1991 World Juniors *in Saskatoon*	7	4	2	6	0

Junior Highlights

Western Collegiate Hockey Assoc. (NCAA) First All-Star Team in 1991, 1992, and 1993
Won Gold Medal at World Junior Championships in 1991
NCAA West First All-American Team in 1991 and 1993
NCAA West Second All-American Team in 1992

Around the Rink

Johnson was traded to Detroit by Philadelphia with Philadelphia's 5th round choice (Frederic Deschenes) in 1994 Entry Draft for Jim Cummins and Philadelphia's 4th round choice (previously acquired by Detroit - later traded to Boston - Boston selected Charles Paquette) in 1993 Entry Draft, June 20, 1993. Traded to Pittsburgh by Detroit for Tomas Sandstrom, January 27, 1997. Traded to Chicago by Pittsburgh for Tuomas Gronman, October 27, 1997. Claimed by Nashville from Chicago in Expansion Draft, June 26, 1998.

Johnston, Greg

Born: January 14, 1965 in Barrie, Ontario
Drafted: By the Boston Bruins from the Toronto Marlboros in 1983, 2nd round, 42nd overall.

Career Junior, NHL and World Junior Statistics

	GP	G	A	PTS	PIM
OHL Regular Season 1982-85	157	78	82	160	180
OHL Playoffs	18	6	5	11	21
NHL Regular Season 1983-92	187	26	29	55	124
NHL Playoffs	22	2	1	3	12
Canada 1985 World Juniors *in Finland*	7	2	0	2	2

Junior Highlights

Won Gold Medal at World Junior Championships in 1985

Around the Rink

Johnston was traded to the New York Rangers by Boston with cash for Chris Nilan, June 28, 1990. Traded to Toronto by the New York Rangers for Tie Domi and Mark LaForest, June 28, 1990. Played in Germany from 1992-2001. Played in Sweden in 2001-02. Did not play in 2002-03.

Joly, Yvan

Born: February 6, 1960 in Hawkesbury, Ontario
Drafted: By the Montreal Canadiens from the Ottawa 67`s in 1979, 5th round, 100th overall.

Career Junior, NHL and World Junior Statistics

	GP	G	A	PTS	PIM
OHL Regular Season 1976-80	256	183	215	398	195
OHL Playoffs	31	11	22	33	43
NHL Regular Season 1979-83	2	0	0	0	0
NHL Playoffs	1	0	0	0	0
Canada 1979 World Juniors *in Sweden*	5	2	0	2	2
Canada 1980 World Juniors *in Finland*	5	3	0	3	8
Canada Totals	**10**	**5**	**0**	**5**	**10**

Junior Highlights

OHL Second All-Star Team in 1979
OHL First All-Star Team in 1980

Around the Rink

Joly played both of his NHL games with Montreal. Spent most of his career with Nova Scotia (AHL) 1980-83. Played for Maine (AHL) in 1983-84 when Montreal moved its farm team from Nova Scotia. Released by Montreal and did not play in 1984-85. Signed as a free agent by Indianapolis (IHL) in 1985. Retired from playing 1986.

Jonathan, Stan

Born: May 9, 1955 in Oshweken, Ontario
Drafted: By the Boston Bruins from the Peterborough Petes in 1975, 5th round, 86th overall. Also Drafted by the Indianapolis Racers (WHA) in 1975, 8th round, 103rd overall.

Career Junior, NHL and World Junior Statistics

	GP	**G**	**A**	**PTS**	**PIM**
OHL Regular Season 1972-75	204	69	107	176	372
OHL Playoffs	22	8	10	18	28
NHL Regular Season 1975-83	411	91	110	201	751
NHL Playoffs	63	8	4	12	137
Canada 1974 World Juniors *in Russia*	5	0	0	0	8

Junior Highlights

Won Bronze Medal at World Junior Championships in 1974

Around the Rink

Jonathan was traded to Pittsburgh by Boston for cash, November 8, 1982. Did not play from 1983-86. Played one game in 1987 with Brantford of the Ontario Senior League and officially retired.

Joseph, Chris

Born: September 10, 1969 in Burnaby, B.C.
Drafted: By the Pittsburgh Penguins from the Seattle Thunderbirds in 1987, 1st round, 5th overall.

Career Junior, NHL and World Junior Statistics

	GP	G	A	PTS	PIM
WHL Regular Season 1985-88	162	22	67	89	254
WHL Playoffs	5	0	3	3	12
NHL Regular Season 1987-2001	510	39	112	151	567
NHL Playoffs	31	3	4	7	24
Canada 1987 World Juniors *in Czech Republic*	6	1	1	2	12
Canada 1988 World Juniors *in Russia*	7	1	2	3	6
Canada Totals	**13**	**2**	**3**	**5**	**18**

Junior Highlights

WHL West Second All-Star Team in 1987
Won Gold Medal at World Junior Championships in 1988

Around the Rink

Joseph was traded to Edmonton by Pittsburgh with Craig Simpson, Dave Hannan and Moe Mantha for Paul Coffey, Dave Hunter and Wayne Van Dorp, November 24, 1987. Traded to Tampa Bay by Edmonton for Bob Beers, November 11, 1993. Claimed by Pittsburgh from Tampa Bay in Waiver Draft, January 18, 1995. Claimed by Vancouver from Pittsburgh in Waiver Draft, September 30, 1996. Signed as a free agent by Philadelphia, September 11, 1997. Signed as a free agent by Ottawa, August 18, 1999. Claimed by Vancouver from Ottawa in Waiver Draft, September 27, 1999. Claimed on waivers by Phoenix from Vancouver, March 14, 2000. Claimed on waivers by Atlanta from Phoenix, February 14, 2001. Signed with Turku in the Finnish league as a free agent in 2001. Signed as a free agent with Manheim in the German league in 2002.

Jovanovski, Ed

Born: June 26, 1976 in Windsor, Ontario
Drafted: By the Florida Panthers from the Windsor Spitfires in 1994, 1st round, 1st overall.

Career Junior, NHL and World Junior Statistics

	GP	G	A	PTS	PIM
OHL Regular Season 1993-95	112	38	77	115	419
OHL Playoffs	13	2	7	9	54
NHL Regular Season 1995-Present	587	71	190	261	963
NHL Playoffs	37	3	13	16	64
Canada 1995 World Juniors *in Alberta*	7	2	0	2	4

Junior Highlights

OHL All-Rookie Team in 1994
OHL Second All-Star Team in 1994
OHL First All-Star Team in 1995
Won Gold Medal at World Junior Championships in 1995

Around the Rink

Jovanovski was dealt to Vancouver by Florida with Dave Gagner, Mike Brown, Kevin Weekes and Florida's 1st round choice (Nathan Smith) in 2000 Entry Draft for Pavel Bure, Bret Hedican, Brad Ference and Vancouver's 3rd round choice (Robert Fried) in 2000 Entry Draft, January 17, 1999.

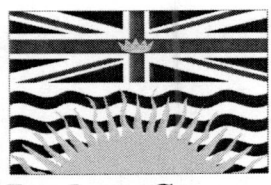

Junker, Steve

Born: June 26, 1972 in Castlegar, B.C.
Drafted: By the New York Islanders from the Spokane Chiefs in 1991, 5th round, 92nd overall.

Career Junior, NHL and World Junior Statistics

	GP	G	A	PTS	PIM
WHL Regular Season 1988-92	266	106	121	227	312
WHL Playoffs	31	11	24	35	26
Memorial Cup 1991	4	0	3	3	2
NHL Regular Season 1992-94	5	0	0	0	0
NHL Playoffs	3	0	1	1	0
Canada 1992 World Juniors *in Germany*	7	2	2	4	4

Junior Highlights

Won Memorial Cup in 1991

Around the Rink

Junker played all of his NHL games with the New York Islanders. Played in the IHL from 1994-96 with Denver, Detroit and Los Angeles. Has played in Germany since 1997.

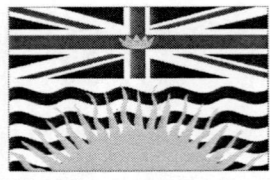

Kariya, Paul

Born: October 16, 1974 in Vancouver, B.C.
Drafted: By the Anaheim Mighty Ducks from the University of Maine in 1993, 1st round, 4th overall.

Career Junior, NHL and World Junior Statistics

	GP	G	A	PTS	PIM
Canadian National Team 1993-94	47	17	52	69	45
NCAA 1992-94	51	33	91	124	16
NHL Regular Season 1994-Present	606	300	369	669	213
NHL Playoffs	14	8	9	17	4
Canada 1992 World Juniors *in Germany*	6	1	1	2	2
Canada 1993 World Juniors *in Sweden*	7	2	6	8	2
Canada World Junior Totals	**13**	**3**	**7**	**10**	**4**

Junior Highlights

World Junior Championship All-Star Team in 1993
Hockey East (NCAA) First All-Star Team in 1993
Hockey East (NCAA) Rookie of the Year in 1993
Hockey East (NCAA) Player of the Year in 1993
NCAA East First All-American Team in 1993
NCAA Championship All-Tournament Team in 1993
Won Hobey Baker Memorial Award (Top U.S. Collegiate Player) in 1993
Won Gold Medal at World Junior Championships in 1993
Won NCAA Championship (Frozen Four) in 1993
Won Silver Medal at Olympics in 1994
Won Gold Medal at World Championships in 1994
World Championship All-Star Team in 1994
Named Best Forward at World Championships in 1994

Around the Rink

Kariya played in two World Junior Championships, two World Championships and an Olympics all before playing one game in the NHL and all before the age of 20. Missed majority of 1997-98 season after failing to come to contract terms with Anaheim and recovering from head injury suffered in game vs. San Jose, February 1, 1998.

Keane, Mike

Born: May 29, 1967 in Winnipeg, Manitoba
Not Drafted: Signed as a Free Agent with Montreal in 1985.

Career Junior, NHL and World Junior Statistics

	GP	**G**	**A**	**PTS**	**PIM**
WHL Regular Season 1983-87	186	76	120	196	410
WHL Playoffs	22	9	17	26	20
NHL Regular Season 1988-Present	1097	160	293	453	861
NHL Playoffs	212	34	40	74	131
Canada 1987 World Juniors *in Czech Republic*	6	0	1	1	4

Junior Highlights

First Put on a Pair of Skates in 1980 Three Years Later Keane was in the WHL

Around the Rink

Keane was an undrafted call up to the Winnipeg Warriors of the WHL for one game in the 1983-84 season from their bantam affiliate the Winnipeg Monarchs of the Manitoba Minor Hockey League. Moose Jaw drafted him in the summer of 1984 where he played the duration of his junior career. Signed as a free agent by Montreal, September 25, 1985. Traded to Colorado by Montreal with Patrick Roy for Andrei Kovalenko, Martin Rucinsky and Jocelyn Thibault, December 6, 1995. Signed as a free agent by NY Rangers July 30, 1997. Traded to Dallas by NY Rangers with Brian Skrudland and NY Rangers' 6th round choice (Pavel Patera) in 1998 Entry Draft for Todd Harvey, Bob Errey and Dallas' 4th round choice (Boyd Kane) in 1998 Entry Draft, March 24, 1998. Signed as a free agent by St. Louis, July 10, 2001. Traded to Colorado by St. Louis for Shjon Podein, February 11, 2002.

Keating, Mike

Born: January 21, 1957 in Toronto, Ontario
Drafted: By the New York Rangers from the St. Catharines Fincups in 1977, 2nd round, 26th overall. Also Drafted by the Winnipeg Jets (WHA) in 1977, 9th round, 80th overall.

Career Junior, NHL and World Junior Statistics

	GP	**G**	**A**	**PTS**	**PIM**
OHL Regular Season 1974-77	184	124	122	246	271
OHL Playoffs	41	15	13	28	68
Memorial Cup 1976	3	1	1	2	0
NHL Regular Season 1977-78	1	0	0	0	0
NHL Playoffs	0	0	0	0	0
Canada 1977 World Juniors *in Czech Republic*	7	0	2	2	4

Junior Highlights

Won Memorial Cup in 1976
Won Silver Medal at World Junior Championships in 1977

Around the Rink

Keating played his first two junior seasons with Hamilton, the team moved to St. Catharines for the 1976-77 season. Played just one NHL game and it was with the New York Rangers, he registered two shots on net and finished the game as a –1. Signed as a free agent with Toledo (IHL) in 1978 and retired from playing in 1980.

Kelly, John-Paul

Born: November 15, 1959 in Edmonton, Alberta
Drafted: By the Los Angeles Kings from the New Westminster Bruins in 1979, 3rd round, 50th overall.

Career Junior, NHL and World Junior Statistics

	GP	G	A	PTS	PIM
WHL Regular Season 1975-79	210	86	76	162	395
WHL Playoffs	30	12	18	30	66
Memorial Cup 1977 and 1978	5	3	0	3	2
NHL Regular Season 1979-86	400	54	70	124	366
NHL Playoffs	18	1	1	2	41
Canada 1979 World Juniors *in Sweden*	5	0	0	0	10

Junior Highlights

Won Memorial Cup in 1977 and 1978

Around the Rink

Kelly played his entire NHL career with Los Angeles. He played just 49 games in the minors with Houston and Rochester from 1980-81. Retired from playing in 1986.

Kennedy, Sheldon

Born: June 15, 1969 in Elkhorn, Manitoba
Drafted: By the Detroit Red Wings from the Swift Current Broncos in 1988, 4th round, 80th overall.

Career Junior, NHL and World Junior Statistics

	GP	G	A	PTS	PIM
WHL Regular Season 1986-89	159	134	153	287	180
WHL Playoffs	26	17	27	44	38
Memorial Cup 1989	5	4	5	9	6
NHL Regular Season 1989-97	310	49	58	107	233
NHL Playoffs	24	6	4	10	20
Canada 1988 World Juniors *in Russia*	7	4	2	6	6
Canada 1989 World Juniors *in United States*	7	3	4	7	14
Canada Totals	**14**	**7**	**6**	**13**	**20**

Junior Highlights

Won Gold Medal at World Junior Championships in 1988
Won Memorial Cup in 1989
WHL East Second All-Star Team in 1989
Memorial Cup All-Star Team in 1989

Around the Rink

Kennedy missed majority of 1990-91 season recovering from arm injury suffered in automobile accident, July 1990. Traded to Winnipeg by Detroit for Winnipeg's 3rd round choice (Darryl Laplante) in 1995 Entry Draft, May 25, 1994. Claimed by Calgary from Winnipeg in NHL Waiver Draft, January 18, 1995. Signed as free agent by Boston, August 7, 1996. Missed entire 1997-98 season recovering from leg injury suffered in cycling accident, July 1997. Retired in 1999 after playing a season in Germany.

Kidd, Trevor

Born: March 26, 1972 in Dugald, Manitoba
Drafted: By the Calgary Flames from the Brandon Wheat Kings in 1990, 1st round, 11th overall.

Career Junior, NHL and World Junior Statistics

	GP	W	L	T	SO	AVG
Canadian National Team 1992	1	1	0	0	1	0.00
WHL Regular Season 1988-91	139	53	67	4	4	4.04
WHL Playoffs	15	14	1	0	2	2.07
Memorial Cup 1991	3	3	0	0	0	1.67
NHL Regular Season 1991-Present	372	134	157	50	18	2.82
NHL Playoffs	9	3	5	0	1	4.06
Canada 1990 World Juniors *in Finland*	0	0	0	0	0	0.00
Canada 1991 World Juniors *in Saskatoon*	6	4	1	0	1	2.25
Canada 1992 World Juniors *in Germany*	7	2	3	2	1	4.29
Canada World Junior Totals	**13**	**6**	**4**	**2**	**2**	**3.31**

Junior Highlights

WHL East First All-Star Team in 1990
Canadian Major Junior Goaltender of the Year in 1990
Won Gold Medal at World Junior Championships in 1990 and 1991
Won Memorial Cup in 1991
Won Silver Medal at Olympics in 1992

Around the Rink

Kidd was traded by Brandon to Spokane after thirty games in 1990-91. Traded to Carolina by Calgary with Gary Roberts for Andrew Cassels and Jean-Sebastien Giguere, August 25, 1997. Claimed by Atlanta from Carolina in Expansion Draft, June 25, 1999. Traded to Florida by Atlanta for Gord Murphy, Herbert Vasiljevs, Daniel Tjarnqvist and Ottawa's 6th round choice (previously acquired, later traded to Dallas - Dallas selected Justin Cox) in 1999 Entry Draft, June 25, 1999. Signed as a free agent by Toronto, August 26, 2002.

Kitchen, Bill

Born: October 2, 1960 in Schomberg, Ontario
Not Drafted: Signed as a Free Agent by the Montreal Canadiens in 1979.

Career Junior, NHL and World Junior Statistics

	GP	G	A	PTS	PIM
OHL Regular Season 1976-80	197	16	41	57	447
OHL Playoffs	30	2	11	13	44
NHL Regular Season 1981-85	41	1	4	5	40
NHL Playoffs	3	0	1	1	0
Canada 1980 World Juniors *in Finland*	5	0	1	1	10

Junior Highlights

Scored a Goal in His First OHL Game in 1976

Around the Rink

Kitchen played two games with Windsor in 1976 as an undrafted bantam call up. Ottawa drafted him in the summer of 1977 where he played the rest of his junior career. Signed as a free agent by Montreal, October 23, 1979. Signed as a free agent by Toronto, August 16, 1984. Retired in 1986 after playing a season in the minors with Toronto's AHL affiliate in St. Catharines.

Klassen, Ralph

Born: September 15, 1955 in Humboldt, Saskatchewan
Drafted: By the California Golden Seals from the Saskatoon Blades in 1975, 1st round, 3rd overall. Also Drafted by the Cleveland Crusaders (WHA) in 1975, 1st round, 5th overall.

Career Junior, NHL and World Junior Statistics

	GP	G	A	PTS	PIM
WHL Regular Season 1970-75	300	81	194	275	317
WHL Playoffs	49	11	34	45	44
NHL Regular Season 1975-84	497	52	93	145	120
NHL Playoffs	26	4	2	6	12
Canada 1975 World Juniors *in Manitoba*	4	0	3	3	0

Junior Highlights

Won Silver Medal at the World Junior Championships in 1975

Around the Rink

Klassen's rights were transferred to Cleveland after California franchise relocated, June 1976. Traded to Colorado by Cleveland with Fred Ahern for Rick Jodzio and Chuck Arnason, January 9, 1978. Claimed by Hartford from Colorado in Expansion Draft, June 13, 1979. Traded to NY Islanders by Hartford for Terry Richardson, June 14, 1979. Traded to St. Louis by NY Islanders as part of three-team transaction that sent Barry Gibbs and Tom Williams to NY Islanders (June 9, 1979) and Tom Williams to LA Kings (August 16, 1979), June 14, 1979. Retired from playing in 1984.

Kluzak, Gord

Born: March 4, 1964 in Climax, Saskatchewan
Drafted: By the Boston Bruins from the Billings Bighorns in 1982, 1st round, 1st overall.

Career Junior, NHL and World Junior Statistics

	GP	G	A	PTS	PIM
WHL Regular Season 1980-82	106	13	58	71	270
WHL Playoffs	5	0	1	1	4
NHL Regular Season 1982-91	299	25	98	123	543
NHL Playoffs	46	6	13	19	129
Canada 1982 World Juniors *in United States*	7	0	1	1	4

Junior Highlights

Won Gold Medal at the World Championships in 1982
WHL Second All-Star Team in 1982
World Junior Championships All-Star Team in 1982
Named Best Defenseman at World Junior Championships in 1982

Around the Rink

Kluzak missed the entire 1984-85 season recovering from knee injury suffered in pre-season game vs. New Jersey, October 7, 1984. Missed entire 1986-87 season recovering from knee surgery, September 1986. Missed majority of 1988-89 season recovering from 8th knee surgery, September 17, 1988. Missed majority of 1989-90 season recovering from 10th knee surgery, October 27, 1989. Retired from playing in 1991.

Photo Gallery Part Two
"All Photos Courtesy of the Hockey Hall of Fame Collection"

1. 1993 Tyler Wright Jersey
2. 1999 Roberto Luongo
3. 1997 Dube, Biron, Denis, Doig and Briere
4. 1991 Eric Lindros
5. 1991 Steven Rice Jersey
6. 1991 Steven Rice Jersey
7. 1977 Bobby Smith
8. 1995 Team Canada Celebration
9. 1996 Jose Theodore

1993 Tyler Wright Jersey

1999 Roberto Luongo

1997 Dube, Biron, Denis, Doig and Briere

1991 Eric Lindros

1991 Steven Rice Jersey

1991 Steven Rice Jersey

1977 Bobby Smith

1995 Team Canada Celebration

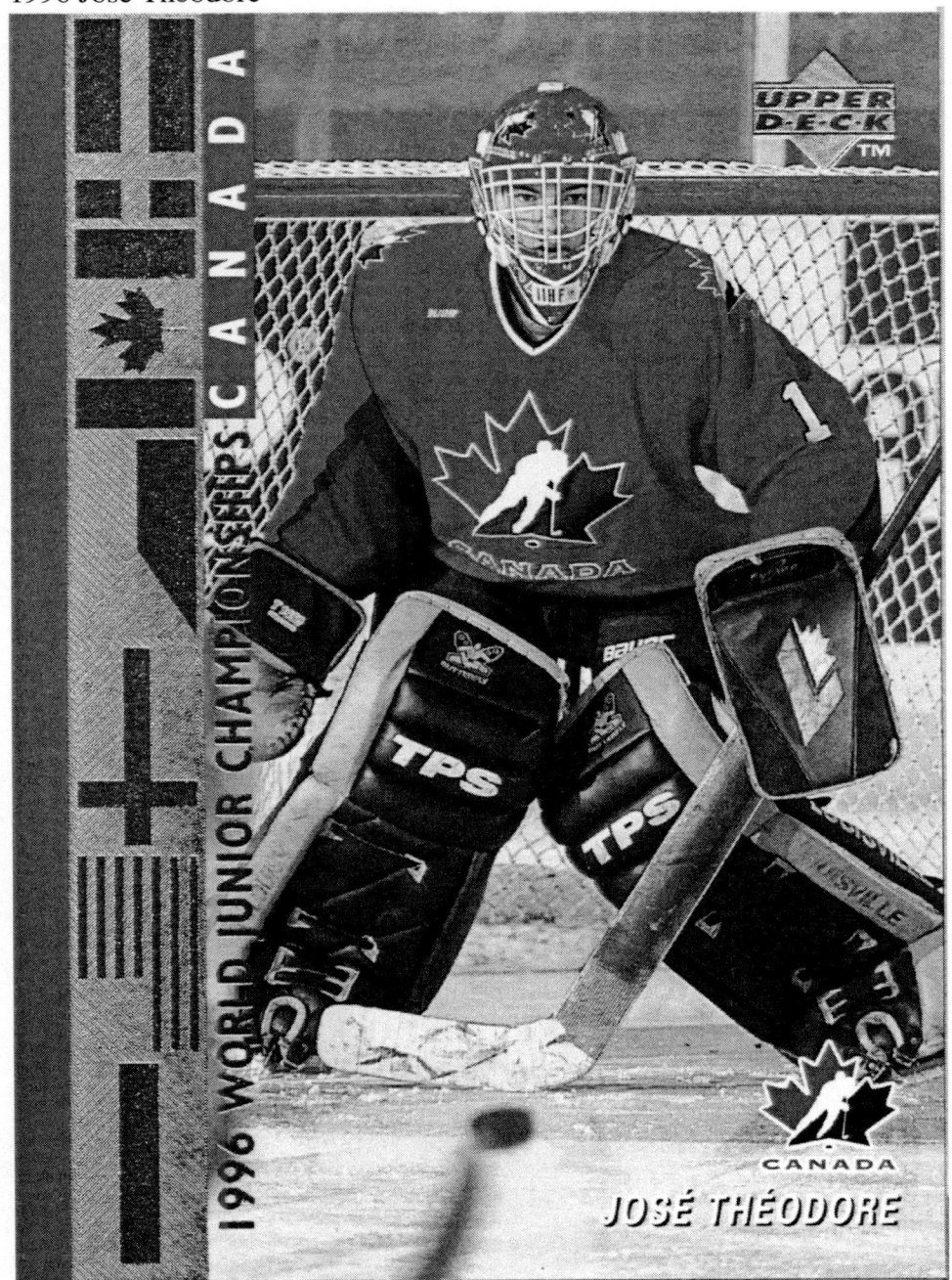

1996 Jose Theodore

Kobasew, Chuck

Born: April 17, 1982 in Osooyoos, B.C.
Drafted: By the Calgary Flames from Boston College in 2001, 1st round, 14th overall.

Career Junior, NHL and World Junior Statistics

	GP	G	A	PTS	PIM
NCAA 2000-01	43	27	22	49	38
WHL Regular Season 2001-02	55	41	21	62	114
WHL Playoffs	15	10	5	15	22
NHL Regular Season 2002-03	23	4	2	6	8
NHL Playoffs	0	0	0	0	0
Canada 2002 World Juniors *in Czech Republic*	7	5	1	6	2

Junior Highlights

Hockey East (NCAA) Rookie of the Year in 2001
NCAA All-Tournament Team in 2001
NCAA Frozen Four Tournament MVP in 2001
Won NCAA Championship (Frozen Four) in 2001
Won Silver Medal at World Junior Championships in 2002

Around the Rink

Kobasew's rights traded to Kelowna by Prince George for Chuck Di Ubaldo and future considerations, Aug. 1, 2001. Played first NHL game on October 10, 2002 versus Vancouver. Scored his first NHL goal on October 14, 2002 against Vancouver, it was the game winner with 4:38 left in the third period.

Komarniski, Zenith

Born: August 13, 1978 in Edmonton, Alberta
Drafted: By the Vancouver Canucks from the Tri-City Americans in 1996, 3rd round, 75th overall.

Career Junior, NHL and World Junior Statistics

	GP	G	A	PTS	PIM
WHL Regular Season 1994-98	212	29	108	137	415
WHL Playoffs	35	5	8	13	96
NHL Regular Season 1999-Present	19	1	1	2	10
NHL Playoffs	0	0	0	0	0
Canada 1998 World Juniors *in Finland*	7	0	0	0	26

Junior Highlights

WHL West First All-Star Team in 1997

Around the Rink

Komarniski was traded to Spokane (WHL) by Tri-City (WHL) for Blake Evans, October 25, 1997. Played 18 games with Vancouver in 1999-00 and one other game in 2002-03. Has spent most of his pro career with Manitoba of the AHL Vancouver`s minor league affiliate.

LaFayette, Nathan

Born: February 17, 1973 in New Westminster, B.C.
Drafted: By the St. Louis Blues from the Cornwall Royals in 1991, 3rd round, 65th overall.

Career Junior, NHL and World Junior Statistics

	GP	G	A	PTS	PIM
OHL Regular Season 1989-93	240	112	126	238	101
OHL Playoffs	20	6	11	17	34
NHL Regular Season 1993-99	187	17	20	37	103
NHL Playoffs	32	2	7	9	8
Canada 1993 World Juniors *in Sweden*	7	3	1	4	0

Junior Highlights

Canadian Major Junior Scholastic Player of the Year in 1992
Won Gold Medal at World Junior Championships in 1993

Around the Rink

LaFayette was traded by Kingston to Cornwall after 35 games in 1990-91. Cornwall moved to Newmarket in 1992 where LaFayette played his last season of junior. Traded to Vancouver by St. Louis with Jeff Brown and Bret Hedican for Craig Janney, March 21, 1994. Traded to NY Rangers by Vancouver for Corey Hirsch, April 7, 1995. Traded to LA Kings by NY Rangers with Ray Ferraro, Mattias Norstrom, Ian Laperriere and NY Rangers' 4th round choice (Sean Blanchard) in 1997 Entry Draft for Marty McSorley, Jari Kurri and Shane Churla, March 14, 1996. Retired in 2000 after playing a full season in the minors with Lowell of the AHL.

LaFerriere, Rick

Born: January 3, 1961 in Hawkesbury, Ontario
Drafted: By the Colorado Rockies from the Peterborough Petes in 1980, 4th round, 64th overall.

Career Junior, NHL and World Junior Statistics

(W-L-T Stats Incomplete)	GP	W	L	T	SO	AVG
OHL Regular Season 1978-82	130	26	23	2	3	3.85
OHL Playoffs	28	12	2	0	0	2.64
Memorial Cup 1980	5	3	2	0	0	4.13
NHL Regular Season 1981-82	1	0	0	0	0	3.00
NHL Playoffs	0	0	0	0	0	0.00
Canada 1980 World Juniors *in Finland*	4	2	2	0	0	3.25

Junior Highlights

OHL Second All-Star Team in 1980
Memorial Cup All-Star Team in 1980
Won Hap Emms Memorial Trophy (Memorial Cup Top Goaltender) in 1980

Around the Rink

LaFerriere was traded from Peterborough to Brantford after 34 games in 1980-81. His only action game when he replaced Chico Resch at start of 3rd period, February 23, 1982. (Detroit 6, Colorado 3). Retired from playing in 1984 after spending two straight season in the IHL.

Lambert, Dan

Born: January 12, 1970 in St. Boniface, Manitoba
Drafted: By the Quebec Nordiques from the Swift Current Broncos in 1989, 6th round, 106th overall.

Career Junior, NHL and World Junior Statistics

	GP	G	A	PTS	PIM
WHL Regular Season 1986-90	244	75	244	319	492
WHL Playoffs	30	14	33	47	78
Memorial Cup 1989	5	2	6	8	12
NHL Regular Season 1990-1992	29	6	9	15	22
NHL Playoffs	0	0	0	0	0
Canada 1991 World Juniors *in Saskatoon*	7	1	2	3	4

Junior Highlights

Won Memorial Cup in 1989
WHL East First All-Star Team in 1989 and 1990
Memorial Cup All-Star Team in 1989
Won Stafford Smythe Memorial Trophy (Memorial Cup MVP) in 1989
Won Gold Medal at World Junior Championships in 1991

Around the Rink

Lambert was traded to Winnipeg by Quebec for Shawn Cronin, August 25, 1992, but he never played a game for Winnipeg. Has played in Germany since 2000 after stints in Finland and the IHL.

Langkow, Daymond

Born: September 27, 1976 in Edmonton, Alberta
Drafted: By the Tampa Bay Lightning from the Tri-City Americans in 1995, 1st round, 5th overall.

Career Junior, NHL and World Junior Statistics

	GP	G	A	PTS	PIM
WHL Regular Season 1991-96	247	159	219	378	515
WHL Playoffs	36	29	30	59	91
NHL Regular Season 1995-Present	544	115	187	302	334
NHL Playoffs	33	8	11	19	27
Canada 1996 World Juniors *in Alberta*	5	3	3	6	2

Junior Highlights

WHL West First All-Star Team in 1995
Canadian Major Junior First All-Star Team in 1995
Won Gold Medal at World Junior Championships in 1996
WHL West Second All-Star Team in 1996

Around the Rink

Langkow was traded to Philadelphia by Tampa Bay with Mikael Renberg for Chris Gratton and Mike Sillinger, December 12, 1998. Traded to Phoenix by Philadelphia for Phoenix's 2nd round choice (later traded to Tampa Bay - later traded to San Jose - San Jose selected Dan Spang) in 2002 Entry Draft and 1st round choice in 2003 Entry Draft, July 2, 2001.

Lanz, Rick

Born: September 16, 1981 in Karlovy Vary, Czech Republic – Raised in Ontario
Drafted: By the Vancouver Canucks from the Oshawa Generals in 1980, 1st round, 7th overall.

Career Junior, NHL and World Junior Statistics

	GP	G	A	PTS	PIM
OHL Regular Season 1977-80	183	30	127	157	190
OHL Playoffs	18	3	8	11	24
NHL Regular Season 1980-92	569	65	221	286	448
NHL Playoffs	28	3	8	11	35
Canada 1980 World Juniors *in Finland*	5	0	1	1	6

Junior Highlights

Averaged More Than a Point Per Game in His Final Year of Junior in 1979-80

Around the Rink

Lanz was traded to Toronto by Vancouver for Jim Benning and Dan Hodgson, December 2, 1986. Signed as a free agent by Chicago, August 13, 1990. Traded to LA Kings by Chicago for cash, November 29, 1991. Retired from playing in 1993 after playing half a season with Atlanta in the IHL. Head Coach of Tri-City from 1997-98. Head Coach of Langley of the BCJHL 1998-Present.

Lapointe, Martin

Born: September 12, 1973 in Ville St. Oierre, Quebec
Drafted: By the Detroit Red Wings from the Laval Titan in 1991, 1st round, 10th overall.

Career Junior, NHL and World Junior Statistics

	GP	G	A	PTS	PIM
QMJHL Regular Season 1989-93	195	149	189	338	316
QMJHL Playoffs	50	32	58	90	134
Memorial Cup 1990 and 1993	9	2	9	11	15
NHL Regular Season 1991-Present	679	133	155	288	1065
NHL Playoffs	97	19	24	43	184
Canada 1991 World Juniors *in Saskatoon*	7	0	3	3	2
Canada 1992 World Juniors *in Germany*	7	4	1	5	10
Canada 1993 World Juniors *in Sweden*	7	5	4	9	6
Canada Totals	**21**	**9**	**8**	**17**	**18**

Junior Highlights

QMJHL First All-Star Team in 1990 and 1993
QMJHL Offensive Rookie of the Year in 1990
Won Gold Medal at World Junior Championships in 1991 and 1993
QMJHL Second All-Star Team in 1991
Memorial Cup All-Star Team in 1993

Around the Rink

Lapointe played his first NHL game on October 5, 1991 against Toronto. Recorded his first NHL with an assist versus Calgary on December 3, 1991. Scored his first NHL goal at St. Louis on November 21, 1993. Signed as a free agent with Boston on July 2, 2001.

Lapointe, Rick

Born: August 2, 1955 in Victoria, B.C.
Drafted: By the Detroit Red Wings from the Victoria Cougars in 1975, 1st round, 5th overall. Also Drafted by the Toronto Toros (WHA) in 1975, 1st round, 11th overall.

Career Junior, NHL and World Junior Statistics

	GP	**G**	**A**	**PTS**	**PIM**
WHL Regular Season 1971-75	176	30	81	111	405
WHL Playoffs	12	1	12	13	26
NHL Regular Season 1975-86	664	44	176	220	831
NHL Playoffs	46	2	7	9	64
Canada 1975 World Juniors *in Manitoba*	5	2	3	5	16

Junior Highlights

Won Silver Medal at World Junior Championships in 1975
World Junior Championships All-Star Team in 1975
WHL First All-Star Team in 1975

Around the Rink

Lapointe was traded to Philadelphia by Detroit with Mike Korney for Terry Murray, Bob Ritchie, Steve Coates and Dave Kelly, February 17, 1977. Traded to St. Louis by Philadelphia with Blake Dunlop for Phil Myre, June 7, 1979. Traded to Quebec by St. Louis for Pat Hickey, August 4, 1982. Signed as a free agent by LA Kings, October 10, 1984. Retired from playing in 1986.

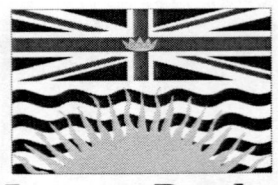

Larsen, Brad

Born: January 28, 1977 in Nakusp, B.C.
Drafted: By the Ottawa Senators from the Swift Current Broncos in 1995, 3rd round, 53rd overall. Also Drafted by the Colorado Avalanche in 1997, 4th round, 87th overall.

Career Junior, NHL and World Junior Statistics

	GP	G	A	PTS	PIM
WHL Regular Season 1993-97	238	105	144	249	238
WHL Playoffs	19	4	5	9	19
NHL Regular Season 1997-Present	65	2	10	12	49
NHL Playoffs	21	1	1	2	13
Canada 1996 World Juniors *in United States*	6	1	1	2	4
Canada 1997 World Juniors *in Switzerland*	7	0	1	1	6
Canada Totals	**13**	**1**	**2**	**3**	**10**

Junior Highlights

Won Gold Medal at World Junior Championships in 1996 and 1997
WHL East Second All-Star Team in 1997

Around the Rink

Larsen's rights were traded to Colorado by Ottawa for Janne Laukkanen, January 26, 1996 but he did not sign with Colorado at that time. First NHL game, March 21, 1998 at San Jose. First NHL point was an assist against Carolina October 23, 2001. First NHL goal March 28, 2002 at San Jose. Missed majority of 1998-99 season recovering from abdominal injury suffered in game vs. Albany (AHL), November 20, 1998.

Latta, David

Born: January 3, 1967 in Thunder Bay, Ontario
Drafted: By the Quebec Nordiques from the Kitchener Rangers in 1985, 1st round, 15th overall.

Career Junior, NHL and World Junior Statistics

	GP	G	A	PTS	PIM
OHL Regular Season 1983-87	223	123	133	256	186
OHL Playoffs	29	12	14	26	30
Memorial Cup 1984	4	0	0	0	0
NHL Regular Season 1985-91	36	4	8	12	4
NHL Playoffs	0	0	0	0	0
Canada 1987 World Juniors *in Czech Republic*	6	4	6	10	12

Junior Highlights

Played on First Place Team that Was Disqualified at World Junior Championships in 1987

Around the Rink

Latta played all of his NHL games with Quebec. Retired from playing in 1998 after playing in England, Germany, the IHL and the WCHL. Head Coach of Tupelo of the WPHL from 1998-99.

Laxdal, Derek

Born: February 21, 1966 in St. Boniface, Manitoba
Drafted: By the Toronto Maple Leafs from the Brandon Wheat Kings in 1984, 8th round, 151st overall.

Career Junior, NHL and World Junior Statistics

	GP	G	A	PTS	PIM
WHL Regular Season 1982-86	238	131	111	242	263
WHL Playoffs	26	0	6	6	12
Memorial Cup 1983	4	0	0	0	0
NHL Regular Season 1984-91	67	12	7	19	88
NHL Playoffs	1	0	2	2	2
Canada 1986 World Juniors *in Hamilton*	7	1	4	5	6

Junior Highlights

Won Memorial Cup in 1983
Won Silver Medal at World Junior Championships in 1986

Around the Rink

Laxdal won a Memorial Cup with Portland and then was traded before the next season to Brandon where he played two and half seasons before being dealt to New Westminster where he finished off his junior career. Traded to the New York Islanders by Toronto with Jack Capuano and Paul Gagne for Mike Stevens and Gilles Thibaudeau, December 20, 1989. Signed as a free agent by Odessa (WPHL), December 9, 1999 after playing five seasons in England and one in Finland. Played in the Roller Hockey League with the Ottawa Loggers in 1995 (22-25-28-53-38) and the Denver Dare Devils in 1996 (16-3-15-18-32). Retired from playing in 2001. Assistant Coach with Odessa (CHL) from 2001-2003, left Odessa to become the Head Coach of Wichita (CHL).

Leach, Jamie

Born: August 25, 1969 in Winnipeg, Manitoba
Drafted: By the Pittsburgh Penguins from the Hamilton Steelhawks in 1987, 3rd round, 47th overall.

Career Junior, NHL and World Junior Statistics

	GP	G	A	PTS	PIM
WHL/OHL Regular Season 1985-89	244	89	107	178	213
OHL Playoffs	40	16	19	35	41
NHL Regular Season 1989-94	81	11	9	20	12
NHL Playoffs	0	0	0	0	0
Canada 1989 World Juniors *in United States*	7	1	4	5	2

Junior Highlights

Had an Incredible 107 Points in Just 58 Games in 1988-89
Son Of Flyer Great Reggie Leach

Around the Rink

Leach played his first season of junior in 1985-86 with New Westminster of the WHL he transferred to Hamilton of the OHL for the following season. Hamilton moved to Niagara Falls in 1988. Claimed on waivers by Hartford from Pittsburgh on November 21, 1992. Signed as a free agent by Florida, August 31, 1993. Played for the Canadian National team in 1994-95. After two years in the minors Leach went to England in 1996 and played there until he officially announced retirement and named Assistant Coach of New Jersey, August 3, 2001.

LeBlanc, Fern

Born: January 12, 1956 in Gaspesie, Quebec
Drafted: By the Detroit Red Wings from the Sherbrooke Beavers in 1976, 7th round, 111th overall. Also Drafted by the Cincinnati Stingers in 1976, 9th round, 96th overall.

Career Junior, NHL and World Junior Statistics

	GP	G	A	PTS	PIM
QMJHL Regular Season 1971-76	180	117	114	231	89
QMJHL Playoffs	Not Available				
NHL Regular Season 1976-79	34	5	6	11	0
NHL Playoffs	0	0	0	0	0
Canada 1976 World Juniors *in Finland*	4	1	1	2	4

Junior Highlights

Won Silver Medal at World Junior Championships in 1976

Around the Rink

LeBlanc did not play from 1979-82. Played in Switzerland from 1982-89 with Chur, Herisau and Ajoie. Retired from playing in 1989.

Lecavalier, Vincent

Born: April 21, 1980 in Ile Bizard, Quebec
Drafted: By the Tampa Bay Lightning from the Rimouski Oceanic in 1998, 1st round, 1st overall.

Career Junior, NHL and World Junior Statistics

	GP	G	A	PTS	PIM
QMJHL Regular Season 1996-98	122	86	131	217	153
QMJHL Playoffs	22	19	29	48	48
NHL Regular Season 1998-Present	386	114	147	261	232
NHL Playoffs	11	3	3	6	22
Canada 1998 World Juniors *in Finland*	7	1	1	2	2

Junior Highlights

Canadian Major Junior Rookie of the Year in 1997
QMJHL All-Rookie Team in 1997
QMJHL Offensive Rookie of the Year in 1997
QMJHL First All-Star Team in 1998
Canadian Major Junior First All-Star Team in 1998

Around the Rink

Lecavalier has never played a game in the minors. Played first NHL game on October 9, 1998 against Florida. Recorded first NHL point with an assist against Pittsburgh on October 21, 1998. Scored first NHL goal on October 25, 1998 versus Vancouver.

Leeb, Brad

Born: August 27, 1979 in Red Deer, Alberta
Not Drafted: Signed as a Free Agent With Vancouver in 1999.

Career Junior, NHL and World Junior Statistics

	GP	G	A	PTS	PIM
WHL Regular Season 1994-99	228	73	96	169	282
WHL Playoffs	38	12	12	24	29
NHL Regular Season 1999-2002	4	0	0	0	2
NHL Playoffs	0	0	0	0	0
Canada 1999 World Juniors *in Winnipeg*	7	3	5	8	2

Junior Highlights

Won Silver Medal at World Junior Championships in 1999
WHL East Second All-Star Team in 1999

Around the Rink

Leeb played his entire junior career with the Red Deer Rebels. Signed as a free agent by Vancouver, October 8, 1999. Played all four of his NHL games with Vancouver. Traded to Toronto by Vancouver for Tomas Mojzis, September 4, 2002. Spent the entire 2002-03 with Toronto's AHL affiliate in St. John's.

Leeman, Gary

Born: February 19, 1964 in Toronto, Ontario
Drafted: By the Toronto Maple Leafs from the Regina Pats in 1982, 2nd round, 24th overall.

Career Junior, NHL and World Junior Statistics

	GP	G	A	PTS	PIM
WHL Regular Season 1981-83	135	43	103	146	200
WHL Playoffs	8	3	7	10	4
NHL Regular Season 1982-97	667	199	267	466	531
NHL Playoffs	36	8	16	24	36
Canada 1983 World Juniors *in Russia*	7	1	2	3	2
Canada 1984 World Juniors *in Sweden*	7	3	6	9	12
Canada Totals	**14**	**4**	**8**	**12**	**14**

Junior Highlights

Won Bronze Medal at World Junior Championships in 1983
WHL First All-Star Team in 1983

Around the Rink

Leeman was traded to Calgary by Toronto with Craig Berube, Alexander Godynyuk, Michel Petit and Jeff Reese for Doug Gilmour, Jamie Macoun, Ric Nattress, Rick Wamsley and Kent Manderville, January 2, 1992. Traded to Montreal by Calgary for Brian Skrudland, January 28, 1993. Signed as a free agent by Vancouver, January 18, 1995. Signed as a free agent by St. Louis, September 26, 1996. Retired from playing in 1999 after spending two seasons in Germany.

Legace, Manny

Born: February 4, 1973 in Toronto, Ontario
Drafted: By the Hartford Whalers from the Niagara Falls Thunder in 1993, 8th round, 188th overall.

Career Junior, NHL and World Junior Statistics

	GP	W	L	T	SO	AVG
OHL Regular Season 1990-93	121	56	46	8	0	3.86
OHL Playoffs	22	9	10	0	0	4.38
NHL Regular Season 1998-Present	105	54	25	13	3	2.26
NHL Playoffs	1	0	0	0	0	5.45
Canada 1993 World Juniors *in Sweden*	6	6	0	0	1	1.67

Junior Highlights

Won Gold Medal at World Junior Championships in 1993
Named Best Goaltender at World Junior Championships in 1993
OHL First All-Star Team in 1993

Around the Rink

Legace's rights were transferred to Carolina after Hartford franchise relocated, June 25, 1997, he never played a game with either franchise. Traded to LA Kings by Carolina for future considerations, July 31, 1998. Signed as a free agent by Detroit, August 9, 1999. Claimed on waivers by Vancouver from Detroit, September 30, 1999. Claimed on waivers by Detroit from Vancouver, October 13, 1999. Recorded his first NHL shutout against Chicago on October 12, 2000.

Lemay, Moe

Born: February 18, 1962 in Saskatoon, Saskatchewan
Drafted: By the Vancouver Canucks from the Ottawa 67's in 1981, 5th round, 105th overall.

Career Junior, NHL and World Junior Statistics

	GP	**G**	**A**	**PTS**	**PIM**
OHL Regular Season 1979-82	187	116	138	254	170
OHL Playoffs	34	14	27	41	54
NHL Regular Season 1981-89	317	72	94	166	442
NHL Playoffs	28	6	3	9	55
Canada 1982 World Juniors *in United States*	7	2	0	2	4

Junior Highlights

Won Gold Medal at World Junior Championships in 1982
OHL First All-Star Team in 1982

Around the Rink

Lemay was traded to Edmonton by Vancouver for Raimo Summanen, March 10, 1987. Traded to Boston by Edmonton for Alan May, March 8, 1988. Traded to Winnipeg by Boston for Ray Neufeld, December 30, 1988. Played in Austria, Switzerland and Germany from 1989-2000. Retired from playing in 2000.

Lemieux, Claude

Born: July 16, 1965 in Buckingham, Quebec
Drafted: By the Montreal Canadiens from the Trois Rivieres Draveurs in 1983, 2nd round, 26th overall.

Career Junior, NHL and World Junior Statistics

	GP	G	A	PTS	PIM
QMJHL Regular Season 1982-85	165	127	149	274	564
QMJHL Playoffs	27	32	29	61	131
Memorial Cup 1984	3	1	3	4	2
NHL Regular Season 1983-Present	1197	379	406	785	1756
NHL Playoffs	226	80	77	157	519
Canada 1985 World Juniors *in Finland*	6	3	2	5	6

Junior Highlights

QMJHL Second All-Star Team in 1984
Won Gold Medal at World Junior Championships in 1985
QMJHL First All-Star Team in 1985

Around the Rink

Lemieux played three years of junior hockey. His first year was with Trois Rivieres, his last two were with the Verdun Junior Canadiens. Missed majority of 1989-90 season recovering from abdominal injury suffered in game vs. Boston, October 9, 1989. Traded to New Jersey by Montreal for Sylvain Turgeon, September 4, 1990. Traded to NY Islanders by New Jersey for Steve Thomas, October 3, 1995. Traded to Colorado by NY Islanders for Wendel Clark, October 3, 1995. Traded to New Jersey by Colorado with Colorado's 1st (David Hale) and 2nd (Matt DeMarchi) round choices in 2000 Entry Draft for Brian Rolston and New Jersey's 1st round choice (later traded to Boston - Boston selected Martin Samuelsson) in 2000 Entry Draft, November 3, 1999. Signed as a free agent by Phoenix, December 5, 2000. Traded by Phoenix to Dallas for Scott Pellerin and a conditional draft pick in the 2004 Entry Draft, January 16, 2003.

Lemieux, Mario

Hockey Hall of Famer Inducted 1997
Born: October 5, 1965 in Montreal, Quebec
Drafted: By the Pittsburgh Penguins from the Laval Titans in 1984, 1st round, 1st overall.

Career Junior, NHL and World Junior Statistics

	GP	**G**	**A**	**PTS**	**PIM**
QMJHL Regular Season 1981-84	200	247	315	561	190
QMJHL Playoffs	44	48	50	98	78
Memorial Cup 1984	3	1	2	3	0
NHL Regular Season 1984-Present	879	682	1010	1692	812
NHL Playoffs	107	76	96	172	87
Canada 1983 World Juniors *in Russia*	7	5	5	10	12

Junior Highlights

Won Bronze Medal at World Junior Championships in 1983
Canadian Major Junior Player of the Year in 1984
All Time QMJHL Points Leader

Around the Rink

Lemieux missed remainder of 1989-90 and majority of 1990-91 seasons recovering from back injury suffered in game vs. NY Rangers, February 14, 1989. Missed most of 1992-93 season after being diagnosed with Hodgkin's Disease, January 12, 1993. Missed majority of 1993-94 season recovering from back injury originally suffered in game vs. Chicago, November 11, 1993. Missed entire 1994-95 season recovering from effects of treatment for Hodgkin's Disease and back injury suffered in game vs. NY Rangers, March 12, 1994. Became third player (Gordie Howe, Guy Lafleur) to appear in NHL game after being inducted into Hockey Hall-of-Fame, December 27, 2000. Missed majority of 2001-02 season recovering from hip injury originally suffered in game vs. Anaheim, October 6, 2001.

Letowski, Trevor

Born: April 5, 1977 in Thunder Bay, Ontario
Drafted: By the Phoenix Coyotes from the Sarnia Sting in 1996, 7th round, 174th overall.

Career Junior, NHL and World Junior Statistics

	GP	G	A	PTS	PIM
OHL Regular Season 1994-97	187	93	155	248	150
OHL Playoffs	26	18	18	36	39
NHL Regular Season 1998-Present	326	48	67	115	109
NHL Playoffs	15	1	3	4	12
Canada 1997 World Juniors *in Switzerland*	7	2	1	3	4

Junior Highlights

Won Gold Medal at World Junior Championships in 1997

Around the Rink

Letowski was traded to Vancouver by Phoenix with Todd Warriner, Tyler Bouck and Phoenix's 3rd round choice in 2003 Entry Draft for Drake Berehowsky and Denis Pederson, December 28, 2001.

Linden, Trevor

Born: April 11, 1970 in Medicine, Alberta
Drafted: By the Vancouver Canucks from the Medicine Hat Tigers in 1988, 1st round, 2nd overall.

Career Junior, NHL and World Junior Statistics

	GP	G	A	PTS	PIM
WHL Regular Season 1985-88	144	62	86	148	135
WHL Playoffs	36	18	16	34	36
Memorial Cup 1987 and 1988	10	5	5	10	6
NHL Regular Season 1988-Present	1079	335	443	778	805
NHL Playoffs	97	31	58	89	86
Canada 1988 World Juniors *in Russia*	7	1	0	1	0

Junior Highlights

Won Memorial Cup in 1987 and 1988
Won Gold Medal at World Junior Championships in 1988
WHL East Second All-Star Team in 1988

Around the Rink

Linden was traded to the New York Islanders by Vancouver for Todd Bertuzzi, Bryan McCabe and NY Islanders' 3rd round choice (Jarkko Ruutu) in 1998 Entry Draft, February 6, 1998. Traded to Montreal by the New York Islanders for Montreal's 1st round choice (Branislav Mezei) in 1999 Entry Draft, May 29, 1999. Traded to Washington by Montreal with Dainius Zubrus and New Jersey's 2nd round choice (previously acquired, later traded to Tampa Bay - Tampa Bay selected Andreas Holmqvist) in 2001 Entry Draft for Richard Zednik, Jan Bulis and Washington's 1st round choice (Alexander Perezhogin) in 2001 Entry Draft, March 13, 2001. Traded to Vancouver by Washington with the New York Islanders' 2nd round choice (previously acquired, Vancouver selected Denis Grot) in 2002 Entry Draft for Vancouver's 1st round choice (Boyd Gordon) in 2002 Entry Draft and 3rd round choice in 2003 Entry Draft, November 10, 2001.

Lindros, Eric

Born: February 28, 1973 in London, Ontario
Drafted: By the Quebec Nordiques from the Oshawa Generals in 1991, 1st round, 1st overall.

Career Junior, NHL and World Junior Statistics

	GP	G	A	PTS	PIM
Canadian National Team 1988-92	45	29	24	53	51
OHL Regular Season 1989-92	95	97	119	216	304
OHL Playoffs	33	36	38	74	169
Memorial Cup 1990	4	0	9	9	12
NHL Regular Season 1992-Present	639	345	439	784	1225
NHL Playoffs	50	24	33	57	118
Canada 1990 World Juniors *in Finland*	7	4	0	4	14
Canada 1991 World Juniors *in Saskatoon*	7	6	11	17	6
Canada 1992 World Juniors *in Germany*	7	2	8	10	12
Canada World Junior Totals	**21**	**12**	**19**	**31**	**32**

Junior Highlights

Memorial Cup All-Star Team in 1990
World Junior Championships All-Star Team in 1991
Named Best Forward at World Junior Championships in 1991
OHL First All-Star Team in 1991
OHL MVP in 1991
Canadian Major Junior Player of the Year in 1991
Won Gold Medal at World Junior Championships in 1990 and 1991
Won Memorial Cup in 1990
Won Canada Cup in 1991
Won Silver Medal at Olympics in 1992

Around the Rink

Lindros was traded to Philadelphia by Quebec for Peter Forsberg, Steve Duchesne, Kerry Huffman, Mike Ricci, Ron Hextall, Philadelphia's 1st round choice (Jocelyn Thibault) in 1993 Entry Draft, $15,000,000 and future considerations (Chris Simon and Philadelphia's 1st round choice in 1994 Entry Draft, July 21, 1992), June 30, 1992. Missed entire 2000-01 season recovering from head injury suffered in game vs. New Jersey, May 26, 2000 and contract dispute with Philadelphia Flyers management. Traded to the New York Rangers by Philadelphia for Kim Johnsson, Jan Havac, Pavel Brendl and the New York Rangers' 3rd round choice in 2003 Entry Draft, August 20, 2001.

Loewen, Darcy

Born: February 26, 1969 in Calgary, Alberta
Drafted: By the Buffalo Sabres from the Spokane Chiefs in 1988, 3rd round, 55th overall.

Career Junior, NHL and World Junior Statistics

	GP	**G**	**A**	**PTS**	**PIM**
Canadian National Team 1988-89	2	0	0	0	0
WHL Regular Season 1985-89	208	78	97	175	175
WHL Playoffs	20	7	5	12	70
NHL Regular Season 1989-94	135	4	8	12	211
NHL Playoffs	0	0	0	0	0
Canada 1989 World Juniors *in United States*	7	1	1	2	12

Junior Highlights

Averaged More Then a Point Per Game in 1987-88

Around the Rink

Loewen was claimed by Ottawa from Buffalo in Expansion Draft, June 18, 1992. Retired in 2001 after playing four seasons in the IHL, three seasons in the WCHL and one season in England.

Lundmark, Jamie

Born: January 16, 1981 in Edmonton, Alberta
Drafted: By the New York Rangers from the Moose Jaw Warriors in 1999, 1st round, 9th overall.

Career Junior, NHL and World Junior Statistics

	GP	G	A	PTS	PIM
WHL Regular Season 1998-01	159	96	120	216	203
WHL Playoffs	20	9	8	17	40
NHL Regular Season 2002-Present	55	8	11	19	16
NHL Playoffs	0	0	0	0	0
Canada 2000 World Juniors *in Sweden*	7	2	3	5	0
Canada 2001 World Juniors *in Russia*	7	4	3	7	6
Canada Totals	**14**	**6**	**6**	**12**	**6**

Junior Highlights

Won Bronze Medal at World Junior Championships in 2000 and 2001

Around the Rink

Lundmark was traded by Moose Jaw to Seattle after the 2000-01 season. Played his first NHL game on October 9, 2002 against Carolina. Recorded his first NHL point with an assist against Toronto on October 15, 2002. Scored his first NHL goal versus Carolina on January 8.

Luongo, Roberto

Born: April 4, 1979 in St. Leonard, Quebec
Drafted: By the New York Islanders from the Val D'Or Foreurs in 1997, 1st round, 4th overall.

Career Junior, NHL and World Junior Statistics

	GP	W	L	T	SO	AVG
QMJHL Regular Season 1995-98	180	85	70	14	10	3.29
QMJHL Playoffs	56	38	15	0	2	2.75
Memorial Cup 1998 and 1999	6	0	6	0	0	5.00
NHL Regular Season 1999-Present	194	55	105	19	16	2.72
NHL Playoffs	0	0	0	0	0	0.00
Canada 1998 World Juniors *in Finland*	3	0	2	0	0	2.89
Canada 1999 World Juniors *in Winnipeg*	7	4	2	1	0	1.93
Canada Totals	**10**	**4**	**4**	**1**	**0**	**2.18**

Junior Highlights

Won Silver Medal at World Junior Championships in 1999
World Junior Championships All-Star Team in 1999
Named Best Goaltender at World Junior Championships in 1999

Around the Rink

Luongo played his first NHL game and recorded his first NHL win with the New York Islanders on November 28, 1999 against Boston. Earned his first NHL shutout on December 27, 1999 versus Boston. Traded to Florida by NY Islanders with Olli Jokinen for Mark Parrish and Oleg Kvasha, June 24, 2000.

Lupul, Gary

Born: April 20, 1959 in Powell River, B.C.
Not Drafted: Signed as a Free Agent With Vancouver in 1979.

Career Junior, NHL and World Junior Statistics

	GP	G	A	PTS	PIM
WHL Regular Season 1975-79	205	129	167	296	282
WHL Playoffs	33	17	29	46	23
NHL Regular Season 1979-86	293	70	75	145	243
NHL Playoffs	25	4	7	11	13
Canada 1979 World Juniors *in Sweden*	5	2	1	3	0

Junior Highlights

Averaged 1.46 Points Per Game in His Last Three Seasons Of Junior 1976-79

Around the Rink

Lupul signed as a free agent by Vancouver, September 14, 1979. Did not play in 1986-87. Retired in 1988 after playing a season in Germany.

MacKenzie, Derek

Born: June 11, 1981 in Sudbury, Ontario
Drafted: By the Atlanta Thrashers from the Sudbury Wolves in 1999, 5th round, 128th overall.

Career Junior, NHL and World Junior Statistics

	GP	G	A	PTS	PIM
OHL Regular Season 1997-01	257	95	158	253	299
OHL Playoffs	38	13	22	35	40
NHL Regular Season 2002-Present	1	0	0	0	2
NHL Playoffs	0	0	0	0	0
Canada 2001 World Juniors *in Russia*	7	1	2	3	4

Junior Highlights

Won Bronze Medal at World Junior Championships in 2001

Around the Rink

MacKenzie played his one and only NHL game on April 12, 2002 against Columbus. Played his first professional hockey game with the Chicago Wolves (AHL) on October 6, 2001 against Utah. Recorded his first professional points with a pair of goals versus Cincinnati, October 10, 2001.

MacLean, John

Born: November 20, 1964 in Oshawa, Ontario
Drafted: By the New Jersey Devils from the Oshawa Generals in 1983, 1st round, 6th overall.

Career Junior, NHL and World Junior Statistics

	GP	G	A	PTS	PIM
OHL Regular Season 1981-84	163	87	109	196	393
OHL Playoffs	36	23	31	54	116
Memorial Cup 1983	5	3	4	7	14
NHL Regular Season 1983-2002	1194	413	429	842	1333
NHL Playoffs	104	35	48	83	152
Canada 1984 World Juniors *in Sweden*	7	7	1	8	4

Junior Highlights

Memorial Cup All-Star Team in 1983

Around the Rink

MacLean missed entire 1991-92 season recovering from knee surgery, June 1991. Traded to San Jose by New Jersey with Ken Sutton for Doug Bodger and Dody Wood, December 7, 1997. Signed as a free agent by the New York Rangers, July 22, 1998. Traded to Dallas by the New York Rangers for future considerations, February 5, 2001. Signed as a free agent by Dallas, February 26, 2002. Officially announced retirement, June 7, 2002 and became an assistant coach with New Jersey.

Mair, Adam

Born: February 15, 1979 in Hamilton, Ontario
Drafted: By the Toronto Maple Leafs from the Owen Sound Platers in 1997, 4th round, 84th overall.

Career Junior, NHL and World Junior Statistics

	GP	G	A	PTS	PIM
OHL Regular Season 1995-99	226	76	118	194	464
OHL Playoffs	37	17	13	30	82
NHL Regular Season 1998-Present	131	8	14	22	229
NHL Playoffs	10	1	0	1	22
Canada 1999 World Juniors *in Winnipeg*	7	1	1	2	29

Junior Highlights

Won Silver Medal at World Junior Championships in 1999

Around the Rink

Mair was traded to the Los Angeles Kings by Toronto with Toronto's 2nd round choice (Mike Cammalleri) in 2001 Entry Draft for Aki Berg, March 13, 2001. Traded to Buffalo by the Los Angeles Kings with the Kings 5th round choice in 2003 Entry Draft for Erik Rasmussen, July 24, 2002.

Malgunas, Stewart

Born: April 21, 1970 in Prince George, B.C.
Drafted: By the Detroit Red Wings from the Seattle Thunderbirds in 1990, 4th round, 66th overall.

Career Junior, NHL and World Junior Statistics

	GP	G	A	PTS	PIM
WHL Regular Season 1987-90	141	26	89	115	167
WHL Playoffs	13	2	9	11	32
NHL Regular Season 1993-99	129	1	5	6	144
NHL Playoffs	0	0	0	0	0
Canada 1990 World Juniors *in Finland*	7	0	1	1	0

Junior Highlights

Won Gold Medal at World Junior Championships in 1990
WHL West First All-Star Team in 1990

Around the Rink

Malgunas played his first junior season with New Westminster in 1987-88, the team moved to Tri-City (Washington State) after the season. He was traded to Seattle before the 1988-89 season. Although drafted by Detroit he never played a game for them. Traded to Philadelphia by Detroit for Philadelphia's 5th round choice (David Arsenault) in 1995 Entry Draft, September 9, 1993. Signed as a free agent by Winnipeg, August 9, 1995. Traded to Washington by Winnipeg for Denis Chasse, February 15, 1996. Traded to Nashville by Washington for future considerations, February 2, 2000. Claimed on waivers by Calgary from Nashville, February 3, 2000. Missed majority of 1999-2000 season recovering from head injury suffered in game vs. Los Angeles, February 14, 2000. Signed as a free agent by Colorado, August 29, 2000. Signed as a free agent by Frankfurt Lions (Germany), March 24, 2001.

Malhotra, Manny

Born: May 18, 1980 in Mississauga, Ontario
Drafted: By the New York Rangers from the Guelph Storm in 1998, 1st round, 7th overall.

Career Junior, NHL and World Junior Statistics

	GP	G	A	PTS	PIM
OHL Regular Season 1996-98	118	32	63	95	55
OHL Playoffs	30	14	13	27	19
Memorial Cup 1998	5	1	6	7	2
NHL Regular Season 1998-Present	281	23	29	52	137
NHL Playoffs	5	1	0	1	0
Canada 2000 World Juniors *in Sweden*	7	0	2	2	8

Junior Highlights

Memorial Cup All-Star Team in 1998
Won George Parsons Trophy (Memorial Cup Most Sportsmanlike Player) in 1998
Won Bronze Medal at World Junior Championships in 2000

Around the Rink

Malhotra played his first NHL game as a member of the New York Rangers against the Montreal Canadiens on October 10, 1998. Recorded his first NHL goal and point versus Edmonton, October 20, 1998. Had his first assist on Novenber 10, 1998 against Tampa Bay. Traded to Dallas by NY Rangers with Barrett Heisten for Martin Rucinsky and Roman Lyashenko, March 12, 2002.

Manderville, Kent

Born: April 12, 1971 in Edmonton, Alberta
Drafted: By the Calgary Flames from Cornell University in 1989, 2nd round, 24th overall.

Career Junior, NHL and World Junior Statistics

	GP	G	A	PTS	PIM
Canadian National Team 1990-92	74	18	28	44	78
NCAA 1989-91	54	28	29	57	88
NHL Regular Season 1991-Present	646	37	67	104	348
NHL Playoffs	67	3	3	6	44
Canada 1990 World Juniors *in Finland*	7	1	2	3	0
Canada 1991 World Juniors *in Saskatoon*	7	1	6	7	0
Canada World Junior Totals	**14**	**2**	**8**	**10**	**0**

Junior Highlights

Won Gold Medal at World Junior Championships in 1990 and 1991
Eastern Collegiate Athletic Conference (NCAA) Rookie of the Year in 1990
Won Silver Medal at Olympics in 1992

Around the Rink

Manderville was drafted by Calgary but never played a game for them. Traded to Toronto by Calgary with Doug Gilmour, Jamie Macoun, Rick Wamsley and Ric Nattress for Gary Leeman, Alexander Godynyuk, Jeff Reese, Michel Petit and Craig Berube, January 2, 1992. Traded to Edmonton by Toronto for Peter White and Edmonton's 4th round choice (Jason Sessa) in 1996 Entry Draft, December 4, 1995. Signed as a free agent by Hartford, October 2, 1996. Transferred to Carolina after Hartford franchise relocated, June 25, 1997. Traded to Philadelphia by Carolina for Sandy McCarthy, March 14, 2000. Missed majority of 2001-02 season recovering from ankle injury originally suffered in game vs. Montreal, October 27, 2001. Traded to Pittsburgh by Philadelphia for Billy Tibbetts, March 17, 2002.

Mann, Cameron

Born: April 20, 1977, Thompson, Manitoba
Drafted: By the Boston Bruins from the Peterborough Petes, 4th round, 99th overall.

Career Junior, NHL and World Junior Statistics

	GP	G	A	PTS	PIM
OHL Regular Season 1993-97	230	101	152	253	257
OHL Playoffs	53	41	43	84	55
Memorial Cup 1996	5	4	2	6	4
NHL Regular Season 1997-01	89	14	10	24	40
NHL Playoffs	1	0	0	0	0
Canada 1997 World Juniors *in Switzerland*	7	3	4	7	10

Junior Highlights

OHL First All-Star Team in 1996 and 1997
Memorial Cup All-Star Team in 1996
Won Stafford Smythe Memorial Trophy (Memorial Cup MVP) in 1996
Won Gold Medal at World Junior Championships in 1997

Around the Rink

Mann was traded to Dallas by Boston for Richard Jackman, June 23, 2001. Traded to Nashville by Dallas with Ed Belfour for David Gosselin and Nashville's 5th round choice in 2003 Entry Draft, June 29, 2002. Has yet to play a game for Dallas as he has played in the AHL since 2001.

Marsh, Brad

Born: March 31, 1958 in London, Ontario
Drafted: By the Atlanta Flames from the London Knights in 1978, 1st round, 11th overall.

Career Junior, NHL and World Junior Statistics

	GP	G	A	PTS	PIM
OHL Regular Season 1973-78	269	22	131	153	659
OHL Playoffs	36	6	17	23	86
NHL Regular Season 1978-93	1086	23	175	198	1241
NHL Playoffs	97	6	18	24	124
Canada 1977 World Juniors *in Czech Republic*	7	1	3	4	18
Canada 1978 World Juniors *in Montreal*	6	0	4	4	2
Canada Totals	**13**	**1**	**7**	**8**	**20**

Junior Highlights

Won Silver Medal at World Junior Championships in 1977
Won Bronze Medal at World Junior Championships in 1978
OHL First All-Star Team in 1978

Around the Rink

Marsh was claimed by Atlanta as a fill-in during Expansion Draft, June 13, 1979. Transferred to Calgary after Atlanta franchise relocated, June 21, 1982. Traded to Philadelphia by Calgary for Mel Bridgman, November 11, 1981. Claimed by Toronto from Philadelphia in Waiver Draft, October 3, 1988. Traded to Detroit by Toronto for Detroit's 8th round choice (Robb McIntyre) in 1991 Entry Draft, February 4, 1991. Traded to Toronto by Detroit for cash, June 10, 1992. Traded to Ottawa by Toronto for future considerations, July 20, 1992. Retired from playing in 1993.

Marsh, Peter

Born: December 21, 1956 in Halifax, Nova Scotia
Drafted: By the Pittsburgh Penguins from the Sherbrooke Beavers in 1976, 2nd round, 29th overall. Also Drafted by the Cincinnati Stingers (WHA) in 1976, 1st round, 2nd overall.

Career Junior, NHL and World Junior Statistics

	GP	G	A	PTS	PIM
QMJHL Regular Season 1973-76	178	118	124	242	281
QMJHL Playoffs	28	19	20	39	51
Memorial Cup 1975	3	0	2	2	0
NHL Regular Season 1979-84	278	48	71	119	224
NHL Playoffs	26	1	5	6	33
Canada 1976 World Juniors *in Finland*	4	4	0	4	8

Junior Highlights

Won Silver Medal at World Junior Championships in 1976
World Junior Championships All-Star Team in 1976
QMJHL West Division First All-Star Team in 1976
QMJHL MVP in 1976

Around the Rink

Marsh played for Cincinnati (WHA) from 1976 to 1978. NHL rights traded to Montreal by Pittsburgh to complete transaction that sent Pete Mahovlich to Pittsburgh (November 29, 1977), December 15, 1977. Reclaimed by Montreal from Cincinnati (WHA) prior to Expansion Draft, June 9, 1979. Claimed by Winnipeg from Montreal in Expansion Draft, June 13, 1979. Traded to Chicago by Winnipeg for Doug Lecuyer and Tim Trimper, December 1, 1980. Retired from playing in 1984.

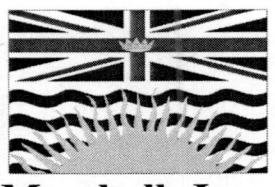

Marshall, Jason

Born: February 22, 1971 in Cranbrook, B.C.
Drafted: By the St. Louis Blues from the Vernon Lakers in 1989, 1st round, 9th overall.

Career Junior, NHL and World Junior Statistics

	GP	G	A	PTS	PIM
Canadian National Team 1988-90	75	1	12	13	57
BCJHL 1988-89	48	10	30	40	197
WHL Regular Season 1990-91	59	10	34	44	236
WHL Playoffs	7	1	2	3	20
NHL Regular Season 1991-Present	479	15	41	56	944
NHL Playoffs	27	2	3	5	22
Canada 1991 World Juniors *in Saskatoon*	7	0	4	4	6

Junior Highlights

Won Gold Medal at World Junior Championships in 1991

Around the Rink

Marshall was traded to Anaheim by St. Louis for Bill Houlder, August 29, 1994. Traded to Washington by Anaheim for Alexei Tezikov and Edmonton's 4th round choice (previously acquired, Anaheim selected Brandon Rogers) in 2001 Entry Draft, March 13, 2001. Signed as a free agent by Minnesota, July 2, 2001.

Matvichuk, Richard

Born: February 5, 1973 in Edmonton, Alberta
Drafted: By the Minnesota North Stars from the Saskatoon Blades in 1991, 1st round, 8th overall.

Career Junior, NHL and World Junior Statistics

	GP	**G**	**A**	**PTS**	**PIM**
WHL Regular Season 1989-92	182	35	100	135	369
WHL Playoffs	32	3	17	20	77
NHL Regular Season 1992-Present	658	37	109	146	548
NHL Playoffs	96	5	16	21	102
Canada 1992 World Juniors *in Germany*	4	0	0	0	2

Junior Highlights

WHL East First All-Star Team in 1992
WHL Best Defenseman in 1991-92

Around the Rink

Matvichuk's rights were transferred to Dallas after Minnesota franchise relocated, June 9, 1993. Played in first NHL game on October 6, 1992 against St. Louis.

Maxwell, Bryan

Born: September 7, 1955 in North Bay, Ontario
Drafted: By the Minnesota North Stars from the Medicine Hat Tigers in 1975, 1st round, 4th overall. Also Drafted by the Indianapolis Racers (WHA) in 1975, 1st round, 2nd overall.

Career Junior, NHL and World Junior Statistics

	GP	G	A	PTS	PIM
WHL Regular Season 1972-75	163	26	117	143	542
WHL Playoffs	27	3	9	12	66
NHL Regular Season 1977-85	331	18	77	95	745
NHL Playoffs	15	1	1	2	86
Canada 1975 World Juniors *in Manitoba*	5	0	0	0	10

Junior Highlights

Won Silver Medal at World Junior Championships in 1975

Around the Rink

Maxwell's rights were transferred to Minnesota (WHA) after Cleveland (WHA) franchise relocated, June 1976. Traded to Cincinnati (WHA) by Minnesota (WHA) for John McKenzie and the rights to Ivan Hlinka, September 1976. Traded to New England (WHA) by Cincinnati (WHA) with Greg Carroll for the rights to Mike Liut, May 1977. Signed as a free agent by Minnesota (NHL) after securing release from New England (WHA), February 1978. Traded to St. Louis by Minnesota with Richie Hansen for St. Louis' 2nd round choice (later traded to Calgary Calgary selected Dave Reierson) in 1982 Entry Draft, June 10, 1979. Traded to Winnipeg by St. Louis with Paul MacLean and Ed Staniowski for Scott Campbell and John Markell, July 3, 1981. Claimed on waivers by Pittsburgh from Winnipeg, October 13, 1983. Retired from playing in 1985. Head Coach of Medicine Hat (WHL) 1986-87. Assistant Coach with the L.A. Kings from 1987-89. Head Coach of Spokane (WHL) 1989-94. Head Coach of Lethbridge (WHL) 1995-2003. Fired by Lethbridge on December 15, 2002, replaced by Mikko Makela.

May, Brad

Born: November 29, 1971 in Toronto, Ontario
Drafted: By the Buffalo Sabres from the Niagara Falls Thunder in 1990, 1st round, 14th overall.

Career Junior, NHL and World Juniors Statistics

	GP	**G**	**A**	**PTS**	**PIM**
OHL Regular Season 1988-91	160	78	104	182	620
OHL Playoffs	47	20	28	48	172
NHL Regular Season 1991-Present	734	115	140	255	1800
NHL Playoffs	41	3	8	11	59
Canada 1991 World Juniors *in Saskatoon*	7	1	0	1	2

Junior Highlights

OHL Second All-Star Team in 1990 and 1991
Won Gold Medal at World Junior Championships in 1991

Around the Rink

May missed majority of 1990-91 season recovering from knee injury suffered at Team Canada Juniors evaluation camp, August 21, 1990. Traded to Vancouver by Buffalo with Buffalo's 3rd round choice (later traded to Tampa Bay - Tampa Bay selected Jimmie Olvestad) in 1999 Entry Draft for Geoff Sanderson, February 4, 1998. Traded to Phoenix by Vancouver for future considerations, June 24, 2000. Traded to Vancouver by Phoenix for a 2003 conditional draft pick, March 11, 2003.

McAmmond, Dean

Born: June 15, 1973 in Grande Cache, Alberta
Drafted: By the Chicago Black Hawks from the Prince Albert Raiders in 1991, 1st round, 22nd overall.

Career Junior, NHL and World Junior Statistics

	GP	G	A	PTS	PIM
WHL Regular Season 1989-93	235	110	142	252	419
WHL Playoffs	43	30	34	64	70
Memorial Cup 1993	4	0	3	3	10
NHL Regular Season 1993-Present	581	118	179	297	336
NHL Playoffs	19	1	4	5	16
Canada 1993 World Juniors *in Sweden*	7	0	1	1	12

Junior Highlights

Won Gold Medal at World Junior Championships in 1993

Around the Rink

McAmmond was traded to Swift Current after 30 games in 1992-93. Traded to Edmonton by Chicago with Igor Kravchuk for Joe Murphy, February 24, 1993. Traded to Chicago by Edmonton with Boris Mironov and Jonas Elofsson for Chad Kilger, Daniel Cleary, Ethan Moreau and Christian Laflamme, March 20, 1999. Traded to Philadelphia by Chicago for Philadelphia's 3rd round choice (later traded to Toronto - Toronto selected Nicolas Corbeil) in 2001 Entry Draft, March 13, 2001. Traded to Calgary by Philadelphia for Calgary's 4th round choice (Rosario Ruggeri) in 2002 Entry Draft, June 24, 2001. Traded by Calgary to Colorado with Derek Morris and Jeff Shantz for Chris Drury and Stephane Yelle, October 1, 2002. Traded by Colorado to Calgary for the Flames 5th round pick in the 2003 entry draft. Suspended by the NHL on March 14, 2003 for the remainder of the season under article 13, subsection 13.36, which states, no NHL team is allowed to reacquire a player that they traded within 4 weeks of the waiver draft in the same season.

McBean, Wayne

Born: February 21, 1969 in Calgary, Alberta
Drafted: By the Los Angeles Kings from the Medicine Hat Tigers in 1987, 1st round, 4th overall.

Career Junior, NHL and World Junior Statistics

	GP	**G**	**A**	**PTS**	**PIM**
WHL Regular Season 1985-88	168	28	85	113	284
WHL Playoffs	61	9	30	39	126
Memorial Cup 1987 and 1988	10	2	5	7	12
NHL Regular Season 1987-94	211	10	39	49	168
NHL Playoffs	2	1	1	2	0
Canada 1988 World Juniors *in Russia*	7	1	0	1	2

Junior Highlights

WHL East First All-Star Team in 1987
Memorial Cup All-Star Team in 1987
Won Stafford Smythe Memorial Trophy (Memorial Cup MVP) in 1987
Won Memorial Cup in 1987 and 1988
Won Gold Medal at World Junior Championships in 1988

Around the Rink

McBean was traded to the New York Islanders by the L.A. Kings with Mark Fitzpatrick and future considerations (Doug Crossman, May 23, 1989) for Kelly Hrudey, February 22, 1989. Missed remainder of 1991-92 season recovering from knee injury suffered in game vs. Pittsburgh, December 23, 1991. Traded to Winnipeg by NY Islanders for Yan Kaminsky, February 1, 1994. Claimed by Pittsburgh from Winnipeg in Waiver Draft, January 18, 1995. Missed entire 1994-95 season recovering from eventual career-ending wrist surgery, October 1994.

McCabe, Bryan

Born: June 8, 1975 in St. Catharines, Ontario
Drafted: By the New York Islanders from the Spokane Chiefs in 1993, 2nd round, 40th overall.

Career Junior, NHL and World Junior Statistics

	GP	G	A	PTS	PIM
WHL Regular Season 1991-95	254	51	192	245	765
WHL Playoffs	31	5	22	27	97
Memorial Cup 1995	4	3	4	7	6
NHL Regular Season 1995-Present	633	60	157	217	1176
NHL Playoffs	36	7	11	18	54
Canada 1994 World Juniors *in Czech Republic*	7	0	0	0	6
Canada 1995 World Juniors *in Alberta*	7	3	9	12	4
Canada Totals	**14**	**3**	**9**	**12**	**10**

Junior Highlights

WHL West Second All-Star Team in1993
Won Gold Medal at World Junior Championships in 1994 and 1995
WHL West First All-Star Team in 1994
World Junior Championships All-Star Team in 1995
Named Best Defenseman at World Junior Championships in 1995
WHL East First All-Star Team in 1995
Memorial Cup All-Star Team in 1995

Around the Rink

McCabe played his first full season of junior with Medicine Hat in 1991-92, traded to Spokane after 14 games in 1992-93. Traded to Brandon after 42 games in 1994-95. Traded to Vancouver by NY Islanders with Todd Bertuzzi and NY Islanders' 3rd round choice (Jarkko Ruutu) in 1998 Entry Draft for Trevor Linden, February 6, 1998. Traded to Chicago by Vancouver with Vancouver's 1st round choice (Pavel Vorobiev) in 2000 Entry Draft for Chicago's 1st round choice (later traded to Tampa Bay - later traded to NY Rangers - NY Rangers selected Pavel Brendl) in 1999 Entry Draft, June 25, 1999. Traded to Toronto by Chicago for Alexander Karpovtsev and Toronto's 4th round choice (Vladimir Gusev) in 2001 Entry Draft, October 2, 2000.

McCarthy, Kevin

Born: July 14, 1957 in Winnipeg, Manitoba
Drafted: By the Philadelphia Flyers from the Winnipeg Monarchs in 1977, 1st round, 17th overall. Also Drafted by the Houston Aeros (WHA) in 1977, 6th round, 48th overall.

Career Junior, NHL and World Junior Statistics

	GP	G	A	PTS	PIM
WHL Regular Season 1973-77	276	80	276	356	437
WHL Playoffs	13	2	13	15	35
NHL Regular Season 1977-87	537	67	191	258	527
NHL Playoffs	13	2	13	15	35
Canada 1975 World Juniors *in Manitoba*	5	1	4	5	6

Junior Highlights

Won Silver Medal at World Junior Championships in 1975
WHL First All-Star Team in 1976 and 1977

Around the Rink

McCarthy played for Winnipeg (WHL) for his entire junior career, the team changed names from the Clubs to the Monarchs in 1976. Traded to Vancouver by Philadelphia with Drew Callander for Dennis Ververgaert, December 29, 1978. Traded to Pittsburgh by Vancouver for Philadelphia's 3rd round choice (previously acquired, later traded back to Philadelphia Philadelphia selected David McClay) in 1984 Entry Draft, January 26, 1984. Signed as a free agent by Philadelphia, July 19, 1985. Retired from playing in 1988 after spending the majority of two seasons in the minors with Hershey (AHL). Assistant Coach with Hershey 1988-89. Head Coach of Hershey from 1989-90. Assistant Coach with Hartford (NHL) 1992-95. Head Coach with Springfield (AHL) 1995-97. Head Coach of New Haven (AHL) from 1997-99. Assistant Coach with Carolina 1999-Present.

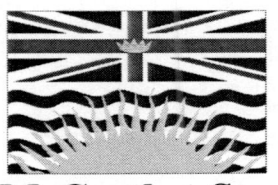

McCarthy, Steve

Born: February 3, 1981 in Trail, B.C.
Drafted: By the Chicago Black Hawks from the Kootenay Ice in 1999, 1st round, 23rd overall.

Career Junior, NHL and World Junior Statistics

	GP	G	A	PTS	PIM
WHL Regular Season 1996-00	154	43	85	128	174
WHL Playoffs	6	0	5	5	8
Memorial Cup 2000	0	0	0	0	0
NHL Regular Season 1999-Present	109	2	10	12	37
NHL Playoffs	6	0	5	5	8
Canada 2000 World Juniors *in Sweden*	7	0	2	2	0

Junior Highlights

Won Bronze Medal at World Junior Championships in 2000

Around the Rink

McCarthy played his first two seasons of junior with the Edmonton Ice, the team moved to Kootenay in 1998. Returned to Kootenay (WHL) by Chicago, October 18, 1999. Suffered season-ending shoulder injury in game vs. Swift Current (WHL), March 3, 2000.

McCauley, Alyn

Born: May 29, 1977 in Brockville, Ontario
Drafted: By the New Jersey Devils from the Ottawa 67's in 1995, 4th round, 79th overall.

Career Junior, NHL and World Junior Statistics

	GP	G	A	PTS	PIM
OHL Regular Season 1993-97	208	119	155	274	70
OHL Playoffs	37	19	36	55	18
NHL Regular Season 1997-Present	320	36	56	92	56
NHL Playoffs	35	5	10	15	12
Canada 1996 World Juniors *in United States*	6	2	3	5	2
Canada 1997 World Juniors *in Switzerland*	7	0	5	5	2
Canada Totals	**13**	**2**	**8**	**10**	**4**

Junior Highlights

Won Gold Medal at World Junior Championships in 1996 and 1997
OHL First All-Star Team in 1996 and 1997
OHL MVP in 1996 and 1997
Canadian Major Junior First All-Star Team in 1997
Canadian Major Junior Player of the Year in 1997

Around the Rink

McCauley was drafted by New Jersey but he never played a game for the Devils. Rights traded to Toronto by New Jersey with Jason Smith and Steve Sullivan for Doug Gilmour, Dave Ellett and New Jersey's 3rd round choice (previously acquired, New Jersey selected Andre Lakos) in 1999 Entry Draft, February 25, 1997. Traded by Toronto to San Jose with Brad Boyes and the Leafs 1st round pick in the 2003 entry draft for Owen Nolan, March 5, 2003.

McCourt, Dale

Born: January 26, 1957 in Falconbridge, Ontario
Drafted: By the Detroit Red Wings from the St. Catharines Fincups in 1977, 1st round, 1st overall. Also Drafted by the Indianapolis Racers (WHA) in 1977, 4th round, 35th overall.

Career Junior, NHL and World Junior Statistics

	GP	G	A	PTS	PIM
OHL Regular Season 1972-77	296	193	286	479	147
OHL Playoffs	49	37	39	76	18
Memorial Cup 1976	3	0	4	4	2
NHL Regular Season 1977-84	532	194	284	478	124
NHL Playoffs	21	9	7	16	6
Canada 1977 World Juniors *in Czech Republic*	7	10	8	18	14

Junior Highlights

OMJHL First All-Star Team in 1976 and 1977
Won Memorial Cup in 1976
Memorial Cup All-Star Team in 1976
Won Stafford Smythe Memorial Trophy (Memorial Cup MVP) in 1976
Won Silver Medal at World Junior Championships in 1977
World Junior Championships All-Star Team in 1977
Named Best Forward at World Junior Championships in 1977
OHL MVP in 1977
Canadian Major Junior Player of the Year in 1977

Around the Rink

McCourt was traded to the Hamilton Red Wings by the Sudbury Wolves after the 1972-73 season. The Red Wings became the Fincups in 1974. The Hamilton Fincups moved to St. Catharines for one season in 1976-77. Rights transferred to LA Kings by Detroit as compensation for Detroit's signing of free agent Rogie Vachon, August 8, 1978. McCourt remained property of Detroit pending result of litigation hearing. Rights traded to Detroit by LA Kings for Andre St. Laurent and Detroit's 1st round choices in 1980 (Larry Murphy) and 1981 (Doug Smith) Entry Drafts, August 22, 1979. Traded to Buffalo by Detroit with Mike Foligno and Brent Peterson for Danny Gare, Jim Schoenfeld and Derek Smith, December 2, 1981. Signed as a free agent by Toronto, October 22, 1983. Played in Switzerland with Ambri-Piotta from 1984-92. Retired from playing in 1992.

McCrimmon, Brad

Born: March 23, 1959 in Dodsland, Saskatchewan
Drafted: By the Boston Bruins from the Brandon Wheat Kings in 1979, 1st round, 15th overall.

Career Junior, NHL and World Junior Statistics

	GP	G	A	PTS	PIM
WHL Regular Season 1976-79	203	61	218	279	480
WHL Playoffs	45	14	40	54	70
Memorial Cup 1979	5	0	5	5	10
NHL Regular Season 1979-97	1222	81	322	403	1416
NHL Playoffs	45	14	40	54	70
Canada 1978 World Juniors *in Montreal*	6	0	2	2	4
Canada 1979 World Juniors *in Sweden*	5	1	2	3	2
Canada Totals	**11**	**1**	**4**	**5**	**6**

Junior Highlights

Won Bronze Medal at World Junior Championships in 1978
WHL First All-Star Team in 1978
WHL First All-Star Team in 1979

Around the Rink

McCrimmon was traded to Philadelphia by Boston for Pete Peeters, June 9, 1982. Traded to Calgary by Philadelphia for Calgary's 3rd round choice (Dominic Roussel) in 1988 Entry Draft and 1st round choice (later traded to Toronto Toronto selected Steve Bancroft) in 1989 Entry Draft, August 26, 1987. Traded to Detroit by Calgary for Detroit's 2nd round choice (later traded to New Jersey New Jersey selected David Harlock) in 1990 Entry Draft, June 15, 1990. Traded to Hartford by Detroit for Detroit's 6th round choice (previously acquired, Detroit selected Tim Spitzig) in 1993 Entry Draft, June 1, 1993. Signed as a free agent by Phoenix, July 16, 1996. Retired from playing in 1997. Assistant Coach with the New York Islanders from 1997-99. Head Coach of the Saskatoon Blades (WHL) 1998-00. Named Assistant Coach by Calgary, August 8, 2000. Fired by Calgary on December 28, 2002.

McDonald, Terry

Born: January 1, 1955 in Coquitlam, B.C.
Drafted: By the Kansas City Scouts from the Kamloops Chiefs in 1975, 5th round, 74th overall.

Career Junior, NHL and World Junior Statistics

	GP	G	A	PTS	PIM
WHL Regular Season 1972-75	183	51	77	128	272
WHL Playoffs	6	3	1	4	2
NHL Regular Season 1975-76	8	0	1	1	6
NHL Playoffs	0	0	0	0	0
Canada 1975 World Juniors *in Manitoba*	3	0	0	0	0

Junior Highlights

Won Silver Medal at World Junior Championships in 1975

Around the Rink

McDonald played his first year of junior hockey with the Vancouver Nationals. Traded to Kamloops Chiefs prior to the 1973-74 season. Played all eight NHL games with Kansas City. Retired in 1979 after playing three straight seasons in the minors.

McIntosh, Paul

Born: March 13, 1954 in Listowel, Ontario
Drafted: By the Buffalo Sabres from the Peterborough Petes in 1974, 4th round, 65th overall. Also Drafted by the Chicago Cougars (WHA) in 1974, 3rd round, 39th overall.

Career Junior, NHL and World Junior Statistics

	GP	G	A	PTS	PIM
OHL Regular Season 1971-74	154	25	68	93	259
OHL Playoffs	19	0	14	14	0
NHL Regular Season 1974-76	48	0	2	2	66
NHL Playoffs	2	0	0	0	7
Canada 1974 World Juniors *in Russia*	5	3	2	5	6

Junior Highlights

Won Bronze Medal at World Junior Championships in 1974
World Junior Championships All-Star Team in 1974
OHL Second All-Star Team in 1974

Around the Rink

McIntosh played all of his NHL games with Buffalo. Retired in 1980 after four seasons in the minors with Hershey (AHL), Springfield (AHL) and Saginaw (IHL).

McIntyre, John

Born: April 29, 1969 in Ravenswood, Ontario
Drafted: By the Toronto Maple Leafs from the Guelph Platers in 1987, 3rd round, 49th overall.

Career Junior, NHL and World Junior Statistics

	GP	G	A	PTS	PIM
OHL Regular Season 1985-89	168	66	72	138	358
OHL Playoffs	27	6	9	15	56
Memorial Cup 1986	4	0	1	1	4
NHL Regular Season 1989-95	351	24	54	78	516
NHL Playoffs	44	0	6	6	54
Canada 1989 World Juniors *in United States*	7	1	0	1	4

Junior Highlights

Won Memorial Cup in 1986

Around the Rink

McIntyre was traded to the L.A. Kings by Toronto for Mike Krushelnyski, November 9, 1990. Traded to the New York Rangers by the L.A. Kings for Mark Hardy and Ottawa's 5th round choice (previously acquired, LA Kings selected Frederick Beaubien) in 1993 Entry Draft, March 22, 1993. Claimed by Vancouver from NY Rangers in Waiver Draft, October 3, 1993. Retired from playing in 1986 after a full season in the minors with Syracuse (AHL).

McKegney, Tony

Born: February 15, 1958 in Montreal, Quebec
Drafted: By the Buffalo Sabres from the Kingston Canadiens in 1978, 2nd round, 32nd overall.

Career Junior, NHL and World Junior Statistics

	GP	G	A	PTS	PIM
OHL Regular Season 1974-78	238	152	230	382	105
OHL Playoffs	34	26	26	52	16
NHL Regular Season 1978-91	912	320	319	639	517
NHL Playoffs	79	24	23	47	56
Canada 1978 World Juniors *in Montreal*	6	2	6	8	0

Junior Highlights

OHL First All-Star Team in 1977
Won Bronze Medal at World Junior Championships in 1978
OHL Second All-Star Team in 1978

Around the Rink

McKegney was traded to Quebec by Buffalo with Andre Savard, Jean-Francois Sauve and Buffalo's 3rd round choice (Iiro Jarvi) in 1983 Entry Draft for Real Cloutier and Quebec's 1st round choice (Adam Creighton) in 1983 Entry Draft, June 8, 1983. Traded to Minnesota by Quebec with Bo Berglund for Brad Maxwell and Brent Ashton, December 14, 1984. Traded to NY Rangers by Minnesota with Curt Giles and Minnesota's 2nd round choice (Troy Mallette) in 1988 Entry Draft for Bob Brooke and Minnesota's 4th round choice (previously acquired, Minnesota selected Jeffrey Stolp) in 1988 Entry Draft, November 13, 1986. Traded to St. Louis by NY Rangers with Rob Whistle for Bruce Bell and future considerations, May 28, 1987. Traded to Detroit by St. Louis with Bernie Federko for Adam Oates and Paul MacLean, June 15, 1989. Traded to Quebec by Detroit for Robert Picard and Greg Adams, December 4, 1989. Traded to Chicago by Quebec for Jacques Cloutier, January 29, 1991. Retired from playing in 1993 after brief stints in Italy, the IHL and Canada's National Team.

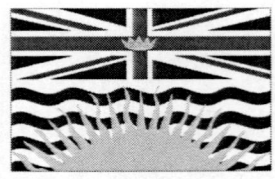

McLean, Brett

Born: August 14, 1978 in Comox, B.C.
Drafted: By the Dallas Stars from the Kelowna Rockets in 1997, 9th round, 242nd overall.

Career Junior, NHL and World Junior Statistics

	GP	G	A	PTS	PIM
WHL Regular Season 1994-99	329	181	225	406	348
WHL Playoffs	28	11	16	27	43
NHL Regular Season 2002-Present	2	0	0	0	0
NHL Playoffs	0	0	0	0	0
Canada 1998 World Juniors *in Finland*	7	1	1	2	4

Junior Highlights

Named Canada's Top Forward at World Junior Championships in 1998

Around the Rink

McLean played his first season of junior with Tacoma in 1994-95, the team moved to Kelowna in 1995. Traded to Brandon mid-way through the 1998-99 season. Since 1999 has played with five different minor league teams. Played both NHL games with Chicago in 2002-03 season.

McLlwain, Dave

Born: January 9, 1967 in Seaforth, Ontario
Drafted: By the Pittsburgh Penguins from the North Bay Centennials in 1986, 9th round, 172nd overall.

Career Junior, NHL and World Junior Statistics

	GP	G	A	PTS	PIM
OHL Regular Season 1984-87	185	96	129	225	101
OHL Playoffs	34	11	22	33	42
NHL Regular Season 1987-97	501	100	107	207	292
NHL Playoffs	20	0	2	2	8
Canada 1987 World Juniors *in Czech Republic*	6	4	3	7	2

Junior Highlights

OHL Second All-Star Team in 1987

Around the Rink

McLlwain was dealt by the Kitchener Rangers to the North Bay Centennials in October 1985. Traded to Winnipeg by Pittsburgh with Randy Cunneyworth and Rick Tabaracci for Jim Kyte, Andrew McBain and Randy Gilhen, June 17, 1989. Traded to Buffalo by Winnipeg with Gord Donnelly, Winnipeg's 5th round choice (Yuri Khmylev) in 1992 Entry Draft and cash for Darrin Shannon, Mike Hartman and Dean Kennedy, October 11, 1991. Traded to NY Islanders by Buffalo with Pierre Turgeon, Uwe Krupp and Benoit Hogue for Pat LaFontaine, Randy Hillier, Randy Wood and NY Islanders' 4th round choice (Dean Melanson) in 1992 Entry Draft, October 25, 1991. Traded to Toronto by NY Islanders with Ken Baumgartner for Daniel Marois and Claude Loiselle, March 10, 1992. Claimed by Ottawa from Toronto in NHL Waiver Draft, October 3, 1993. Traded to Pittsburgh by Ottawa for Pittsburgh's 8th round choice (Erich Goldmann) in 1996 Entry Draft, March 1, 1996. Signed as a free agent by NY Islanders, July 29, 1996. Has been playing in Europe since 1997, two seasons in Switzerland and four in Germany.

Mellanby, Scott

Born: June 11, 1966 in Montreal, Quebec
Drafted: By the Philadelphia Flyers from the University of Wisconsin in 1984, 2nd round, 27th overall.

Career Junior, NHL and World Junior Statistics

	GP	G	A	PTS	PIM
NCAA 1984-86	72	35	47	82	149
NHL Regular Season 1985-Present	1223	326	413	739	2285
NHL Playoffs	128	24	28	52	214
Canada 1986 World Juniors *in Hamilton*	7	5	4	9	6

Junior Highlights

Won Silver Medal at World Junior Championships in 1986

Around the Rink

Mellanby was traded to Edmonton by Philadelphia with Craig Fisher and Craig Berube for Dave Brown, Corey Foster and Jari Kurri, May 30, 1991. Claimed by Florida from Edmonton in Expansion Draft, June 24, 1993. Traded to St. Louis by Florida for rights to Dave Morisset and St. Louis' 5th round choice (Vince Bellissimo) in 2002 Entry Draft, February 9, 2001.

Melnyk, Larry

Born: February 21, 1960 in Saskatoon, Saskatchewan
Drafted: By the Boston Bruins from the New Westminster Bruins in 1979, 4th round, 78th overall.

Career Junior, NHL and World Junior Statistics

	GP	G	A	PTS	PIM
WHL Regular Season 1977-80	182	23	93	116	449
WHL Playoffs	8	1	4	5	14
Memorial Cup 1978	5	1	3	4	7
NHL Regular Season 1980-90	432	11	63	74	686
NHL Playoffs	66	2	9	11	129
Canada 1979 World Juniors *in Sweden*	5	1	1	2	2

Junior Highlights

Won Memorial Cup in 1978

Around the Rink

Melnyk was traded to Edmonton by Boston for John Blum, March 6, 1984. Traded to the New York Rangers by Edmonton with Todd Strueby for Mike Rogers, December 20, 1985. Traded to Vancouver by the New York Rangers with Willie Huber for Michel Petit, November 4, 1987. Retired from playing in 1990.

Metcalfe, Scott

Born: January 6, 1967 in Toronto, Ontario
Drafted: By the Edmonton Oilers from the Kingston Canadiens in 1985, 1st round, 20th overall.

Career Junior, NHL and World Junior Statistics

	GP	G	A	PTS	PIM
OHL Regular Season 1983-87	249	113	182	295	623
OHL Playoffs	23	8	11	19	48
NHL Regular Season 1987-90	19	1	2	3	18
NHL Playoffs	0	0	0	0	0
Canada 1987 World Juniors *in Czech Republic*	6	2	5	7	12

Junior Highlights

Played on First Place World Junior Team That Was Disqualified in 1987

Around the Rink

Metcalfe was traded by Kingston to Windsor mid-way through the 1986-87 season. Traded to Buffalo by Edmonton with Edmonton's 9th round choice (Donald Audette) in 1989 Entry Draft for Steve Dykstra and Buffalo's 7th round choice (Davis Payne) in 1989 Entry Draft, February 11, 1988. From 1990-2000 he has played in England, Germany and the AHL. Signed as a free agent by Adirondack (UHL), September 29, 2001.

Micalef, Corrado

Born: April 20, 1961 in Montreal, Quebec
Drafted: By the Detroit Red Wings from the Sherbrooke Beavers in 1981, 3rd round, 44th overall.

Career Junior, NHL and World Junior Statistics

	GP	W	L	T	SO	AVG
QMJHL Regular Season 1978-81	170	72	43	10	3	4.29
QMJHL Playoffs	32	17	12	0	1	3.49
Memorial Cup 1981	3	3	0	0	0	2.57
NHL Regular Season 1981-86	113	26	59	15	2	4.24
NHL Playoffs	3	0	0	0	0	9.80
Canada 1981 World Juniors *in Germany*	5	1	2	1	0	5.79

Junior Highlights

QMJHL Second All-Star Team in 1980
Won Memorial Cup With The Cornwall Royals in 1981
QMJHL First All-Star Team in 1981
Memorial Cup All-Star Team in 1981
Won Hap Emms Memorial Trophy (Memorial Cup Top Goaltender) in 1981

Around the Rink

Micalef was loaned to Cornwall (QMJHL) by Sherbrooke (QMJHL) for Memorial Cup Tournament, May 1981. Played in the Roller Hockey League with the Montreal Roadrunners in 1994 (18-4-4-0-527-79-0-7.19) and 1995 (13-7-3-1-566-61-0-5.17); Orlando Rollergators in 1996 (5-2-1-0-161-31-0-9.24) and San Jose Rhinos in 1997 (16-8-4-1-592-72-0-5.84) Has played in Europe since 1987 in France, Italy, Germany and Switzerland.

Michaud, Olivier

Born: September 14, 1983 in Beloeil, Quebec
Not Drafted: Signed as a Free Agent by the Montreal Canadiens in 2001.

Career Junior, NHL and World Junior Statistics

	GP	W	L	T	SO	AVG
QMJHL Regular Season 1999-Present	126	72	34	12	8	2.85
QMJHL Playoffs	27	15	12	0	0	2.92
NHL Regular Season 2001-02	1	0	0	0	0	0.00
NHL Playoffs	0	0	0	0	0	0.00
Canada 2002 World Juniors *in Czech Rep.*	2	1	1	0	0	2.50

Junior Highlights

Won Silver Medal at World Junior Championships in 2002

Around the Rink

Michaud was signed as a free agent by the Montreal Canadiens, from the Shawinigan Cataractes (QMJHL) on September 18, 2001. Recalled by Montreal from the Shawinigan (QMJHL) under emergency conditions, October 26, 2001. Returned to Shawinigan (QMJHL) by Montreal, November 5, 2001. Traded by Shawinigan with Jean-Francois David to the Baie-Comeau Drakkar for Michel Bergevin-Robinson and Benoit Mondu on December 14, 2002.

Mills, Craig

Born: August 27, 1976 in Toronto, Ontario
Drafted: By the Winnipeg Jets from the Belleville Bulls in 1994, 5th round, 108th overall.

Career Junior, NHL and World Junior Statistics

	GP	G	A	PTS	PIM
OHL Regular Season 1993-96	173	64	78	142	305
OHL Playoffs	39	13	15	28	51
NHL Regular Season 1995-99	31	0	5	5	36
NHL Playoffs	1	0	0	0	0
Canada 1996 World Juniors *in United States*	6	0	0	0	4

Junior Highlights

Won Gold Medal at World Junior Championships in 1996
Canadian Major Junior Humanitarian Player of the Year in 1996

Around the Rink

Mills rights were transferred to Phoenix after Winnipeg franchise relocated, July 1, 1996. Traded to Chicago by Phoenix with Alexei Zhamnov and Phoenix's 1st round choice (Ty Jones) in 1997 Entry Draft for Jeremy Roenick, August 16, 1996. Traded to Phoenix by Chicago for cash, September 11, 1999. Traded to Toronto by Phoenix with Robert Reichel and Travis Green for Danny Markov, June 12, 2001.

Miner, John

Born: August 28, 1965 in Moose Jaw, Saskatchewan
Drafted: By the Edmonton Oilers from the Regina Pats in 1983, 11th round, 220th overall.

Career Junior, NHL and World Junior Statistics

	GP	G	A	PTS	PIM
WHL Regular Season 1981-85	217	68	120	188	397
WHL Playoffs	53	14	36	50	111
NHL Regular Season 1987-88	14	2	3	5	16
NHL Playoffs	0	0	0	0	0
Canada 1985 World Juniors *in Finland*	7	0	2	2	12

Junior Highlights

Won Gold Medal at World Junior Championships in 1985
WHL East First All-Star Team in 1985

Around the Rink

Miner was traded to the Los Angeles Kings by Edmonton for Craig Redmond, August 10, 1988. Played all of his NHL games with Edmonton. Has played in Europe since 1992 in Austria, Switzerland and Germany.

Moffat, Mike

Born: February 4, 1962 in Galt, Ontario
Drafted: By the Boston Bruins from the Kingston Canadiens in 1980, 8th round, 165th overall.

Career Junior, NHL and World Junior Statistics

	GP	W	L	T	SO	AVG
OHL Regular Season 1979-82	124	59	49	8	1	3.95
OHL Playoffs	20	6	8	0	0	4.35
NHL Regular Season 1981-84	19	7	7	2	0	4.29
NHL Playoffs	11	6	5	0	0	3.44
Canada 1982 World Juniors *in U.S.A.*	4	3	0	1	1	1.75

Junior Highlights

OHL Second All-Star Team in 1981
Won Gold Medal at World Junior Championships in 1982
World Junior Championships All-Star Team in 1982
Named Best Goaltender at World Junior Championships in 1982

Around the Rink

Moffat officially announced his retirement from the NHL, October 15, 1984. Played for Wilfrid Laurier University from 1985-87. Retired from playing in 1987 after six games with Canada's National Team.

Moller, Mike

Born: June 16, 1962 in Calgary, Alberta
Drafted: By the Buffalo Sabres from the Lethbridge Broncos in 1980, 2nd round, 41st overall.

Career Junior, NHL and World Junior Statistics

	GP	G	A	PTS	PIM
WHL Regular Season 1979-82	191	110	191	301	164
WHL Playoffs	25	11	28	39	21
NHL Regular Season 1980-87	134	15	28	43	41
NHL Playoffs	3	0	1	1	0
Canada 1982 World Juniors *in United States*	7	5	9	14	4

Junior Highlights

WHL First All-Star Team in 1981 and 1982
Won Gold Medal at World Junior Championships in 1982
World Junior Championships All-Star Team in 1982

Around the Rink

Moller was traded to Pittsburgh by Buffalo with Randy Cunneyworth for Pat Hughes, October 4, 1985. Traded to Edmonton by Pittsburgh for Pat Hughes, October 4, 1985. Retired from playing in 1990 after three seasons in the AHL and a season with the Canadian National Team. Assistant Coach with the Red Deer Rebels (WHL) from 1993-95.

Moller, Randy

Born: August 23, 1963 in Red Deer, Alberta
Drafted: By the Quebec Nordiques from the Lethbridge Broncos in 1981, 1st round, 11th overall.

Career Junior, NHL and World Junior Statistics

	GP	G	A	PTS	PIM
WHL Regular Season 1979-82	108	24	76	100	429
WHL Playoffs	21	4	10	14	89
NHL Regular Season 1981-95	815	45	180	225	1692
NHL Playoffs	78	6	16	22	199
Canada 1982 World Juniors *in United States*	7	0	3	3	4

Junior Highlights

Won Gold Medal at World Junior Championships in 1982
WHL Second All-Star Team in 1982

Around the Rink

Moller played his first two junior games with the Billings Bighorns before completing it with Lethbridge. Traded to the New York Rangers by Quebec for Michel Petit, October 5, 1989. Traded to Buffalo by the New York Rangers for Jay Wells, March 9, 1992. Signed as a free agent by Florida, July 11, 1994. Retired from playing in 1995.

Morrison, Dave

Born: June 12, 1962 in Toronto, Ontario
Drafted: By the Los Angeles Kings from the Peterborough Petes in 1980, 2nd round, 34th overall.

Career Junior, NHL and World Junior Statistics

	GP	G	A	PTS	PIM
OHL Regular Season 1979-82	163	95	103	198	144
OHL Playoffs	14	6	9	15	38
NHL Regular Season 1980-85	39	3	3	5	4
NHL Playoffs	0	0	0	0	0
Canada 1982 World Juniors *in United States*	7	1	2	3	0

Junior Highlights

Won Gold Medal at World Junior Championships in 1982

Around the Rink

Morrison signed as a free agent by Vancouver, October 28, 1983. Did not play from 1986-91. Played in Europe from 1992-99 in Germany and England. Announced retirement to become scout with Vancouver Canucks, April 15, 1999.

Morrison, Mark

Born: March 11, 1963 in Delta, B.C.
Drafted: By the New York Rangers from the Victoria Cougars in 1981, 3rd round, 51st overall.

Career Junior, NHL and World Junior Statistics

	GP	G	A	PTS	PIM
WHL Regular Season 1979-83	244	159	235	394	229
WHL Playoffs	47	19	35	54	49
Memorial Cup 1981	4	3	3	6	2
NHL Regular Season 1981-84	10	1	1	2	0
NHL Playoffs	0	0	0	0	0
Canada 1982 World Juniors *in United States*	7	3	7	10	0
Canada 1983 World Juniors *in Russia*	7	3	2	5	0
Canada Totals	**14**	**6**	**9**	**15**	**0**

Junior Highlights

Won George Parsons Trophy (Memorial Cup Most Sportsmanlike Player) in 1981
Won Gold Medal at World Junior Championships in 1982
Won Bronze Medal at World Junior Championships in 1983

Around the Rink

Morrison was traded to Edmonton by the New York Rangers for cash, November 27, 1984. Played all of his NHL games with New York. Since 1984 has played with the Canadian National Team, in Italy, Switzerland and the past eight seasons with Fife in Britain.

Morrow, Brenden

Born: January 16, 1979 in Carlyle, Saskatchewan
Drafted: By the Dallas Stars from the Portland Winter Hawks in 1997, 1st round, 25th overall.

Career Junior, NHL and World Junior Statistics

	GP	G	A	PTS	PIM
WHL Regular Season 1995-99	265	127	157	284	671
WHL Playoffs	33	12	13	25	95
Memorial Cup 1998	4	1	2	3	20
NHL Regular Season 1999-Present	289	72	83	155	452
NHL Playoffs	43	5	12	17	50
Canada 1999 World Juniors *in Winnipeg*	7	1	7	8	4

Junior Highlights

Won Memorial Cup in 1998
Won Silver Medal at World Junior Championships in 1999
WHL West First All-Star Team in 1999

Around the Rink

Morrow played his first NHL game on November 18, 1999 against Philadelphia. Recorded his first NHL goal and point on November 22, 1999 versus Colorado.

Muller, Kirk

Born: February 8, 1966 in Kingston, Ontario
Drafted: By the New Jersey Devils from the Guelph Platers in 1984, 1st round, 2nd overall.

Career Junior, NHL and World Junior Statistics

	GP	G	A	PTS	PIM
Canadian National Team 1983-84	21	4	3	7	6
OHL Regular Season 1980-84	199	95	162	257	95
OHL Playoffs	4	5	1	6	4
NHL Regular Season 1984-Present	1349	357	602	959	1223
NHL Playoffs	127	33	36	69	153
Canada 1984 World Juniors *in Sweden*	7	2	1	3	16

Junior Highlights

Represented Canada at Olympics in 1984

Around the Rink

Muller was traded by Kingston to Guelph prior to the start of the 1982-83 season. Traded to Montreal by New Jersey with Rollie Melanson for Stephane Richer and Tom Chorske, September 20, 1991. Traded to NY Islanders by Montreal with Mathieu Schneider and Craig Darby for Pierre Turgeon and Vladimir Malakhov, April 5, 1995. Traded to Toronto by NY Islanders with Don Beaupre to complete transaction that sent Damian Rhodes and Ken Belanger to NY Islanders (January 23, 1996), January 23, 1996. Traded to Florida by Toronto for Jason Podollan, March 18, 1997. Signed as a free agent by Dallas, December 15, 1999. Claimed by Columbus from Dallas in Waiver Draft, September 28, 2001. Traded to Dallas by Columbus for the rights to Evgeny Petrochinin, September 28, 2001.

Murphy, Joe

Born: October 16, 1967 in London, Ontario
Drafted: By the Detroit Red Wings from Michigan State University in 1986, 1st round, 1st overall.

Career Junior, NHL and World Junior Statistics

	GP	G	A	PTS	PIM
Canadian National Team 1985-86	8	3	3	6	2
NCAA 1985-86	35	24	37	61	50
NHL Regular Season 1986-01	779	233	295	528	810
NHL Playoffs	120	34	43	77	185
Canada 1986 World Juniors *in Hamilton*	7	4	10	14	2

Junior Highlights

Won Silver Medal at World Junior Championships in 1986
Won NCAA Frozen Four Championship in 1986
NCAA (Central Collegiate Hockey Association) Rookie of the Year in 1986

Around the Rink

Murphy was traded to Edmonton by Detroit with Petr Klima, Adam Graves and Jeff Sharples for Jimmy Carson, Kevin McClelland and Edmonton's 5th round choice (later traded to Montreal - Montreal selected Brad Layzell) in 1991 Entry Draft, November 2, 1989. Missed majority of 1992-93 season after failing to come to contract terms with Edmonton. Traded to Chicago by Edmonton for Igor Kravchuk and Dean McAmmond, February 24, 1993. Signed as a free agent by St. Louis, July 8, 1996. Traded to San Jose by St. Louis for Todd Gill, March 24, 1998. Signed as a free agent by Boston, November 12, 1999. Claimed on waivers by Washington from Boston, February 10, 2000. Retired from playing in 2001.

Murphy, Larry

Born: March 8, 1961 in Scarborough, Ontario
Drafted: By the Los Angeles Kings from the Peterborough Petes in 1980, 1st round, 4th overall.

Career Junior, NHL and World Junior Statistics

	GP	**G**	**A**	**PTS**	**PIM**
OHL Regular Season 1978-80	134	27	89	116	170
OHL Playoffs	33	5	22	27	62
Memorial Cup 1979 and 1980	10	1	8	9	12
NHL Regular Season 1980-01	1615	287	919	1216	1086
NHL Playoffs	33	5	22	27	62
Canada 1980 World Juniors *in Finland*	5	1	0	1	4

Junior Highlights

Won Memorial Cup in 1979
OHL First All-Star Team in 1980

Around the Rink

Murphy was traded to Washington by the Los Angeles Kings for Ken Houston and Brian Englblom, October 18, 1983. Traded to Minnesota by Washington with Mike Gartner for Dino Ciccarelli and Bob Rouse, March 7, 1989. Traded to Pittsburgh by Minnesota with Peter Taglianetti for Chris Dahlquist and Jim Johnson, December 11, 1990. Traded to Toronto by Pittsburgh for Dmitri Mironov and Toronto's 2nd round choice (later traded to New Jersey - New Jersey selected Josh DeWolf) in 1996 Entry Draft, July 8, 1995. Traded to Detroit by Toronto for future considerations, March 18, 1997. Retired from playing in 2001.

Murphy, Rob

Born: April 7, 1969 in Hull, Quebec
Drafted: By the Vancouver Canucks from the Laval Titan in 1987, 2nd round, 24th overall.

Career Junior, NHL and World Junior Statistics

	GP	G	A	PTS	PIM
QMJHL Regular Season 1986-89	155	75	132	207	225
QMJHL Playoffs	35	8	22	30	80
Memorial Cup 1988	3	2	0	2	0
NHL Regular Season 1988-94	125	9	12	21	152
NHL Playoffs	4	0	0	0	2
Canada 1989 World Juniors *in United States*	7	1	0	1	8

Junior Highlights

QMJHL Offensive Rookie of the Year in 1987

Around the Rink

Murphy was dealt by Laval to Drummondville after the 1986-87 season. Claimed by Ottawa from Vancouver in Expansion Draft, June 18, 1992. Signed as a free agent by the Los Angeles Kings, August 2, 1993. Has played in Germany since 1997 after three seasons in the IHL.

Murray, Marty

Born: February 16, 1975 in Deloraine, Manitoba
Drafted: By the Calgary Flames from the Brandon Wheat Kings in 1993, 4th round, 96th overall.

Career Junior, NHL and World Junior Statistics

	GP	G	A	PTS	PIM
WHL Regular Season 1991-95	264	132	260	392	158
WHL Playoffs	36	16	37	53	30
Memorial Cup 1995	4	0	3	3	2
NHL Regular Season 1995-Present	176	26	33	59	29
NHL Playoffs	9	0	1	1	4
Canada 1994 World Juniors *in Czech Republic*	7	1	3	4	4
Canada 1995 World Juniors *in Alberta*	7	6	9	15	0
Canada Totals	**14**	**7**	**12**	**19**	**4**

Junior Highlights

Canadian Major Junior Second All-Star Team in 1994
Won Gold Medal at World Junior Championships in 1994 and 1995
WHL East First All-Star Team in 1994 and 1995
World Junior Championships All-Star Team in 1995
Named Best Forward at World Junior Championships in 1995
WHL MVP in 1995

Around the Rink

Signed as a free agent by Philadelphia, July 9, 2001.

Murray, Troy

Born: July 31, 1962 in Calgary, Alberta
Drafted: By the Chicago Black Hawks from the St. Albert Saints in 1980, 3rd round, 57th overall.

Career Junior, NHL and World Junior Statistics

	GP	G	A	PTS	PIM
AJHL 1978-80	120	86	94	180	192
WHL Regular Season 1979-80	2	1	1	2	2
WHL Playoffs	0	0	0	0	0
NCAA 1980-82	64	46	62	108	90
NHL Regular Season 1981-96	914	230	354	584	875
NHL Playoffs	113	17	26	43	145
Canada 1982 World Juniors *in United States*	7	4	4	8	6

Junior Highlights

NCAA (Western Collegiate Hockey Association) Second All-Star Team in 1981 and 1982
Won Gold Medal at World Junior Championships in 1982
Won NCAA Frozen Four Championship in 1982

Around the Rink

Murray was an emergency call up to Lethbridge from St. Albert's of the Alberta Junior Hockey League as an undrafted player in 1979-80 for two games. Traded to Winnipeg by Chicago with Warren Rychel for Bryan Marchment and Chris Norton, July 22, 1991. Traded to Chicago by Winnipeg for Steve Bancroft and future considerations, February 21, 1993. Traded to Ottawa by Chicago with Chicago's 11th round choice (Antti Tormanen) in 1994 Entry Draft for Ottawa's 11th round choice (Rob Mara) in 1994 Entry Draft, March 11, 1994. Traded to Pittsburgh by Ottawa with Norm Maciver for Martin Straka, April 7, 1995. Signed as a free agent by Colorado, August 7, 1995. Retired in 1997 after a full season with the Chicago Wolves of the IHL.

Nash, Rick

Born: June 16, 1984 in Brampton, Ontario
Drafted: By the Columbus Blue Jackets from the London Knights in 2002, 1st round, 1st overall.

Career Junior, NHL and World Junior Statistics

	GP	G	A	PTS	PIM
OHL Regular Season 2000-02	112	63	75	138	144
OHL Playoffs	16	13	12	25	29
NHL Regular Season 2002-Present	74	17	22	39	78
NHL Playoffs	0	0	0	0	0
Canada 2002 World Juniors *in Czech Republic*	7	1	2	3	2

Junior Highlights

CHL Rookie of the Year in 2001
OHL All Rookie Team in 2001
CHL All Rookie Team in 2001
Won Silver Medal at World Junior Championships in 2002

Around the Rink

Nash played his first NHL game on October 10, 2002 against Chicago. His first NHL point and goal came in that game when he scored at 7:35 of the second period beating Chicago goalie Jocelyn Thibault.

Needham, Mike

Born: April 4, 1970 in Calgary, Alberta
Drafted: By the Pittsburgh Penguins from the Kamloops Blazers in 1989, 6th round, 126th overall.

Career Junior, NHL and World Junior Statistics

	GP	G	A	PTS	PIM
WHL Regular Season 1986-90	176	115	131	246	223
WHL Playoffs	49	15	24	39	33
Memorial Cup 1990	3	1	2	3	2
NHL Regular Season 1991-94	86	9	5	14	16
NHL Playoffs	14	2	0	2	4
Canada 1990 World Juniors *in Finland*	7	3	4	7	2

Junior Highlights

Won Gold Medal at World Junior Championships in 1990
WHL West First All-Star Team in 1990

Around the Rink

Needham was traded to Dallas by Pittsburgh for Jim McKenzie, March 21, 1994. Retired from playing in 1996 after two seasons in the minors.

Nelson, Jeff

Born: December 18, 1972 in Prince Albert, Saskatchewan
Drafted: By the Washington Capitals from the Prince Albert Raiders in 1991, 2nd round, 36th overall.

Career Junior, NHL and World Junior Statistics

	GP	G	A	PTS	PIM
WHL Regular Season 1988-92	279	152	265	417	295
WHL Playoffs	30	10	29	39	36
NHL Regular Season 1994-99	52	3	8	11	20
NHL Playoffs	3	0	0	0	4
Canada 1992 World Juniors *in Germany*	7	1	1	2	2

Junior Highlights

Canadian Major Junior Scholastic Player of the Year in 1989 and 1990
WHL East Second All-Star Team in 1991 and 1992

Around the Rink

Nelson signed as a free agent by Grand Rapids (IHL), September 9, 1996. Signed as a free agent by Nashville, August 19, 1998. Traded to Washington by Nashville for cash, June 21, 1999. Signed as a free agent by Schwenningen (Germany), July 17, 2001.

Nemeth, Steve

Born: February 11, 1967 in Calgary, Alberta
Drafted: By the New York Rangers from the Lethbridge Broncos in 1985, 10th round, 196th overall.

Career Junior, NHL and World Junior Statistics

	GP	G	A	PTS	PIM
Canadian National Team 1986-87	43	14	7	21	12
WHL Regular Season 1982-87	218	113	149	262	119
WHL Playoffs	32	19	18	37	33
NHL Regular Season 1987-88	12	2	0	2	2
NHL Playoffs	0	0	0	0	0
Canada 1987 World Juniors *in Czech Republic*	6	4	4	8	4

Junior Highlights

Assistant Captain of Canada at World Junior Championships in 1987

Around the Rink

Nemeth played all twelve of his NHL games with the New York Rangers. Rejoined the Canadian National Team from 1988-91. Played in England from 1991-97. Came back to North America and played in two minor pro-leagues from 1997-99 and then retired from playing.

Niedermayer, Rob

Born: December 28, 1974 in Cassiar, B.C.
Drafted: By the Florida Panthers from the Medicine Hat Tigers in 1993, 1st round, 5th overall.

Career Junior, NHL and World Junior Statistics

	GP	**G**	**A**	**PTS**	**PIM**
WHL Regular Season 1990-95	207	108	121	229	166
WHL Playoffs	16	5	10	15	4
NHL Regular Season 1993-Present	641	117	191	308	541
NHL Playoffs	41	10	7	17	36
Canada 1993 World Juniors *in Sweden*	7	0	2	2	2

Junior Highlights

Won Gold Medal at World Junior Championships in 1993
WHL East First All-Star Team in 1993

Around the Rink

Niedermayer missed the majority of 1997-98 season recovering from thumb (vs. Boston, November 26, 1997) and head (vs. Buffalo, March 19, 1998) injuries. Traded to Calgary by Florida with Philadelphia's 2nd round choice (previously acquired, Calgary selected Andrei Medvedev) in 2001 Entry Draft for Valeri Bure and Jason Wiemer, June 23, 2001. Traded to Anaheim by Calgary for J.F. Damphousse and Mike Commodore, March 11, 2003.

Niedermayer, Scott

Born: August 31, 1973 in Edmonton, Alberta – Raised in Cranbrook, B.C.
Drafted: By the New Jersey Devils from the Kamloops Blazers in 1991, 1st round, 3rd overall.

Career Junior, NHL and World Junior Statistics

	GP	G	A	PTS	PIM
WHL Regular Season 1989-92	156	47	143	190	177
WHL Playoffs	34	11	28	39	63
Memorial Cup 1990 and 1992	8	3	6	9	8
NHL Regular Season 1991-Present	811	98	324	422	401
NHL Playoffs	122	15	33	48	86
Canada 1991 World Juniors *in Saskatoon*	7	0	0	0	0
Canada 1992 World Juniors *in Germany*	7	0	0	0	10
Canada Totals	**14**	**0**	**0**	**0**	**10**

Junior Highlights

Won Gold Medal at World Junior Championships in 1991
WHL West First All-Star Team in 1991 and 1992
Canadian Major Junior Scholastic Player of the Year in 1991
World Junior Championships All-Star Team in 1992
Memorial Cup All-Star Team in 1992
Won Stafford Smythe Memorial Trophy (Memorial Cup MVP) in 1992
Won Memorial Cup in 1992

Around the Rink

Niedermayer has played all of his NHL games with New Jersey. Never played game in the minor leagues. Signed to 25-game try-out contract by Utah (IHL) while holding out from the New Jersey Devils, October 19, 1998.

Nielsen, Chris

Born: February 16, 1980 in Moshi, Tanzania – Raised in Goodlands, Manitoba
Drafted: By the New York Islanders from the Calgary Hitmen in 1998, 2nd round, 36th overall.

Career Junior, NHL and World Junior Statistics

	GP	G	A	PTS	PIM
WHL Regular Season 1995-00	268	93	103	196	201
WHL Playoffs	52	27	18	45	58
Memorial Cup 1999	4	2	1	3	0
NHL Regular Season 2000-02	52	6	8	14	8
NHL Playoffs	0	0	0	0	0
Canada 1999 World Juniors *in Winnipeg*	2	1	0	1	4
Canada 2000 World Juniors *in Sweden*	7	3	0	3	8
Canada Totals	**9**	**4**	**0**	**4**	**12**

Junior Highlights

Won Silver Medal at World Junior Championships in 1999
Won Bronze Medal at World Junior Championships in 2000

Around the Rink

Nielsen played his first NHL game on December 14, 2000 against San Jose. Scored his first NHL goal on December 16, 2000 versus Vancouver. Traded to Columbus by the New York Islanders for Columbus' 4th (later traded to Anaheim - Anaheim selected Jonas Ronnqvist) and 9th (Dmitri Altarev) round choices in 2000 Entry Draft, May 11, 2000. Traded to Atlanta with Petteri Nummelin from Columbus for Tomi Kallio and Pauli Levokari on Dec. 2, 2002. Traded by Atlanta with Chris Herperger to Vancouver in exchange for Jeff Farkas, January 20, 2003. Did not play in the NHL in 2002-03.

Nieuwendyk, Joe

Born: September 10, 1966 in Oshawa, Ontario
Drafted: By the Calgary Flames from Cornell University in 1985, 2nd round, 27th overall.

Career Junior, NHL and World Junior Statistics

	GP	G	A	PTS	PIM
NCAA 1984-87	73	68	71	139	101
NHL Regular Season 1986-Present	1113	511	501	1012	601
NHL Playoffs	143	59	48	107	85
Canada 1986 World Juniors *in Hamilton*	7	5	7	12	6

Junior Highlights

NCAA (Eastern Collegiate Athletic Conference) Rookie of the Year in 1985
NCAA (ECAC) First All-Star Team in 1986 and 1987
NCAA East First All-American Team in 1986 and 1987
Won Silver Medal at World Junior Championships in 1986
NCAA (ECAC) Player of the Year in 1987

Around the Rink

Nieuwendyk was traded to Dallas by Calgary for Corey Millen and Jarome Iginla, December 19, 1995. Traded to New Jersey by Dallas with Jamie Langenbrunner for Jason Arnott, Randy McKay and New Jersey's 1st round choice (later traded to Columbus - later traded to Buffalo - Buffalo selected Dan Paille) in 2002 Entry Draft, March 19, 2002.

Norris, Dwayne

Born: January 8, 1970 in St. John's, Newfoundland
Drafted: By the Quebec Nordiques from Michigan State University in 1990, 7th round, 127th overall.

Career Junior, NHL and World Junior Statistics

	GP	G	A	PTS	PIM
NCAA 1988-92	167	105	113	218	192
NHL Regular Season 1993-96	20	2	4	6	8
NHL Playoffs	0	0	0	0	0
Canada 1990 World Juniors *in Finland*	7	2	4	6	2

Junior Highlights

Won Gold Medal at World Junior Championships in 1990
NCAA (Central Collegiate Hockey Association) First All-Star Team in 1992
NCAA (CCHA) Player of the Year in 1992
NCAA West First All-American Team in 1992

Around the Rink

Norris signed as a free agent by Anaheim, November 3, 1995. Has played in Germany since 1996 with the Cologne Sharks.

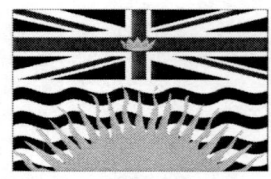

Nylund, Gary

Born: October 28, 1963 in Surrey, B.C.
Drafted: By the Toronto Maple Leafs from the Portland Winter Hawks in 1982, 1st round, 3rd overall.

Career Junior, NHL and World Junior Statistics

	GP	G	A	PTS	PIM
WHL Regular Season 1978-82	209	18	120	138	512
WHL Playoffs	32	4	24	28	93
Memorial Cup 1982	4	0	2	2	10
NHL Regular Season 1982-93	608	32	139	171	1235
NHL Playoffs	24	0	6	6	63
Canada 1982 World Juniors *in United States*	7	1	3	4	0

Junior Highlights

Won Gold Medal at World Junior Championships in 1982
WHL First All-Star Team in 1982
Memorial Cup All-Star Team in 1982

Around the Rink

Nylund signed as a free agent by Chicago, August 27, 1986. Traded to the New York Islanders by Chicago with Marc Bergevin for Steve Konroyd and Bob Bassen, November 25, 1988. Retired from playing in 1993.

Odelein, Selmar

Born: April 11, 1966 in Quill Lake, Saskatchewan
Drafted: By the Edmonton Oilers from the Regina Pats in 1984, 1st round, 21st overall.

Career Junior, NHL and World Junior Statistics

	GP	G	A	PTS	PIM
WHL Regular Season 1982-86	172	46	105	151	223
WHL Playoffs	39	11	15	26	82
NHL Regular Season 1985-89	18	0	2	2	35
NHL Playoffs	0	0	0	0	0
Canada 1985 World Juniors *in Finland*	7	1	5	6	8
Canada 1986 World Juniors *in Hamilton*	7	0	1	1	6
Canada Totals	**14**	**1**	**6**	**7**	**14**

Junior Highlights

Won Gold Medal at World Junior Championships in 1985
WHL Second All-Star Team in 1985
Won Silver Medal at World Junior Championships in 1986

Around the Rink

Odelein suffered a knee injury in a game against Adirondack (AHL), October 17, 1986 and missed the remainder of the season. Played for Canadian National Team in 1989-90 and then went to Europe for three seasons before retiring from playing in 1994.

Ogrodnick, John

Born: June 20, 1959 in Ottawa, Ontario
Drafted: By the Detroit Red Wings from the New Westminster Bruins in 1979, 4th round, 66th overall.

Career Junior, NHL and World Junior Statistics

	GP	G	A	PTS	PIM
WHL Regular Season 1976-79	158	109	69	178	85
WHL Playoffs	41	19	10	29	20
Memorial Cup 1977 and 1978	10	5	1	6	2
NHL Regular Season 1979-93	928	402	425	827	260
NHL Playoffs	41	18	8	26	6
Canada 1979 World Juniors *in Sweden*	5	3	0	3	4

Junior Highlights

Won Memorial Cup in 1977 and 1978
WHL Rookie of the Year (Co-winner with Keith Brown) in 1978

Around the Rink

Ogrodnick was traded to Quebec by Detroit with Basil McRae and Doug Shedden for Brent Ashton, Gilbert Delorme and Mark Kumpel, January 17, 1987. Traded to NY Rangers by Quebec with David Shaw for Jeff Jackson and Terry Carkner, September 30, 1987. Signed as a free agent by Detroit, September 29, 1992. Retired from playing in 1993.

O'Neill, Jeff

Born: February 23, 1976 in Richmond Hill, Ontario
Drafted: By the Hartford Whalers from the Guelph Storm in 1994, 1st round, 5th overall.

Career Junior, NHL and World Junior Statistics

	GP	G	A	PTS	PIM
OHL Regular Season 1992-95	188	120	209	329	239
OHL Playoffs	28	12	31	43	71
NHL Regular Season 1995-Present	606	184	198	382	492
NHL Playoffs	34	9	8	17	37
Canada 1995 World Juniors *in Alberta*	7	2	4	6	2

Junior Highlights

OHL All-Rookie Team in 1993
OHL Rookie of the Year in 1993
Won Gold Medal at World Junior Championships in 1995
OHL First All-Star Team in 1995

Around the Rink

O'Neill's rights were transferred to Carolina after Hartford franchise relocated, June 25, 1997. Played his first NHL game with Hartford on October 7, 1995 against the New York Rangers. Recorded his first NHL point and goal versus the Rangers on October 16, 1995.

Orleski, Dave

Born: December 26, 1959 in Edmonton, Alberta
Drafted: By the Montreal Canadiens from the New Westminster Bruins in 1979, 4th round, 79th overall.

Career Junior, NHL and World Junior Statistics

	GP	G	A	PTS	PIM
WHL Regular Season 1976-79	197	50	198	148	262
WHL Playoffs	36	18	17	35	38
Memorial Cup 1977 and 1978	5	2	2	4	0
NHL Regular Season 1980-82	2	0	0	0	0
NHL Playoffs	0	0	0	0	0
Canada 1979 World Juniors *in Sweden*	5	2	0	2	0

Junior Highlights

Won Memorial Cup in 1977 and 1978

Around the Rink

Orleski played both of his NHL games with the Montreal Canadiens. Retired from playing in 1985 after three seasons in the minors.

Ott, Steve

Born: August 19, 1982 in Summerside, P.E.I.
Drafted: By the Dallas Stars from the Windsor Spitfires in 2000, 1st round, 25th overall.

Career Junior, NHL and World Junior Statistics

	GP	G	A	PTS	PIM
OHL Regular Season 1999-02	174	116	121	237	473
OHL Playoffs	35	12	23	35	97
NHL Regular Season 2002-Present	26	3	4	7	31
NHL Playoffs	1	0	0	0	0
Canada 2001 World Juniors *in Russia*	7	2	1	3	6
Canada 2002 World Juniors *in Czech Republic*	7	3	3	6	8
Canada Totals	**14**	**5**	**4**	**9**	**14**

Junior Highlights

Won Bronze Medal at World Junior Championships in 2001
OHL Second All Star Team in 2001
Won Silver Medal at World Junior Championships in 2002
OHL Western Conference All Star Team in 2002
OHL Third All Star Team in 2002

Around the Rink

Ott played his first NHL game on December 13, 2002 against Atlanta. Recorded his first point and goal versus Edmonton on December 31, 2002.

Ouellet, Maxime

Born: June 17, 1981 in Beauport, Quebec
Drafted: By the Philadelphia Flyers from the Quebec Remparts in 1999, 1st round, 22nd overall.

Career Junior, NHL and World Junior Statistics

	GP	W	L	T	SO	AVG
QMJHL Regular Season 1997-01	161	101	41	12	6	2.76
QMJHL Playoffs	39	20	16	0	3	2.95
NHL Regular Season 2000-01	2	0	1	0	0	2.37
NHL Playoffs	0	0	0	0	0	0.00
Canada 2000 World Juniors *in Sweden*	6	3	1	2	0	1.83
Canada 2001 World Juniors *in Russia*	7	4	2	1	1	1.51
Canada Totals	**13**	**7**	**3**	**3**	**1**	**1.66**

Junior Highlights

Won Jacques Plante Trophy (fewest goals against - QMJHL) in 1999
QMJHL Second All-Star Team in 1999, 2000 and 2001
Won Bronze Medal at World Junior Championships in 2000 and 2001

Around the Rink

Ouellet was traded by Quebec to Rouyn-Noranda after the 1999-00 season. Played both of his NHL games with Philadelphia. Returned to Rouyn-Noranda (QMJHL) by Philadelphia, October 27, 2000. Traded to Washington by Philadelphia with Philadelphia's 1st (later traded to Dallas - Dallas selected Martin Vagner), 2nd (Maxime Daigneault) and 3rd (Derek Krestanovich) round choices in 2002 Entry Draft for Adam Oates, March 19, 2002.

Pachal, Clayton

Born: April 21, 1956 in Yorkton, Saskatchewan
Drafted: By the Boston Bruins from the New Westminster Bruins in 1976, 1st round, 16th overall. Also Drafted by the Winnipeg Jets (WHA) in 1976, 2nd round, 17th overall.

Career Junior, NHL and World Junior Statistics

	GP	G	A	PTS	PIM
WHL Regular Season 1972-76	234	68	100	168	910
WHL Playoffs	48	13	15	28	156
Memorial Cup 1975 and 1976	8	4	1	5	18
NHL Regular Season 1976-79	35	2	3	5	95
NHL Playoffs	0	0	0	0	0
Canada 1975 World Juniors *in Manitoba*	3	0	0	0	2

Junior Highlights

Won Silver Medal at World Junior Championships in 1975

Around the Rink

Pachal was traded to Colorado by Boston for Mark Suzor, October 11, 1978. Signed as a free agent by Edmonton, July 1979 but never played a game for the Oilers. Retired from playing in 1980 after a season split between the IHL and CHL. Coached in the Saskatchewan Hockey League from 1980-84.

Paterson, Mark

Born: February 22, 1964 in Ottawa, Ontario
Drafted: By the Hartford Whalers from the Ottawa 67's in 1982, 2nd round, 35th overall.

Career Junior, NHL and World Junior Statistics

	GP	G	A	PTS	PIM
OHL Regular Season 1981-84	166	19	43	62	313
OHL Playoffs	39	4	16	20	87
Memorial Cup 1984	5	0	2	2	8
NHL Regular Season 1982-86	29	3	3	6	33
NHL Playoffs	0	0	0	0	0
Canada 1984 World Juniors *in Sweden*	7	0	2	2	10

Junior Highlights

Won Memorial Cup in 1984

Around the Rink

Paterson played all of his NHL games with Hartford. Traded to Calgary by Hartford for Yves Courteau, October 7, 1986. Retired from playing in 1989 after three seasons in the minors with Moncton (AHL) and Saginaw (IHL).

Paterson, Rick

Born: February 10, 1958 in Kingston, Ontario
Drafted: By the Chicago Black Hawks from the Cornwall Royals in 1978, 3rd round, 46th overall.

Career Junior, NHL and World Junior Statistics

	GP	G	A	PTS	PIM
QMJHL Regular Season 1973-78	342	128	237	365	309
QMJHL Playoffs	21	9	16	25	49
NHL Regular Season 1979-87	430	50	43	93	136
NHL Playoffs	61	7	10	17	51
Canada 1978 World Juniors *in Montreal*	6	1	2	3	0

Junior Highlights

Won Bronze Medal at World Junior Championships in 1978

Around the Rink

Paterson played all of his NHL games with Chicago. Retired from playing in 1988 after a full season with Saginaw (IHL). Assistant Coach with Pittsburgh from 1988-93. Head Coach of the Cleveland Lumberjacks (IHL) from 1993-97. Assistant Coach with Tampa Bay from 1997-99.

Patrick, James

Born: June 14, 1963 in Winnipeg, Manitoba
Drafted: By the New York Rangers from the Prince Albert Raiders in 1981, 1st round, 9th overall.

Career Junior, NHL and World Junior Statistics

	GP	G	A	PTS	PIM
SJHL 1980-81	59	21	61	82	162
NCAA 1981-83	78	17	60	77	55
NHL Regular Season 1983-Present	1225	145	483	628	747
NHL Playoffs	117	6	32	38	86
Canada 1982 World Juniors *in United States*	7	0	2	2	6
Canada 1983 World Juniors *in Russia*	7	0	2	2	4
Canada Totals	**14**	**0**	**4**	**4**	**10**

Junior Highlights

Won Gold Medal at World Junior Championships in 1982
NCAA (Western Collegiate Hockey Association) Second All-Star Team in 1982
NCAA (WCHA) Freshman of the Year in 1982
NCAA Chamionship All-Tournament Team in 1982
Won NCAA Frozen Four Championship in 1982
Won Bronze Medal at World Junior Championships in 1983
NCAA (WCHA) First All-Star Team in 1983
NCAA West All American Team in 1983

Around the Rink

Patrick played one season in the Saskatchewan Junior Hockey League before accepting a scholarship to the University of North Dakota. Traded to Hartford by the New York Rangers with Darren Turcotte for Steve Larmer, Nick Kypreos, Barry Richter and Hartford's 6th round choice (Yuri Litvinov) in 1994 Entry Draft, November 2, 1993. Traded to Calgary by Hartford with Zarley Zalapski and Michael Nylander for Gary Suter, Paul Ranheim and Ted Drury, March 10, 1994. Missed majority of 1996-97 season recovering from knee injury originally suffered in game vs. Pittsburgh, October 24, 1996. Signed as a free agent by Buffalo, October 7, 1998.

Peca, Mike

Born: March 26, 1974 in Toronto, Ontario
Drafted: By the Vancouver Canucks from the Ottawa 67's in 1992, 2nd round, 40th overall.

Career Junior, NHL and World Junior Statistics

	GP	G	A	PTS	PIM
OHL Regular Season 1990-94	238	126	205	331	298
OHL Playoffs	33	14	32	46	43
NHL Regular Season 1993-Present	546	140	191	331	489
NHL Playoffs	64	9	14	23	52
Canada 1994 World Juniors *in Czech Republic*	7	2	2	4	8

Junior Highlights

Won Gold Medal at World Junior Championships in 1994

Around the Rink

Peca was traded by the Sudbury Wolves to the Ottawa 67's mid-way through the 1991-92 season. Traded to Buffalo by Vancouver with Mike Wilson and Vancouver's 1st round choice (Jay McKee) in 1995 Entry Draft for Alexander Mogilny and Buffalo's 5th round choice (Todd Norman) in 1995 Entry Draft, July 8, 1995. Missed entire 2000-01 season after failing to come to contract terms with Buffalo. Rights traded to the New York Islanders by Buffalo for Tim Connolly and Taylor Pyatt, June 24, 2001.

Pederson, Denis

Born: September 10, 1975 in Prince Albert, Saskatchewan
Drafted: By the New Jersey Devils from the Prince Albert Raiders in 1993, 1st round, 13th overall.

Career Junior, NHL and World Junior Statistics

	GP	G	A	PTS	PIM
WHL Regular Season 1991-95	216	116	209	325	419
WHL Playoffs	22	11	15	26	27
NHL Regular Season 1995-Present	435	57	71	128	398
NHL Playoffs	27	1	5	6	8
Canada 1995 World Juniors *in Alberta*	7	2	2	4	0

Junior Highlights

Won Gold Medal at World Junior Championships in 1995
WHL East Second All-Star Team in 1994

Around the Rink

Pederson was traded to Vancouver by New Jersey with Brendan Morrison for Alexander Mogilny, March 14, 2000. Traded to Phoenix by Vancouver with Drake Berehowsky for Todd Warriner, Trevor Letowski, Tyler Bouck and Phoenix's 3rd round choice in 2003 Entry Draft, December 28, 2001. Signed as a free agent by Nashville, July 24, 2002.

Pederson, Mark

Born: January 14, 1968 in Prelate, Saskatchewan
Drafted: By the Montreal Canadiens from the Medicine Hat Tigers in 1986, 1st round, 15th overall.

Career Junior, NHL and World Junior Statistics

	GP	G	A	PTS	PIM
WHL Regular Season 1983-88	277	197	204	401	222
WHL Playoffs	71	47	21	68	55
Memorial Cup 1987 and 1988	10	5	7	12	10
NHL Regular Season 1989-94	169	35	50	85	77
NHL Playoffs	2	0	0	0	0
Canada 1988 World Juniors *in Russia*	7	1	2	3	4

Junior Highlights

WHL East First All-Star Team in 1987
Won Gold Medal at World Junior Championships in 1988
WHL East Second All-Star Team in 1988

Around the Rink

Pederson was dealt to Philadelphia by Montreal for Philadelphia's 2nd round choice (Jim Campbell) in 1991 Entry Draft, March 15, 1991. Traded to San Jose by Philadelphia with future considerations for Dave Snuggerud, December 19, 1992. Signed as a free agent by Detroit, August 23, 1993. Played in Europe from 1995-2002. Returned to North America and signed with San Diego of the West Coast Hockey League for the 2002-03 season.

Pellerin, Scott

Born: January 9, 1970 in Shediac, New Brunswick
Drafted: By the New Jersey Devils from the University of Maine in 1989, 3rd round, 47th overall.

Career Junior, NHL and World Junior Statistics

	GP	**G**	**A**	**PTS**	**PIM**
NCAA 1988-92	167	106	117	223	274
NHL Regular Season 1992-Present	534	72	126	198	318
NHL Playoffs	37	1	2	3	26
Canada 1990 World Juniors *in Finland*	7	2	0	2	2

Junior Highlights

NCAA - Hockey East Rookie of the Year (Shared with Rob Gaudreau) in 1989
Won Gold Medal at World Junior Championships in 1990
NCAA - Hockey East First All-Star Team in 1992
NCAA - Hockey East Player of the Year in 1992
NCAA East First All-American Team in 1992
Won Hobey Baker Memorial Award (Top U.S. Collegiate Player) in 1992

Around the Rink

Pellerin signed as a free agent by St. Louis, July 10, 1996. Selected by Minnesota from St. Louis in Expansion Draft, June 23, 2000. Traded to Carolina by Minnesota for Askhat Rakhmatullin, Carolina's 3rd round choice (later traded to NY Rangers - NY Rangers selected Garth Murray) in 2001 Entry Draft and Carolina's compensatory 5th round choice (Armands Berzins) in 2002 Entry Draft, March 1, 2001. Signed as a free agent by Boston, July 26, 2001. Claimed on waivers by Dallas from Boston, January 12, 2002. Traded to Phoenix by Dallas with a 2004 conditional draft pick for Claude Lemieux on January 16, 2003.

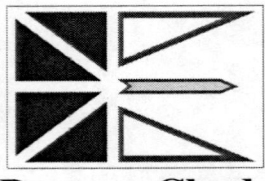

Penney, Chad

Born: September 18, 1973 in Labrador City, Newfoundland
Drafted: By the Ottawa Senators from the North Bay Centennials in 1992, 2nd round, 25th overall.

Career Junior, NHL and World Junior Statistics

	GP	G	A	PTS	PIM
OHL Regular Season 1990-93	189	95	112	207	235
OHL Playoffs	49	22	33	55	39
Memorial Cup 1993	4	5	2	7	6
NHL Regular Season 1993-94	3	0	0	0	2
NHL Playoffs	0	0	0	0	0
Canada 1992 World Juniors *in Germany*	7	0	0	0	2

Junior Highlights

Won Memorial Cup in 1993
Memorial Cup All-Star Team in 1993

Around the Rink

Penney was traded from North Bay to the Sault Ste. Marie Greyhounds after 18 games in 1992. Played all three of his NHL games with Ottawa and was a –2. Retired from playing in 1999 after four seasons in the minors and a year in Europe.

Pettinger, Matt

Born: October 22, 1980 in Edmonton, Alberta
Drafted: By the Washington Capitals from the Calgary Hitmen in 2000, 2nd round, 43rd overall.

Career Junior, NHL and World Junior Statistics

	GP	**G**	**A**	**PTS**	**PIM**
NCAA 1998-00	57	8	20	28	101
WHL Regular Season 1999-00	27	14	6	20	41
WHL Playoffs	11	2	6	8	30
NHL Regular Season 2000-Present	72	7	3	10	46
NHL Playoffs	0	0	0	0	0
Canada 1999 World Juniors *in Winnipeg*	2	1	0	1	2
Canada 2000 World Juniors *in Sweden*	7	4	0	4	4
Canada Totals	**9**	**5**	**0**	**5**	**6**

Junior Highlights

Won Silver Medal at World Junior Championships in 1999
Won Bronze Medal at World Junior Championships in 2000

Around the Rink

Pettinger left the University of Denver and signed as a free agent with Calgary (WHL), January 10, 2000. Has played all of his NHL games with Washington. Played just one NHL game in 2002-03.

Phillips, Chris

Born: March 9, 1978 in Calgary, Alberta
Drafted: By the Ottawa Senators from the Prince Albert Raiders in 1996, 1st round, 1st overall.

Career Junior, NHL and World Junior Statistics

	GP	G	A	PTS	PIM
WHL Regular Season 1995-97	119	17	71	88	183
WHL Playoffs	37	6	33	39	50
Memorial Cup 1997	5	2	3	5	14
NHL Regular Season 1997-Present	385	24	72	96	240
NHL Playoffs	45	2	6	8	26
Canada 1996 World Juniors *in United States*	6	0	0	0	0
Canada 1997 World Juniors *in Switzerland*	7	0	1	1	4
Canada Totals	**13**	**0**	**1**	**1**	**4**

Junior Highlights

Won Gold Medal at World Junior Championships in 1996 and 1997
World Junior Championships All-Star Team in 1997
WHL East First All-Star Team in 1997
Canadian Major Junior First All-Star Team in 1997

Around the Rink

Phillips missed the majority of 1998-99 season recovering from ankle injury suffered in game versus Buffalo, December 30, 1998. He has played all of his NHL games with Ottawa and has never played in the minors.

Plantery, Mark

Born: August 14, 1959 in St. Catharines, Ontario
Not Drafted: Signed as a Free Agent with the Winnipeg Jets in 1979.

Career Junior, NHL and World Junior Statistics

	GP	G	A	PTS	PIM
OHL Regular Season 1976-79	169	8	63	71	344
OHL Playoffs	36	1	4	5	59
NHL Regular Season 1980-81	25	1	5	6	14
NHL Playoffs	0	0	0	0	0
Canada 1977 World Juniors *in Czech Republic*	7	0	1	1	6

Junior Highlights

Won Silver Medal at World Junior Championships in 1977

Around the Rink

Plantery started his junior career with the St. Catharines Fincups in 1976, the team moved to Hamilton in 1977, and then relocated to Brantford in 1978 and became the Alexanders. He was traded by Brantford to Windsor halfway through the 1978-79 season. Signed as a free agent by Winnipeg, October 5, 1979. Played all of his NHL games with the Jets. Retired from playing in 1986 after four seasons in the minors.

Plavsic, Adrien

Born: January 13, 1970 in Montreal, Quebec
Drafted: By the St. Louis Blues from the University of New Hampshire in 1988, 2nd round, 30th overall.

Career Junior, NHL and World Junior Statistics

	GP	G	A	PTS	PIM
Canadian National Team 1988-89	62	5	10	15	25
NCAA 1987-88	30	5	6	11	45
NHL Regular Season 1989-97	214	16	56	72	161
NHL Playoffs	13	1	7	8	4
Canada 1990 World Juniors *in Finland*	7	0	1	1	8

Junior Highlights

Won Gold Medal at World Junior Championships in 1990

Around the Rink

Plavsic was traded to Vancouver by St. Louis with Montreal's 1st round choice (previously acquired, Vancouver selected Shawn Antoski) in 1990 Entry Draft and St. Louis' 2nd round choice (later traded to Montreal Montreal selected Craig Darby) in 1991 Entry Draft for Rich Sutter, Harold Snepsts and St. Louis' 2nd round choice (previously acquired, St. Louis selected Craig Johnson) in 1990 Entry Draft, March 6, 1990. Traded to Tampa Bay by Vancouver for Tampa Bay's 5th round choice (David Darguzas) in 1997 Entry Draft, March 23, 1995. Signed as a free agent by Anaheim, September 6, 1996. Retired from playing in 2002 after one season in Germany and four years in Switzerland.

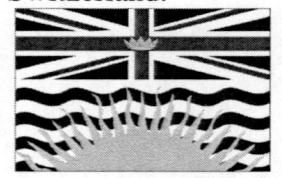

Podollan, Jason

Born: February 18, 1976 in Vernon, B.C.
Drafted: By the Florida Panthers from the Spokane Chiefs in 1994, 2nd round, 31st overall.

Career Junior, NHL and World Junior Statistics

	GP	G	A	PTS	PIM
WHL Regular Season 1991-96	271	145	136	281	423
WHL Playoffs	52	36	24	60	78
NHL Regular Season 1996-2002	41	1	5	6	19
NHL Playoffs	0	0	0	0	0
Canada 1996 World Juniors *in United States*	6	2	3	5	2

Junior Highlights

Won Gold Medal at World Junior Championships in 1996
WHL West Second All-Star Team in 1996

Around the Rink

Podollan was traded to Toronto by Florida for Kirk Muller, March 18, 1997. Traded to Los Angeles by Toronto with Toronto's 3rd round choice (Cory Campbell) in 1999 Entry Draft for Yanic Perreault, March 23, 1999. Claimed by Tampa Bay from LA Kings in Waiver Draft, September 29, 2000. Signed as a free agent by NY Islanders, August 24, 2001. Signed as a free agent by Mannheim (Germany), July 29, 2002.

Potvin, Felix

Born: June 23, 1971 in Anjou, Quebec
Drafted: By the Toronto Maple Leafs from the Chicoutimi Sagueneens in 1990, 2nd round, 31st overall.

Career Junior, NHL and World Junior Statistics

	GP	W	L	T	SO	AVG
QMJHL Regular Season 1988-91	181	89	72	7	10	3.81
QMJHL Playoffs	16	11	5	0	0	2.78
Memorial Cup 1991	3	1	2	0	0	2.76
NHL Regular Season 1991-Present	607	254	252	79	28	2.77
NHL Playoffs	72	35	37	0	8	2.64
Canada 1991 World Juniors *in Saskatoon*	2	1	0	0	0	3.75

Junior Highlights

QMJHL All-Rookie Team in 1989
QMJHL Second All-Star Team in 1990
Won Gold Medal at World Junior Championships in 1991
QMJHL First All-Star Team in 1991
Canadian Major Junior Goaltender of the Year in 1991
Memorial Cup All-Star Team in 1991
Won Hap Emms Memorial Trophy (Memorial Cup Top Goaltender) in 1991

Around the Rink

Potvin was traded to the New York Islanders by Toronto with Toronto's 6th round choice (later traded to Tampa Bay - Tampa Bay selected Fedor Fedorov) in 1999 Entry Draft for Bryan Berard and the Islanders' 6th round choice (Jan Sochor) in 1999 Entry Draft, January 9, 1999. Traded to Vancouver by the New York Islanders with the Islanders compensatory 2nd (later traded to New Jersey - New Jersey selected Teemu Laine) and 3rd (Thatcher Bell) round choices in 2000 Entry Draft for Kevin Weekes, Dave Scatchard and Bill Muckalt, December 19, 1999. Traded to the L.A. Kings by Vancouver for future considerations, February 15, 2001.

Poulin, Patrick

Born: April 23, 1973 in Vanier, Quebec
Drafted: By the Hartford Whalers from the St. Hyacinthe Lasers in 1991, 1st round, 9th overall.

Career Junior, NHL and World Junior Statistics

	GP	G	A	PTS	PIM
QMJHL Regular Season 1989-92	172	109	150	259	195
QMJHL Playoffs	21	3	13	16	32
NHL Regular Season 1991-02	634	101	134	235	299
NHL Playoffs	32	6	2	8	8
Canada 1992 World Juniors *in Germany*	7	2	2	4	2

Junior Highlights

QMJHL All-Rookie Team in 1990
QMJHL First All-Star Team in 1992
Canadian Major Junior Player of the Year in 1992

Around the Rink

Poulin was dealt to Chicago by Hartford with Eric Weinrich for Steve Larmer and Bryan Marchment, November 2, 1993. Traded to Tampa Bay by Chicago with Igor Ulanov and Chicago's 2nd round choice (later traded to New Jersey - New Jersey selected Pierre Dagenais) in 1996 Entry Draft for Enrico Ciccone and Tampa Bay's 2nd round choice (Jeff Paul) in 1996 Entry Draft, March 20, 1996. Traded to Montreal by Tampa Bay with Mick Vukota and Igor Ulanov for Stephane Richer, Darcy Tucker and David Wilkie, January 15, 1998. Did not play in 2002-03.

Pronger, Chris

Born: October 10, 1974 in Dryden, Ontario
Drafted: By the Hartford Whalers from the Peterborough Petes in 1993, 1st round, 3rd overall.

Career Junior, NHL and World Junior Statistics

	GP	G	A	PTS	PIM
OHL Regular Season 1991-93	124	32	107	139	198
OHL Playoffs	31	16	33	49	79
Memorial Cup 1993	5	1	5	6	8
NHL Regular Season 1993-Present	642	80	266	346	1010
NHL Playoffs	80	10	40	50	194
Canada 1993 World Juniors *in Sweden*	7	1	3	4	6

Junior Highlights

OHL All-Rookie Team in 1992
Won Gold Medal at World Junior Championships in 1993
OHL First All-Star Team in 1993
Canadian Major Junior First All-Star Team in 1993
Canadian Major Junior Defenseman of the Year in 1993

Around the Rink

Pronger was traded to St. Louis by Hartford for Brendan Shanahan, July 27, 1995.
Missed most of the 2002-03 season after off season wrist surgery.

Propp, Brian

Born: February 15, 1959 in Lanigan, Saskatchewan
Drafted: By the Philadelphia Flyers from the Brandon Wheat Kings in 1979, 1st round, 14th overall.

Career Junior, NHL and World Junior Statistics

	GP	G	A	PTS	PIM
WHL Regular Season 1976-79	213	219	292	511	374
WHL Playoffs	46	36	41	77	57
Memorial Cup 1978 and 1979	5	4	7	11	6
NHL Regular Season 1979-93	1016	425	579	1004	830
NHL Playoffs	160	64	84	148	151
Canada 1979 World Juniors *in Sweden*	5	2	1	3	2

Junior Highlights

WHL Rookie of the Year in 1977
Won Memorial Cup in 1978 and 1979
WHL First All-Star Team in 1978
WHL First All-Star Team in 1979

Around the Rink

Propp was injured in 1978 and did not play in Memorial Cup. Traded to Boston by Philadelphia for Boston's 2nd round choice (Terran Sandwith) in 1990 Entry Draft, March 2, 1990. Signed as a free agent by Minnesota, July 25, 1990. Signed as a free agent by Hartford, October 4, 1993. Retired in 1995 after a season of playing in France.

Racine, Yves

Born: February 7, 1969 in Matane, Quebec
Drafted: By the Detroit Red Wings from the Longueuil Chevaliers in 1987, 1st round, 11th overall.

Career Junior, NHL and World Junior Statistics

	GP	G	A	PTS	PIM
QMJHL Regular Season 1986-89	202	40	212	252	295
QMJHL Playoffs	41	6	41	47	68
Memorial Cup 1987	5	0	0	0	0
NHL Regular Season 1989-98	508	37	194	231	439
NHL Playoffs	25	5	4	9	37
Canada 1989 World Juniors *in United States*	7	0	0	0	6

Junior Highlights

QMJHL First-All Star Team in 1988 and 1989

Around the Rink

Racine was traded by Longueuil to Victoriaville after the 1986-87 season. Traded to Philadelphia by Detroit with Detroit's 4th round choice (Sebastien Vallee) in 1994 Entry Draft for Terry Carkner, October 5, 1993. Traded to Montreal by Philadelphia for Kevin Haller, June 29, 1994. Claimed on waivers by San Jose from Montreal, January 23, 1996. Traded to Calgary by San Jose for cash, December 17, 1996. Signed as a free agent by Tampa Bay, July 16, 1997. Played in Finland in 1998-99 and has played in Germany from 1999 to present with Manheim.

Ramage, Rob

Born: January 11, 1959 in Byron, Ontario
Drafted: By the Colorado Rockies from the London Knights in 1979, 1st round, 1st overall.

Career Junior, NHL and World Junior Statistics

	GP	G	A	PTS	PIM
OHL Regular Season 1975-78	189	44	136	180	452
OHL Playoffs	36	7	17	24	95
NHL Regular Season 1979-94	1044	139	425	564	2224
NHL Playoffs	84	8	42	50	218
Canada 1977 World Juniors *in Czech Republic*	7	0	1	1	6
Canada 1978 World Juniors *in Montreal*	6	1	3	4	6
Canada Totals	**13**	**1**	**4**	**5**	**12**

Junior Highlights

Won Silver Medal at World Junior Championships in 1977
Won Bronze Medal at World Junior Championships in 1978
OHL First All-Star Team in 1978

Around the Rink

Ramage signed as an underage free agent by Birmingham (WHA), June 1978. Traded to St. Louis by New Jersey for St. Louis' 1st round choice (John MacLean) in 1983 Entry Draft, June 9, 1982. Traded to Calgary by St. Louis with Rick Wamsley for Brett Hull and Steve Bozek, March 7, 1988. Traded to Toronto by Calgary for Toronto's 2nd round choice (Kent Manderville) in 1989 Entry Draft June 16, 1989. Claimed by Minnesota from Toronto in Expansion Draft, May 30, 1991. Claimed by Tampa Bay from Minnesota in Expansion Draft, June 18, 1992. Traded to Montreal by Tampa Bay for Eric Charron, Alain Cote and future considerations (Donald Dufresne, June 18, 1993), March 20, 1993. Traded to Philadelphia by Montreal for cash, November 28, 1993. Retired from playing in 1994.

Rathje, Mike

Born: May 11, 1974 in Mannville, Alberta
Drafted: By the San Jose Sharks from the Medicine Hat Tigers in 1992, 1st round, 3rd overall.

Career Junior, NHL and World Junior Statistics

	GP	G	A	PTS	PIM
OHL Regular Season 1990-93	188	24	76	100	230
OHL Playoffs	26	3	8	11	16
NHL Regular Season 1993-Present	591	25	111	136	393
NHL Playoffs	54	8	9	17	32
Canada 1993 World Juniors *in Sweden*	7	2	2	4	12

Junior Highlights

WHL East Second All-Star Team in 1992 and 1993
Won Gold Medal at World Junior Championships in 1993
World Junior Championships Second Team All-Star in 1993

Around the Rink

Rathje has played his entire NHL career with San Jose. Missed majority of 1996-97 season recovering from groin injury suffered in game versus Dallas, November 8, 1996. Played his first NHL game on October 16, 1993 against Boston and recorded his first NHL point with an assist. Scored first NHL goal on March 29, 1994 versus Winnipeg.

Ratushny, Dan

Born: October 29, 1970 in Nepean, Ontario
Drafted: By the Winnipeg Jets from Cornell University in 1989, 2nd round, 25th overall.

Career Junior, NHL and World Junior Statistics

	GP	G	A	PTS	PIM
Canadian National Team 1989-90	2	0	0	0	2
NCAA 1988-91	80	14	51	65	156
NHL Regular Season 1992-93	1	0	1	1	2
NHL Playoffs	0	0	0	0	0
Canada 1990 World Juniors *in Finland*	7	2	2	4	4

Junior Highlights

Won Gold Medal at World Junior Championships in 1990
NCAA (Eastern Collegiate Athletic Conference) First All-Star Team in 1990 and 1991

Around the Rink

Ratushny played his only NHL game with Vancouver. Traded to Vancouver by Winnipeg for Vancouver's 9th round choice (Harijs Vitolinsh) in 1993 Entry Draft, March 22, 1993. After spending 1993-99 in the minors, Ratushny moved on to play in Japan, Finland and presently in Scotland.

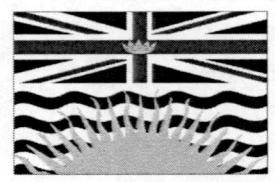

Rausse, Errol

Born: May 18, 1959 in Quesnel, B.C.
Drafted: By the Washington Capitals from the Seattle Breakers in 1979, 2nd round, 24th overall.

Career Junior, NHL and World Junior Statistics

	GP	G	A	PTS	PIM
WHL Regular Season 1976-79	211	149	157	306	98
WHL Playoffs	5	0	2	2	0
NHL Regular Season 1979-82	31	7	3	10	0
NHL Playoffs	0	0	0	0	0
Canada 1979 World Juniors *in Sweden*	5	1	1	2	2

Junior Highlights

Won Consolation Round at World Junior Championships in 1979

Around the Rink

Rausse played all of his NHL games with Washington. Played in Italy from 1984 until his retirement from play in 1994.

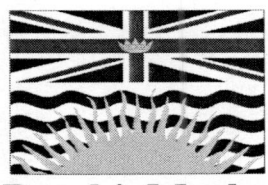

Recchi, Mark

Born: Fabruary 1, 1968 in Kamloops, B.C.
Drafted: By the Pittsburgh Penguins from the Kamloops Blazers in 1988, 4th round, 67th overall.

Career Junior, NHL and World Junior Statistics

	GP	**G**	**A**	**PTS**	**PIM**
WHL Regular Season 1984-88	178	108	184	292	193
WHL Playoffs	30	13	37	50	35
NHL Regular Season 1988-Present	1091	430	696	1126	733
NHL Playoffs	92	36	55	91	55
Canada 1988 World Juniors *in Russia*	7	0	5	5	4

Junior Highlights

Won Gold Medal at World Junior Championships in 1988
WHL West First All-Star Team in 1988

Around the Rink

Recchi played his first two seasons of junior with the New Westminster Bruins, he was traded to Kamloops prior to the 1986-87 season. Traded to Philadelphia by Pittsburgh with Brian Benning and LA Kings' 1st round choice (previously acquired, Philadelphia selected Jason Bowen) in 1992 Entry Draft for Rick Tocchet, Kjell Samuelsson, Ken Wregget and Philadelphia's 3rd round choice (Dave Roche) in 1993 Entry Draft, February 19, 1992. Traded to Montreal by Philadelphia with Philadelphia's 3rd round choice (Martin Hohenberger) in 1995 Entry Draft for Eric Desjardins, Gilbert Dionne and John LeClair, February 9, 1995. Traded to Philadelphia by Montreal for Danius Zubrus, Philadelphia's 2nd round choice (Matt Carkner) in 1999 Entry Draft and the New York Islanders 6th round choice (previously acquired, Montreal selected Scott Selig) in 2000 Entry Draft, March 10, 1999.

Redden, Wade

Born: June 12, 1977 in Lloydminster, Saskatchewan
Drafted: By the New York Islanders from the Brandon Wheat Kings in 1995, 1st round, 2nd overall.

Career Junior, NHL and World Junior Statistics

	GP	**G**	**A**	**PTS**	**PIM**
WHL Regular Season 1993-96	178	27	126	153	236
WHL Playoffs	51	12	24	36	37
Memorial Cup 1995 and 1996	8	1	6	7	4
NHL Regular Season 1996-Present	548	61	182	243	338
NHL Playoffs	41	5	12	17	18
Canada 1995 World Juniors *in Alberta*	7	3	2	5	0
Canada 1996 World Juniors *in United States*	6	0	2	2	2
Canada Totals	**13**	**3**	**4**	**7**	**2**

Junior Highlights

WHL Rookie of the Year in 1994
Won Gold Medal at World Junior Championships in 1995 and 1996
WHL East Second All-Star Team in 1995
WHL East First All-Star Team in 1996
Memorial Cup All-Star Team in 1996

Around the Rink

Redden has played all of his NHL games with Ottawa and has never played a game in the minors. Traded to Ottawa by the New York Islanders with Damian Rhodes for Don Beaupre, Martin Straka and Bryan Berard, January 23, 1996.

Reeds, Mark

Born: January 24, 1960 in Toronto, Ontario
Drafted: By the St. Louis Blues from the Peterborough Petes in 1979, 5th round, 86th overall.

Career Junior, NHL and World Junior Statistics

	GP	G	A	PTS	PIM
OHL Regular Season 1976-80	206	76	104	180	220
OHL Playoffs	33	10	16	26	50
Memorial Cup 1978, 1979 and 1980	13	3	6	9	13
NHL Regular Season 1981-89	365	45	114	159	135
NHL Playoffs	53	8	9	17	23
Canada 1980 World Juniors *in Finland*	5	1	0	1	2

Junior Highlights

Won Memorial Cup in 1979
Memorial Cup All-Star Team in 1980

Around the Rink

Reeds played his first season of junior with the Toronto Marlboros, he was dealt to Peterborough after the 1976-77 season. Traded to Hartford by St. Louis for Hartford's 3rd round choice (later traded back to Hartford - Hartford selected Blair Atcheynum) in 1989 Entry Draft, October 5, 1987. Played in Italy from 1989-91. Did not play in 1991-92. Player/Assistant Coach with the Peoria Rivermen (IHL) in 1992-93. Retired from playing in 1993 and continued to be the Assistant Coach of Peoria until 1996 when he was named Head Coach. Left Peoria in 1999 to become the Head Coach of the Missouri River Otters (UHL).

Regehr, Robyn

Born: April 19, 1980 in Recife, Brazil – Raised in Saskatchewan
Drafted: By the Colorado Avalanche from the Kamloops Blazers in 1998, 1st round, 19th overall.

Career Junior, NHL and World Junior Statistics

	GP	G	A	PTS	PIM
WHL Regular Season 1996-99	183	20	49	69	346
WHL Playoffs	12	1	8	9	47
NHL Regular Season 1999-Present	281	8	28	36	296
NHL Playoffs	0	0	0	0	0
Canada 1999 World Juniors *in Winnipeg*	7	0	0	0	2

Junior Highlights

Won Silver Medal at World Junior Championships in 1999
WHL West First All-Star Team in 1999

Around the Rink

Regehr has played all of his NHL games with Calgary. Traded to Calgary by Colorado with Rene Corbet, Wade Belak and Colorado's 2nd round compensatory choice (Jarret Stoll) in 2000 Entry Draft for Theoren Fleury and Chris Dingman, February 28, 1999. Played his first NHL game on October 28, 1999 against Ottawa. Recorded first NHL point with an assist versus Florida on November 6, 1999. Scored his first NHL goal against the San Jose Sharks, November 10, 1999.

Reid, Brandon

Born: March 9, 1981 in Kirkland, Quebec
Drafted: By the Vancouver Canucks from the Halifax Mooseheads in 2000, 7th round, 208th overall.

Career Junior, NHL and World Junior Statistics

	GP	G	A	PTS	PIM
QMJHL Regular Season 1997-01	256	134	207	341	67
QMJHL Playoffs	41	23	42	65	33
Memorial Cup 2000 and 2001	11	4	11	15	0
NHL Regular Season 2003-Present	7	2	3	5	0
NHL Playoffs	9	0	1	1	0
Canada 2000 World Juniors *in Sweden*	7	4	5	9	4
Canada 2001 World Juniors *in Russia*	7	1	3	4	0
Canada Totals	**14**	**5**	**8**	**13**	**4**

Junior Highlights

Memorial Cup All-Star Team in 2000
Won Bronze Medal at World Junior Championships in 2000 and 2001
Assistant Captain of Canada at World Junior Championships in 2001

Around the Rink

Reid was traded by Halifax to the Val D'Or Foreurs in 2000. Played his first NHL game and recorded first point with an assist on March 1, 2003 against Montreal. Scored his first NHL goal versus Nashville, March 20, 2003.

Ribeiro, Mike

Born: February 10, 1980 in Montreal, Quebec
Drafted: By the Montreal Canadiens from the Rouyn-Noranda Huskies in 1998, 2nd round, 45th overall.

Career Junior, NHL and World Junior Statistics

	GP	G	A	PTS	PIM
QMJHL Regular Season 1997-00	159	125	216	341	222
QMJHL Playoffs	28	11	32	43	50
NHL Regular Season 1999-Present	116	14	23	37	22
NHL Playoffs	0	0	0	0	0
Canada 2000 World Juniors *in Sweden*	7	0	2	2	0

Junior Highlights

QMJHL Second All-Star Team in 1998
QMJHL First All-Star Team in 1999
Canadian Major Junior First All-Star Team in 1999
Won Bronze Medal at World Junior Championships in 2000

Around the Rink

Ribeiro was assigned to Rouyn-Noranda by Montreal, (NHL) January 5, 2000. Traded to Quebec (QMJHL) by Rouyn-Noranda for Guillaume Lefebvre and future considerations, January 9, 2000. Played his first career NHL game against Toronto on October 2, 1999. Scored his first NHL goal versus Toronto, October 23, 1999.

Ricci, Mike

Born: October 27, 1971 in Scarborough, Ontario
Drafted: By the Philadelphia Flyers from the Peterborough Petes in 1990, 1st round, 4th overall.

Career Junior, NHL and World Junior Statistics

	GP	G	A	PTS	PIM
OHL Regular Season 1987-90	161	130	153	283	102
OHL Playoffs	41	31	29	60	48
Memorial Cup 1989	5	3	1	4	8
NHL Regular Season 1990-Present	943	226	336	562	861
NHL Playoffs	93	21	40	61	73
Canada 1989 World Juniors *in United States*	7	5	2	7	6
Canada 1990 World Juniors *in Finland*	5	0	4	4	0
Canada Totals	**12**	**5**	**6**	**11**	**6**

Junior Highlights

OHL Second All-Star Team in 1989
Won Gold Medal at World Junior Championships in 1990
OHL First All-Star Team in 1990
OHL MVP in 1990
Canadian Major Junior Player of the Year in 1990
OHL First All-Star Team in 1990

Around the Rink

Ricci was traded to Quebec by Philadelphia with Steve Duchesne, Peter Forsberg, Kerry Huffman, Ron Hextall, Philadelphia's 1st round choice (Jocelyn Thibault) in 1993 Entry Draft, $15,000,000 and future considerations (Chris Simon and Philadelphia's 1st round choice (later traded to Toronto - later traded to Washington - Washington selected Nolan Baumgartner) in 1994 Entry Draft, July 21, 1992) for Eric Lindros, June 30, 1992. Transferred to Colorado after Quebec franchise relocated, June 21, 1995. Traded to San Jose by Colorado with Colorado's 2nd round choice (later traded to Buffalo - Buffalo selected Jaroslav Kristek) in 1998 Entry Draft for Shean Donovan and San Jose's 1st round choice (Alex Tanguay) in 1998 Entry Draft, November 21, 1997.

Rice, Steven

Born: May 26, 1971 in Kitchener, Ontario
Drafted: By the New York Rangers from the Kitchener Rangers in 1989, 1st round, 20th overall.

Career Junior, NHL and World Junior Statistics

	GP	G	A	PTS	PIM
OHL Regular Season 1987-91	210	116	111	227	230
OHL Playoffs	31	11	16	27	34
Memorial Cup 1990	5	4	4	8	10
NHL Regular Season 1990-98	329	64	61	125	275
NHL Playoffs	2	2	1	3	6
Canada 1990 World Juniors *in Finland*	7	2	0	2	16
Canada 1991 World Juniors *in Saskatoon*	7	4	1	5	8
Canada Totals	**14**	**6**	**1**	**7**	**24**

Junior Highlights

Won Gold Medal at World Junior Championships in 1990 and 1991
Memorial Cup All-Star Team in 1990
OHL Second All-Star Team in 1991

Around the Rink

Rice was traded to Edmonton by the New York Rangers with Bernie Nicholls and Louie DeBrusk for Mark Messier and future considerations (Jeff Beukeboom for David Shaw, November 12, 1991), October 4, 1991. Signed as a free agent by Hartford, August 18, 1994. Transferred to Carolina after Hartford franchise relocated, June 25, 1997. Retired from playing in 1998.

Richardson, Luke

Born: March 26, 1969 in Ottawa, Ontario
Drafted: By the Toronto Maple Leafs from the Peterborough Petes in 1987, 1st round, 7th overall.

Career Junior, NHL and World Junior Statistics

	GP	G	A	PTS	PIM
OHL Regular Season 1985-87	122	19	50	69	127
OHL Playoffs	28	2	6	8	74
NHL Regular Season 1987-Present	1183	31	142	173	1877
NHL Playoffs	69	0	8	8	130
Canada 1987 World Juniors *in Czech Republic*	6	0	0	0	0

Junior Highlights

Second Youngest Player on Canada at World Junior Championships in 1987

Around the Rink

Richardson was traded to Edmonton by Toronto with Vincent Damphousse, Peter Ing and Scott Thornton for Grant Fuhr, Glenn Anderson and Craig Berube, September 19, 1991. Signed as a free agent by Philadelphia, July 23, 1997. Signed as a free agent by Columbus, July 4, 2002.

Richer, Stephane

Born: June 7, 1966 in Buckingham, Quebec
Drafted: By the Montreal Canadiens from the Granby Bisons in 1984, 2nd round, 29th overall.

Career Junior, NHL and World Junior Statistics

	GP	G	A	PTS	PIM
QMJHL Regular Season 1983-85	124	100	96	196	129
QMJHL Playoffs	15	14	14	28	29
NHL Regular Season 1984-02	1054	421	398	819	614
NHL Playoffs	134	53	45	98	61
Canada 1985 World Juniors *in Finland*	7	4	3	7	2

Junior Highlights

QMJHL Offensive Rookie of the Year in 1984
Won Gold Medal at World Junior Championships in 1985
QMJHL Second All-Star Team in 1985

Around the Rink

Richer was traded by Granby to the Chicoutimi Saguneens halfway through the 1984-85 season. Traded to New Jersey by Montreal with Tom Chorske for Kirk Muller and Rollie Melanson, September 20, 1991. Traded to Montreal by New Jersey for Lyle Odelein, August 22, 1996. Traded to Tampa Bay by Montreal with Darcy Tucker and David Wilkie for Patrick Poulin, Mick Vukota and Igor Ulanov, January 15, 1998. Traded to St. Louis by Tampa Bay for Rich Parent and Chris McAlpine, January 13, 2000. Signed as a free agent by Washington, August 25, 2000 did not play a game in 2000-01. Signed as a free agent by Pittsburgh, October 2, 2001. Traded to New Jersey by Pittsburgh for a conditional choice in 2003 Entry Draft, March 19, 2002. Retired from playing in 2002.

Rioux, Pierre

Born: February 1, 1962 in Quebec City, Quebec
Not Drafted: Signed as a Free Agent with Calgary in 1982.

Career Junior, NHL and World Junior Statistics

	GP	G	A	PTS	PIM
QMJHL Regular Season 1979-82	192	136	190	326	123
QMJHL Playoffs	26	19	31	50	18
NHL Regular Season 1982-83	14	1	2	3	4
NHL Playoffs	0	0	0	0	0
Canada 1982 World Juniors *in United States*	7	3	3	6	4

Junior Highlights

Won Gold Medal at World Junior Championships in 1982
QMJHL First All-Star Team in 1982

Around the Rink

Rioux signed as a free agent by Calgary, August 24, 1982. Played all 14 games of his NHL career with Calgary. After three years in the minors Rioux went to play in Germany for seven seasons. Retired from playing in 2001 after a year in the Quebec Senior League.

Rivers, Jamie

Born: March 16, 1975 in Ottawa, Ontario
Drafted: By the St. Louis Blues from the Sudbury Wolves in 1993, 3rd round, 63rd overall.

Career Junior, NHL and World Junior Statistics

	GP	G	A	PTS	PIM
OHL Regular Season 1991-95	228	56	201	257	128
OHL Playoffs	50	15	54	69	40
NHL Regular Season 1995-Present	340	13	36	49	270
NHL Playoffs	13	1	1	2	6
Canada 1995 World Juniors *in Alberta*	7	3	3	6	2

Junior Highlights

OHL First All-Star Team in 1994
Canadian Major Junior Second All-Star Team in 1994
Won Gold Medal at World Juniors in 1995
OHL Second All-Star Team in 1995

Around the Rink

Rivers was claimed by the New York Islanders from the St. Louis Blues in waiver draft, September 27, 1999. Signed as a free agent by Ottawa, November 30, 2000. Claimed on waivers by Boston from Ottawa, October 13, 2001. Signed as a free agent by Florida, December 16, 2002.

Roberts, Gary
Born: May 23, 1966 in North York, Ontario
Drafted: By the Calgary Flames from the Ottawa 67's in 1984, 1st round, 12th overall.

Career Junior, NHL and World Junior Statistics

	GP	G	A	PTS	PIM
OHL Regular Season 1982-86	207	127	140	267	561
OHL Playoffs	43	31	28	59	134
Memorial Cup 1984 and 1986	9	5	5	10	32
NHL Regular Season 1986-Present	958	369	388	757	2261
NHL Playoffs	101	24	53	77	288
Canada 1986 World Juniors in *Hamilton*	7	6	3	9	6

Junior Highlights

Won Memorial Cup in 1984 and 1986
OHL Second All-Star Team in 1985 and 1986
Won Silver Medal at World Junior Championships in 1986

Around the Rink

Roberts was traded by Ottawa to the Guelph Platers midway through the 1985-86 season. Missed remainder of 1994-95 and majority of 1995-96 seasons recovering from neck injury suffered in game versus Toronto, February 4, 1995. Missed remainder of 1995-96 and entire 1996-97 seasons recovering from neck injury suffered in game versus Vancouver, April 3, 1996. Traded to Carolina by Calgary with Trevor Kidd for Andrew Cassels and Jean-Sebastien Giguere, August 25, 1997. Signed as a free agent by Toronto, July 4, 2000. Missed majority of the 2002-03 season recovering from surgery on both shoulders.

Robitaille, Luc

Born: February 17, 1966 in Montreal, Quebec
Drafted: By the Los Angeles Kings from the Hull Olympiques in 1984, 9th round, 171st overall.

Career Junior, NHL and World Junior Statistics

	GP	G	A	PTS	PIM
QMJHL Regular Season 1983-86	197	155	269	424	256
QMJHL Playoffs	20	21	29	50	55
Memorial Cup 1986	5	8	5	13	8
NHL Regular Season 1986-Present	1286	631	688	1319	1069
NHL Playoffs	159	58	69	127	174
Canada 1986 World Juniors *in Hamilton*	7	3	5	8	2

Junior Highlights

QMJHL Second All-Star Team in 1985
Won Silver Medal at World Junior Championships in 1986
QMJHL First All-Star Team in 1986
Canadian Major Junior Player of the Year in 1986

Around the Rink

Robitaille was traded to Pittsburgh by LA Kings for Rick Tocchet and Pittsburgh's 2nd round choice (Pavel Rosa) in 1995 Entry Draft, July 29, 1994. Traded to the New York Rangers by Pittsburgh with Ulf Samuelsson for Petr Nedved and Sergei Zubov, August 31, 1995. Traded to L.A. Kings by the New York Rangers for Kevin Stevens, August 28, 1997. Signed as a free agent by Detroit, July 5, 2001. Released by Detroit, May 5, 2003.

Rossiter, Kyle

Born: June 9, 1980 in Edmonton, Alberta
Drafted: By the Florida Panthers from the Spokane Chiefs in 1998, 2nd round, 30th overall.

Career Junior, NHL and World Junior Statistics

	GP	**G**	**A**	**PTS**	**PIM**
WHL Regular Season 1996-00	245	21	57	78	616
WHL Playoffs	39	1	7	8	59
NHL Regular Season 2001-Present	5	0	0	0	2
NHL Playoffs	0	0	0	0	0
Canada 2000 World Juniors *in Sweden*	7	0	0	0	20

Junior Highlights

Canadian Major Junior Scholastic Player of the Year in 1998
Won Bronze Medal at World Junior Championships in 2000

Around the Rink

Rossiter has played all of his NHL games with Florida. Has split his pro career between Florida, Lousiville (AHL), Utah (AHL), and San Antonio (AHL).

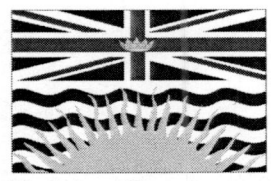

Sakic, Joe

Born: July 7, 1969 in Burnaby, B.C.
Drafted: By the Quebec Nordiques from the Swift Current Broncos in 1987, 1st round, 15th overall.

Career Junior, NHL and World Junior Statistics

	GP	G	A	PTS	PIM
Canadian National Team 1986-87	1	0	0	0	0
WHL Regular Season 1985-88	139	138	155	293	95
WHL Playoffs	14	11	14	25	12
NHL Regular Season 1988-Present	1074	509	806	1315	440
NHL Playoffs	142	71	86	157	64
Canada 1988 World Juniors *in Russia*	7	3	1	4	2

Junior Highlights

WHL East Second All-Star Team in 1987
WHL East Rookie of the Year in 1987
WHL East MVP in 1987
Won Gold Medal at World Junior Championships in 1988
WHL East First All-Star Team in 1988
WHL MVP in 1988
Canadian Major Junior Player of the Year in 1988
Shared Bobby Clarke Trophy (Top Scorer - WHL) with Theo Fleury in 1988

Around the Rink

Sakic played in his first NHL game on October 6, 1988 against Hartford, also recorded his first NHL point in that game with an assist. Scored first NHL goal on October 8, 1988 versus New Jersey. Transferred to Colorado after Quebec franchise relocated, June 21, 1995.

Sandlak, Jim

Born: December 12, 1966 in Kitchener, Ontario
Drafted: By the Vancouver Canucks from the London Knights in 1985, 1st round, 4th overall.

Career Junior, NHL and World Junior Statistics

	GP	G	A	PTS	PIM
OHL Regular Season 1982-86	143	71	56	127	309
OHL Playoffs	21	6	16	22	51
NHL Regular Season 1985-96	549	110	119	229	821
NHL Playoffs	33	7	10	17	30
Canada 1985 World Juniors *in Finland*	5	1	0	1	6
Canada 1986 World Juniors *in Hamilton*	7	5	7	12	16
Canada Totals	**12**	**6**	**7**	**13**	**22**

Junior Highlights

Won Gold Medal at World Junior Championships in 1985
Won Silver Medal at World Junior Championships in 1986
Named Best Forward at World Junior Championships in 1986

Around the Rink

Sandlak played one game for the Kitchener Rangers in 1982-83 as an undrafted emergency call up from their midget affiliate the Kitchener Dutchman. Drafted in the summer of 1983 by the London Knights. Traded to Hartford by Vancouver to complete transaction that sent Murray Craven to Vancouver (March 22, 1993), May 17, 1993. Signed as a free agent by Vancouver, October 1, 1995. Retired from playing in 1998 after a season in the IHL and a season in Germany.

Sands, Mike

Born: April 6, 1963 in Mississauga, Ontario
Drafted: By the Minnesota North Stars from the Sudbury Wolves in 1981, 2nd round, 31st overall.

Career Junior, NHL and World Junior Statistics

	GP	W	L	T	SO	AVG
OHL Regular Season 1980-83	146	39	88	3	2	5.31
OHL Playoffs	0	0	0	0	0	0.00
NHL Regular Season 1984-87	6	0	5	0	0	5.16
NHL Playoffs	0	0	0	0	0	0.00
Canada 1983 World Juniors *in Russia*	5	2	2	1	1	3.51

Junior Highlights

Won Bronze Medal at World Junior Championships in 1983

Around the Rink

Sands played all of his NHL games with Minnesota. After four games in 1987-88 he was suspended for remainder of the season by Minnesota for leaving Baltimore (AHL) without permission, October 1987. Signed as a free agent by Kalamazoo (IHL) after release by Minnesota, March 1988. Retired in 1989 after a season with the Canadian National Team.

Sanipass, Everett

Born: February 13, 1968 in Big Cove, New Brunswick
Drafted: By the Chicago Black Hawks from the Verdun Jr. Canadiens in 1986, 1st round, 14th overall.

Career Junior, NHL and World Junior Statistics

	GP	**G**	**A**	**PTS**	**PIM**
QMJHL Regular Season 1984-87	140	70	125	195	624
QMJHL Playoffs	25	8	11	19	130
Memorial Cup 1985	2	1	0	1	2
NHL Regular Season 1986-91	164	25	34	59	358
NHL Playoffs	5	2	0	2	4
Canada 1987 World Juniors *in Czech Republic*	6	3	2	5	8

Junior Highlights

QMJHL First All-Star Team in 1987

Around the Rink

Sanipass was dealt by Verdun to the Granby Bisons after twenty-three games in the 1986-87 season. Traded to Quebec by Chicago with Mario Doyon and Dan Vincelette for Greg Millen, Michel Goulet and Quebec's 6th round choice (Kevin St. Jacques) in 1991 Entry Draft, March 5, 1990. Suffered season ending back injury in game versus Philadelphia, January 17, 1991. Retired from playing in 1995 after three seasons in the minors.

Sarich, Cory

Born: August 16, 1978 in Saskatoon, Saskatchewan
Drafted: By the Buffalo Sabres from the Saskatoon Blades in 1996, 2nd round, 27th overall.

Career Junior, NHL and World Junior Statistics

	GP	G	A	PTS	PIM
WHL Regular Season 1994-98	169	19	85	104	353
WHL Playoffs	6	0	1	1	4
NHL Regular Season 1998-Present	290	6	34	40	351
NHL Playoffs	11	0	2	2	6
Canada 1997 World Juniors *in Switzerland*	7	0	0	0	6
Canada 1998 World Juniors *in Finland*	7	0	1	1	6
Canada Totals	**14**	**0**	**1**	**1**	**12**

Junior Highlights

Won Gold Medal at World Junior Championships in 1997
WHL West Second All-Star Team in 1998

Around the Rink

Sarich was traded by Saskatoon to the Seattle Thunderbirds halfway through the 1997-98 season. Traded to Tampa Bay by Buffalo with Wayne Primeau, Brian Holzinger and Buffalo's 3rd round choice (Alexander Kharitonov) in 2000 Entry Draft for Chris Gratton and Tampa Bay's 2nd round choice (Derek Roy) in 2001 Entry Draft, March 9, 2000.

Savage, Reggie

Born: May 1, 1970 in Montreal, Quebec
Drafted: By the Washington Capitals from the Victoriaville Tigres in 1988, 1st round, 15th overall.

Career Junior, NHL and World Junior Statistics

	GP	**G**	**A**	**PTS**	**PIM**
QMJHL Regular Season 1987-90	185	177	152	329	334
QMJHL Playoffs	37	30	26	56	100
NHL Regular Season 1990-94	34	5	7	12	28
NHL Playoffs	0	0	0	0	0
Canada 1989 World Juniors *in United States*	7	4	5	9	4

Junior Highlights

Finished Second in Team Scoring at World Junior Championships in 1989

Around the Rink

Savage was traded to Quebec by Washington with Paul MacDermid for Mike Hough, June 20, 1993. Signed as a free agent by Phoenix, August 28, 1996. Signed as a free agent by Vancouver June 17, 1999. Signed as a free agent by Columbus, June 2, 2000. Signed as a free agent by Biel-Bienne (Swiss-2), June 21, 2001.

Scamurra, Peter

Born: February 23, 1955 in Buffalo, New York – Raised in Ontario
Drafted: By the Washington Capitals from the Peterborough Petes in 1975, 2nd round, 19th overall. Also Drafted by the Cleveland Crusaders (WHL) in 1975, 4th round, 50th overall.

Career Junior, NHL and World Junior Statistics

	GP	G	A	PTS	PIM
NCAA 1973-74	13	2	1	3	12
OHL Regular Season 1973-75	97	15	51	66	57
OHL Playoffs	11	2	5	7	12
NHL Regular Season 1975-80	132	8	25	33	59
NHL Playoffs	0	0	0	0	0
Canada 1974 World Juniors *in Russia*	5	1	0	1	8

Junior Highlights

Won Bronze Medal at World Junior Championships in 1974
OHL Second All-Star Team in 1975

Around the Rink

Scamurra left the University of Wisconsin in 1973 and signed as a free agent with the Peterborough Petes. Played all of his NHL games with Washington. Retired from playing in 1981 after a season in Finland.

Schneider, Andy

Born: March 29, 1972 in Edmonton, Alberta
Not Drafted: Signed as a Free Agent with Ottawa in 1992.

Career Junior, NHL and World Junior Statistics

	GP	G	A	PTS	PIM
WHL Regular Season 1988-93	309	108	259	367	442
WHL Playoffs	32	19	36	55	52
Memorial Cup 1993	4	2	5	7	4
NHL Regular Season 1993-94	10	0	0	0	15
NHL Playoffs	0	0	0	0	0
Canada 1992 World Juniors *in Germany*	7	0	0	0	6

Junior Highlights

WHL East Second All-Star Team in 1993

Around the Rink

Schneider was traded by the Seattle Thunderbirds to the Swift Current Broncos at the midway point of the 1989-90 season. Signed as a free agent by Ottawa, October 9, 1992. Played all of his NHL games with Ottawa. Has played in Germany for the past seven years.

Schultz, Nick

Born: August 25, 1982 in Strasbourg, Saskatchewan
Drafted: By the Minnesota Wild from the Prince Albert Raiders in 2000, 2nd round, 33rd overall.

Career Junior, NHL and World Junior Statistics

	GP	G	A	PTS	PIM
WHL Regular Season 1998-01	189	33	81	114	195
WHL Playoffs	20	0	10	10	2
NHL Regular Season 2001-Present	127	7	13	20	37
NHL Playoffs	9	0	0	0	4
Canada 2001 World Juniors *in Russia*	7	0	0	0	2
Canada 2002 World Juniors *in Czech Republic*	7	0	2	2	4
Canada Totals	**14**	**0**	**2**	**2**	**6**

Junior Highlights

Won Bronze Medal at World Junior Championships in 2001
WHL Eastern Conference All-Star Team in 2001
Won Silver Medal at World Junior Championships in 2002

Around the Rink

Schultz played his first NHL game against the Edmonton Oilers on October 14, 2001. Scored his first NHL goal on November 29, 2001 versus Florida.

Secord, Al

Born: March 3, 1958 in Sudbury, Ontario
Drafted: By the Boston Bruins from the Hamilton Fincups in 1978, 1st round, 16th overall.

Career Junior, NHL and World Junior Statistics

	GP	G	A	PTS	PIM
OHL Regular Season 1975-78	179	69	89	138	645
OHL Playoffs	46	12	16	28	141
Memorial Cup 1976	3	0	0	0	5
NHL Regular Season 1978-90	723	273	222	495	2093
NHL Playoffs	102	21	34	55	382
Canada 1977 World Juniors *in Czech Republic*	7	2	2	4	8

Junior Highlights

Won Memorial Cup in 1976
Won Silver Medal at World Junior Championships in 1977

Around the Rink

Secord was traded to Chicago by Boston for Mike O'Connell, December 18, 1980. Traded to Toronto by Chicago with Ed Olczyk for Rick Vaive, Steve Thomas and Bob McGill, September 3, 1987. Traded to Philadelphia by Toronto for Philadelphia's 5th round choice (Keith Carney) in 1989 Entry Draft, February 7, 1989. Signed as a free agent by Chicago, August 7, 1989. Retired from playing in 1990. Came out of retirement and signed as a free agent by Chicago Wolves (IHL), September 10, 1994. Played in the Roller Hockey Internationals Chicago Cheetahs in 1994 (18-11-14-25-45). Retired from playing a second time in 1996.

Seiling, Ric

Born: December 15, 1957 in Elmira, Ontario
Drafted: By the Buffalo Sabres from the St. Catharines Fincups in 1977, 1st round, 14th overall. Also Drafted by the Winnipeg Jets (WHA) in 1977, 6th round, 55th overall.

Career Junior, NHL and World Junior Statistics

	GP	G	A	PTS	PIM
OHL Regular Season 1974-77	189	117	142	259	226
OHL Playoffs	45	33	24	57	80
Memorial Cup 1976	3	3	6	9	2
NHL Regular Season 1977-87	738	179	208	387	573
NHL Playoffs	62	14	14	28	36
Canada 1977 World Juniors *in Czech Republic*	7	3	1	4	10

Junior Highlights

Won Memorial Cup in 1976
Memorial Cup All-Star Team in 1976
Won Silver Medal at World Junior Championships in 1977

Around the Rink

Seiling was traded to Detroit by Buffalo for future considerations, October 7, 1986. Retired from playing in 1988. Came out of retirement in 1994 and played one game in the Colonial League with the Utica Blizzard where he was Head Coach from 1994-95. Head Coach of the Tulsa Oilers from 1997-99.

Sevigny, Pierre

Born: September 8, 1971 in Trois Rivieres, Quebec
Drafted: By the Montreal Canadiens from the Verdun Jr. Canadiens in 1989, 3rd round, 51st overall.

Career Junior, NHL and World Junior Statistics

	GP	**G**	**A**	**PTS**	**PIM**
QMJHL Regular Season 1988-91	191	110	161	271	496
QMJHL Playoffs	12	8	8	16	42
NHL Regular Season 1993-98	78	4	5	9	64
NHL Playoffs	3	0	1	1	0
Canada 1991 World Juniors *in Saskatoon*	7	4	2	6	8

Junior Highlights

QMJHL All-Rookie Team in 1989
QMJHL Second All-Star Team in 1990 and 1991
Won Gold Medal at World Junior Championships in 1991

Around the Rink

Sevigny played his first season of junior with the Verdun Jr. Canadiens, traded to St. Hyacinthe after the 1988-89 season. Signed as a free agent by the New York Rangers, August 26, 1997. Signed as a free agent by ERC Straubing (German-2), July 24, 2002.

Sevigny, Richard

Born: November 4, 1957 in Montreal, Quebec
Drafted: By the Montreal Canadiens from the Sherbrooke Beavers in 1977, 7th round, 124th overall.

Career Junior, NHL and World Junior Statistics

	GP	W	L	T	SO	AVG
QMJHL Regular Season 1974-77	122	Not Avaliable			4	3.96
QMJHL Playoffs	33	Not Available			2	3.81
Memorial Cup 1977	4	0	4	0	0	4.75
NHL Regular Season 1979-87	176	80	54	20	5	3.21
NHL Playoffs	4	0	3	0	0	3.75
Canada 1976 World Juniors *in Finland*	3	1	2	0	0	7.67

Junior Highlights

Won Silver Medal at World Junior Championships in 1976
QMJHL West First All-Star Team in 1976

Around the Rink

Sevigny signed as a free agent by Quebec July 4, 1984. Retired from playing in 1991 after two seasons in France.

Shanahan, Brendan

Born: January 23, 1969 in Mimico, Ontario
Drafted: By the New Jersey Devils from the London Knights in 1987, 1st round, 2nd overall.

Career Junior, NHL and World Junior Statistics

	GP	G	A	PTS	PIM
OHL Regular Season 1985-87	115	67	87	154	198
OHL Playoffs	5	5	5	10	5
NHL Regular Season 1987-Present	1186	533	565	1098	2156
NHL Playoffs	139	51	60	111	231
Canada 1987 World Juniors *in Czech Republic*	6	4	3	7	4

Junior Highlights

Finished 6th in Team Scoring at the World Junior Championships in 1987

Around the Rink

Shanahan signed as a free agent by St. Louis, July 25, 1991. Traded to Hartford by St. Louis for Chris Pronger, July 27, 1995. Traded to Detroit by Hartford with Brian Glynn for Paul Coffey, Keith Primeau and Detroit's 1st round choice (Nikos Tselios) in 1997 Entry Draft, October 9, 1996.

Shannon, Darrin

Born: December 8, 1969 in Barrie, Ontario
Drafted: By the Pittsburgh Penguins from the Windsor Spitfires in 1988, 1st round, 4th overall.

Career Junior, NHL and World Junior Statistics

	GP	G	A	PTS	PIM
OHL Regular Season 1986-89	157	83	130	213	127
OHL Playoffs	30	11	24	35	19
Memorial Cup 1988	4	2	3	5	16
NHL Regular Season 1988-98	506	87	163	250	344
NHL Playoffs	45	7	10	17	38
Canada 1989 World Juniors *in United States*	7	1	3	4	10

Junior Highlights

Canadian Major Junior Scholastic Player of the Year in 1988

Around the Rink

Shannon was traded to Buffalo by Pittsburgh with Doug Bodger for Tom Barrasso and Buffalo's 3rd round choice (Joe Dziedzic) in 1990 Entry Draft, November 12, 1988. Traded to Winnipeg by Buffalo with Mike Hartman and Dean Kennedy for Dave McLlwain, Gord Donnelly, Winnipeg's 5th round choice (Yuri Khmylev) in 1992 Entry Draft and future considerations, October 11, 1991. Transferred to Phoenix after Winnipeg franchise relocated July 1, 1996. Missed majority of 1998-99 and 1999-2000 seasons recovering from knee surgery, June 1998. Signed as a free agent by Grand Rapids (IHL), February 18, 1999. Signed as a free agent by Toronto, August 25, 1999 but never played a game with the Leafs. Retired from playing in 2000.

Shantz, Jeff

Born: October 10, 1973 in Duchess, Alberta
Drafted: By the Chicago Black Hawks from the Regina Pats in 1992, 2nd round, 36th overall.

Career Junior, NHL and World Junior Statistics

	GP	**G**	**A**	**PTS**	**PIM**
WHL Regular Season 1989-93	206	84	125	209	132
WHL Playoffs	21	4	14	18	16
NHL Regular Season 1993-Present	642	72	139	211	341
NHL Playoffs	44	5	8	13	24
Canada 1993 World Juniors *in Sweden*	7	2	4	6	2

Junior Highlights

Won Gold Medal at World Junior Championships in 1993
WHL East First All-Star Team in 1993

Around the Rink

Shantz was traded to Calgary by Chicago with Steve Dubinsky for Marty McInnis, Jamie Allison and Eric Andersson, October 27, 1998. Traded by Calgary to Colorado with Dean McAmmond and Derek Morris for Chris Drury and Stephane Yelle, October 1, 2002.

Shaw, Brad

Born: April 28, 1964 in Cambridge, Ontario
Drafted: By the Detroit Red Wings from the Ottawa 67's in 1982, 5th round, 86th overall.

Career Junior, NHL and World Junior Statistics

	GP	G	A	PTS	PIM
OHL Regular Season 1981-84	199	36	196	232	123
OHL Playoffs	37	5	49	54	17
Memorial Cup 1984	5	1	4	5	2
NHL Regular Season 1985-99	377	22	137	159	208
NHL Playoffs	23	4	8	12	6
Canada 1983 World Juniors *in Russia*	7	1	1	2	2
Canada 1984 World Juniors *in Sweden*	7	0	2	2	0
Canada Totals	**14**	**1**	**3**	**4**	**2**

Junior Highlights

Won Bronze Medal at World Junior Championships in 1983
OHL First All-Star Team in 1984
Won Memorial Cup in 1984

Around the Rink

Shaw was traded to Hartford by Detroit for Hartford's 8th round choice (Urban Nordin) in 1984 Entry Draft, May 29, 1984. Traded to New Jersey by Hartford for cash, June 13, 1992. Claimed by Ottawa from New Jersey in Expansion Draft, June 18, 1992. Signed as a free agent by Ottawa, March 8, 1999. Claimed on waivers by Washington from Ottawa March 10, 1999. Traded to St. Louis by Washington with Washington's 8th round choice (Colin Hemingway) in 1999 Entry Draft for St. Louis' 6th round choice (Kyle Clark) in 1999 Entry Draft, March 18, 1999. Retired from playing in 1999. Named Head Coach of Detroit Vipers (IHL), May 24, 2000. Named Head Coach of Cincinnati (AHL), July 19, 2002.

Sherven, Gord

Born: August 21, 1963 in Weyburn, Saskatchewan
Drafted: By the Edmonton Oilers from the University of North Dakota in 1981, 10th round 197th overall.

Career Junior, NHL and World Junior Statistics

	GP	G	A	PTS	PIM
NCAA 1981-84	92	35	51	86	36
NHL Regular Season 1983-88	97	13	22	35	33
NHL Playoffs	3	0	0	0	0
Canada 1983 World Juniors *in Russia*	7	1	3	4	0

Junior Highlights

Won Bronze Medal at World Junior Championships in 1983

Around the Rink

Sherven was traded to Minnesota by Edmonton with Terry Martin for Mark Napier, January 24, 1985. Traded to Edmonton by Minnesota with Don Biggs for Marc Habscheid, Don Barber and Emanuel Viveiros, December 20, 1985. Claimed by Hartford from Edmonton in Waiver Draft, October 6, 1986. Played in Germany from 1989 until his retirement in 2000.

Sillinger, Mike

Born: June 29, 1971 in Regina, Saskatchewan
Drafted: By the Detroit Red Wings from the Regina Pats in 1989, 1st round, 11th overall.

Career Junior, NHL and World Junior Statistics

	GP	G	A	PTS	PIM
WHL Regular Season 1987-91	266	178	241	419	152
WHL Playoffs	23	20	21	41	6
NHL Regular Season 1990-Present	752	153	221	374	439
NHL Playoffs	28	5	4	9	8
Canada 1991 World Juniors *in Saskatoon*	7	4	2	6	2

Junior Highlights

WHL East Second All-Star Team in 1990
Won Gold Medal at World Junior Championships in 1991
WHL East First All-Star Team in 1991

Around the Rink

Sillinger was traded to Anaheim by Detroit with Jason York for Stu Grimson, Mark Ferner and Anaheim's 6th round choice (Magnus Nilsson) in 1996 Entry Draft, April 4, 1995. Traded to Vancouver by Anaheim for Roman Oksiuta, March 15, 1996. Traded to Philadelphia by Vancouver for Philadelphia's 5th round choice (later traded back to Philadelphia - Philadelphia selected Garrett Prosofsky) in 1998 Entry Draft, February 5, 1998. Traded to Tampa Bay by Philadelphia with Chris Gratton for Mikael Renberg and Daymond Langkow, December 12, 1998. Traded to Florida by Tampa Bay for Ryan Johnson and Dwayne Hay, March 14, 2000. Traded to Ottawa by Florida for future considerations, March 13, 2001. Signed as a free agent by Columbus, July 7, 2001.

Slaney, John

Born: February 7, 1972 in St. John's, Newfoundland
Drafted: By the Washington Capitals from the Cornwall Royals in 1990, 1st round, 9th overall.

Career Junior, NHL and World Junior Statistics

	GP	G	A	PTS	PIM
OHL Regular Season 1988-92	198	94	168	262	154
OHL Playoffs	30	11	32	43	21
NHL Regular Season 1993-Present	264	22	67	89	99
NHL Playoffs	14	2	1	3	4
Canada 1991 World Juniors *in Saskatoon*	7	1	2	3	6
Canada 1992 World Juniors *in Germany*	7	1	3	4	6
Canada Totals	**14**	**2**	**5**	**7**	**12**

Junior Highlights

OHL First All-Star Team in 1990
Canadian Major Junior Defenseman of the Year in 1990
Won Gold Medal at World Junior Championships in 1991
OHL Second All-Star Team in 1991

Around the Rink

Slaney was traded to Colorado by Washington for Philadelphia's 3rd round choice (previously acquired, Washington selected Shawn McNeil) in 1996 Entry Draft, July 12, 1995. Traded to LA Kings by Colorado for Winnipeg's 6th round choice (previously acquired, Colorado selected Brian Willsie) in 1996 entry draft, December 28, 1995. Signed as a free agent by Phoenix, August 19, 1997. Claimed by Nashville from Phoenix in Expansion Draft, June 26, 1998. Signed as a free agent by Pittsburgh, September 30, 1999. Traded to Philadelphia by Pittsburgh for Kevin Stevens, January 14, 2001.

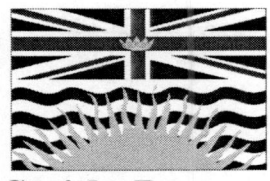

Smith, Barry

Born: April 25, 1955 in Surrey, B.C.
Drafted: By the Boston Bruins from the New Westminster Bruins in 1975, 2nd round, 32nd overall. Also Drafted by the Edmonton Oilers (WHA) in 1975, 3rd round, 36th overall.

Career Junior, NHL and World Junior Statistics

	GP	G	A	PTS	PIM
WHL Regular Season 1971-75	242	50	63	113	219
WHL Playoffs	34	9	7	16	26
Memorial Cup 1975	3	1	2	3	0
NHL Regular Season 1975-81	114	7	7	14	10
NHL Playoffs	0	0	0	0	0
Canada 1975 World Juniors *in Manitoba*	5	1	2	3	2

Junior Highlights

Won Silver Medal at World Junior Championships in 1975
Memorial Cup All-Star Team in 1975
Won Stafford Smythe Memorial Trophy (Memorial Cup Tournament MVP) in 1975

Around the Rink

Smith signed as a free agent by Colorado, September 14, 1979. Retired from playing in 1981. Head Coach of the Knoxville Cherokees (ECHL) from 1992-97. Head Coach of the San Angelo Outlaws (WPHL) in 2000-01.

Smith, Bobby

Born: February 12, 1958 in North Sydney, Nova Scotia
Drafted: By the Minnesota North Stars from the Ottawa 67's in 1978, 1st round, 1st overall.

Career Junior, NHL and World Junior Statistics

	GP	G	A	PTS	PIM
OHL Regular Season 1975-78	187	158	227	385	117
OHL Playoffs	47	33	32	65	43
Memorial Cup 1977	5	6	6	12	4
NHL Regular Season 1978-93	1077	357	679	1036	917
NHL Playoffs	184	64	96	160	245
Canada 1978 World Juniors *in Montreal*	3	1	4	5	0

Junior Highlights

OHL Second All-Star Team in 1976 and 1977
Memorial Cup All-Star Team in 1977
Won George Parsons Trophy (Memorial Cup Most Sportsmanlike Player) in 1977
Won Bronze Medal at World Junior Championships in 1978
OHL First All-Star Team in 1978
OHL MVP in 1978
Canadian Major Junior Player of the Year in 1978

Around the Rink

Smith was traded to Montreal by Minnesota for Keith Acton, Mark Napier and Toronto's 3rd round choice (previously acquired, Minnesota selected Ken Hodge Jr.) in 1984 Entry Draft, October 28, 1983. Traded to Minnesota by Montreal for Minnesota's 4th round choice (Louis Bernard) in 1992 Entry Draft, August 7, 1990. Retired from playing in 1993.

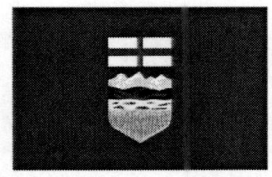

Smith, Geoff

Born: March 7, 1969 in Edmonton, Alberta
Drafted: By the Edmonton Oilers from the St. Albert Saints in 1987, 3rd round, 63rd overall.

Career Junior, NHL and World Junior Statistics

	GP	**G**	**A**	**PTS**	**PIM**
AJHL 1986-87	57	7	28	35	101
NCAA 1987-89	51	4	13	17	48
WHL Regular Season 1988-89	32	4	31	35	29
WHL Playoffs	6	1	3	4	12
NHL Regular Season 1989-99	462	18	73	91	282
NHL Playoffs	13	0	1	1	8
Canada 1989 World Juniors *in United States*	7	0	1	1	4

Junior Highlights

WHL West Second All-Star Team in 1989

Around the Rink

Smith left the University of North Dakota and signed as a free agent with Kamloops in 1988. Traded to Florida by Edmonton with Edmonton's 4th round choice (David Nemirovsky) in 1994 entry draft for Florida's 3rd round choice (Corey Neilson) in 1994 Entry Draft and St.Louis' 6th round choice (previously acquired by Florida - later traded to Winnipeg - Winnipeg selected Chris Kibermanis) in 1994 entry draft December 6, 1993. Signed as a free agent by the New York Rangers, September 29, 1997. Traded to St. Louis by NY Rangers with Jeff Finley for future considerations (Chris Kenady, February 22, 1999), February 13, 1999. Retired from playing in 1999.

Smith, Jason

Born: November 2, 1973 in Calgary, Alberta
Drafted: By the New Jersey Devils from the Regina Pats in 1992, 1st round, 18th overall.

Career Junior, NHL and World Junior Statistics

	GP	G	A	PTS	PIM
WHL Regular Season 1990-93	128	23	81	104	320
WHL Playoffs	17	4	8	12	41
NHL Regular Season 1993-Present	642	26	85	111	681
NHL Playoffs	27	0	4	4	40
Canada 1993 World Juniors *in Sweden*	7	1	3	4	10

Junior Highlights

Won Gold Medal at World Junior Championships in 1993
WHL East First All-Star Team in 1993
Canadian Major Junior First All-Star Team in 1993

Around the Rink

Smith missed the majority of the 1994-95 season recovering from knee injury suffered in practice, November 5, 1994. Traded to Toronto by New Jersey with Steve Sullivan and the rights to Alyn McCauley for Doug Gilmour, Dave Ellett and New Jersey's 4th round choice (previously acquired, New Jersey selected Andre Lakos) in 1999 Entry Draft, February 25, 1997. Traded to Edmonton by Toronto for Edmonton's 4th round choice (Jonathon Zion) in 1999 Entry Draft and 2nd round choice (Kris Vernarsky) in 2000 Entry Draft, March 23, 1999.

Smith, Stuart

Born: March 17, 1960 in Toronto, Ontario
Drafted: By the Hartford Whalers from the Peterborough Petes in 1979, 2nd round, 39th overall.

Career Junior, NHL and World Junior Statistics

	GP	G	A	PTS	PIM
OHL Regular Season 1977-80	192	18	93	111	403
OHL Playoffs	54	3	23	26	112
Memorial Cup 1978, 1979 and 1980	15	2	5	7	33
NHL Regular Season 1979-83	77	2	10	12	95
NHL Playoffs	0	0	0	0	0
Canada 1980 World Juniors *in Finland*	5	0	1	1	10

Junior Highlights

Won Memorial Cup in 1979

Around the Rink

Smith signed as a free agent by the L.A. Kings, November 8, 1984 but never played a game for the Kings. Played all of his NHL games with Hartford. Retired from playing in 1985.

Smyl, Stan

Born: January 28, 1958 in Glendon, Alberta
Drafted: By the Vancouver Canucks from the New Westminster Bruins in 1978, 3rd round, 40th overall.

Career Junior, NHL and World Junior Statistics

	GP	G	A	PTS	PIM
WHL Regular Season 1975-78	197	96	120	216	580
WHL Playoffs	55	28	34	62	167
Memorial Cup 1976, 1977 and 1978	12	9	11	20	27
NHL Regular Season 1978-91	896	262	411	673	1556
NHL Playoffs	41	16	17	33	64
Canada 1978 World Juniors *in Montreal*	6	1	1	2	6

Junior Highlights

Won Memorial Cup in 1977 and 1978
Won Bronze Medal at World Junior Championships in 1978
Memorial Cup All-Star Team in 1978
Won Stafford Smythe Memorial Trophy (Memorial Cup MVP) in 1978

Around the Rink

Smyl played all of his NHL games with the Vancouver Canucks. Played only three games in the minors throughout his career. Retired from playing in 1991. Assistant Coach with Vancouver from 1991-99. Named Head Coach of Manitoba (AHL), June 28, 2001.

Smyth, Ryan

Born: February 21, 1976 in Banff, Alberta
Drafted: By the Edmonton Oilers from the Moose Jaw Warriors in 1994, 1st round, 6th overall.

Career Junior, NHL and World Junior Statistics

	GP	G	A	PTS	PIM
WHL Regular Season 1991-95	188	110	114	224	213
WHL Playoffs	10	6	9	15	22
NHL Regular Season 1994-Present	560	175	196	371	435
NHL Playoffs	44	15	12	27	54
Canada 1995 World Juniors *in Alberta*	7	2	5	7	4

Junior Highlights

Won Gold Medal at World Junior Championships in 1995
WHL East Second All-Star Team in 1995

Around the Rink

Smyth has played his entire NHL career with Edmonton. Played first NHL game on January 22, 1995 against Los Angeles. Scored his first NHL goal on November 24, 1995 versus Calgary.

Snell, Chris

Born: July 12, 1971 in Regina, Saskatchewan
Drafted: By the Buffalo Sabres from the Ottawa 67's in 1991, 7th round, 145th overall.

Career Junior, NHL and World Junior Statistics

	GP	G	A	PTS	PIM
OHL Regular Season 1988-91	195	52	169	221	110
OHL Playoffs	31	8	23	31	12
NHL Regular Season 1993-95	34	2	7	9	24
NHL Playoffs	0	0	0	0	0
Canada 1991 World Juniors in Saskatoon	7	0	4	4	0

Junior Highlights

OHL First All-Star Team in 1990 and 1991
Won Gold Medal at World Junior Championships in 1991

Around the Rink

Snell signed as a free agent by Toronto, August 3, 1993. Traded to L.A. Kings by Toronto with Eric Lacroix and Toronto's 4th round choice (Eric Belanger) in 1996 Entry Draft for Dixon Ward, Guy Leveque and Kelly Fairchild, October 3, 1994. Traded to the New York Rangers by L.A. Kings for Steve Larouche, January 14, 1996. Signed as a free agent by Chicago, August 16, 1996 but never played a game for the Black Hawks. Has played in Germany since 1997.

Soetaert, Doug

Born: April 21, 1956 in Edmonton, Alberta
Drafted: By the New York Rangers from the Edmonton Oil Kings in 1975, 2nd round, 30th overall.

Career Junior, NHL and World Junior Statistics

(WHL W-L-T Incomplete)	GP	W	L	T	SO	AVG
WHL Regular Season 1971-75	184	31	27	5	6	4.12
WHL Playoffs	15	Not Available			0	4.19
NHL Regular Season 1975-87	284	110	104	42	6	3.97
NHL Playoffs	5	1	2	0	0	4.67
Canada 1975 World Juniors *in Manitoba*	2	1	1	0	0	2.50

Junior Highlights

Won Silver Medal at World Junior Championships in 1975

Around the Rink

Soetaert was traded to Winnipeg by the New York Rangers for Winnipeg's 3rd round choice (Vesa Salo) in 1983 Entry Draft, September 8, 1981. Traded to Montreal by Winnipeg for Mark Holden, October 9, 1984. Signed as a free agent by the New York Rangers, July 24, 1986. Retired from playing in 1987. Head Coach of the Kansas City Blades in 1990-91.

Sorochan, Lee

Born: September 9, 1975 in Edmonton, Alberta
Drafted: By the New York Rangers from the Lethbridge Hurricaines in 1993, 2nd round, 34th overall.

Career Junior, NHL and World Junior Statistics

	GP	G	A	PTS	PIM
WHL Regular Season 1991-95	235	24	96	120	642
WHL Playoffs	28	7	12	19	68
NHL Regular Season 1998-99	3	0	0	0	0
NHL Playoffs	0	0	0	0	0
Canada 1995 World Juniors *in Alberta*	7	0	1	1	6

Junior Highlights

Won Gold Medal at World Junior Championships in 1995

Around the Rink

Sorochan was traded to Calgary by the NewYork Rangers for Chris O'Sullivan, March 23, 1999. Signed as a free agent by London (Britain), October 18, 2000. Signed as a free agent by Belfast (Britain), August 14, 2002.

Spezza, Jason

Born: June 13, 1983 in Brampton, Ontario
Drafted: By the Ottawa Senators in 2001, 1st round, 2nd overall.

Career Junior, NHL and World Junior Statistics

	GP	G	A	PTS	PIM
Canadian National Team 1998-00	16	6	6	12	14
OHL Regular Season 1998-02	228	124	222	346	136
OHL Playoffs	20	9	11	20	28
NHL Regular Season 2002-Present	33	7	14	21	8
NHL Playoffs	0	0	0	0	0
Canada 2000 World Juniors *in Sweden*	7	0	2	2	2
Canada 2001 World Juniors *in Russia*	7	3	3	6	2
Canada 2002 World Juniors *in Czech Republic*	7	0	4	4	8
Canada World Junior Totals	**21**	**3**	**9**	**12**	**12**

Junior Highlights

Won Bronze Medal at World Junior Championships in 2000 and 2001
Won Silver Medal at World Junior Championships in 2002

Around the Rink

Spezza was traded by the Brampton Batallion to the Mississauga Ice Dogs in 1999. Traded by Mississauga to the Windsor Spitfires in 2000. Traded by Windsor to the Belleveille Bulls in 2001. Played first NHL game on October 24, 2002 against Philadelphia, also recorded first NHL point in that game with an assist. Scored first goal against the Florida Panthers, October 29, 2002.

Stajan, Matthew

Born: December 19, 1983 in Mississauga, Ontario
Drafted: By the Toronto Maple Leafs from the Belleville Bulls in 2002, 2nd round, 57th overall.

Career Junior, NHL and World Junior Statistics

	GP	G	A	PTS	PIM
OHL Regular Season 2000-03	182	76	130	206	152
OHL Playoffs	25	9	22	31	35
NHL Regular Season 2003-Present	1	1	0	1	0
NHL Playoffs	0	0	0	0	0
Canada 2003 World Juniors *in Nova Scotia*	6	1	1	2	0

Junior Highlights

Won Silver Medal at World Junior Championships in 2003

Around the Rink

Stajan played his first NHL game on April 5, 2003 against Ottawa and he recorded his first NHL goal in that game, scoring the only goal for Toronto.

Stajduhar, Nick

Born: December 6, 1974 in Kitchener, Ontario
Drafted: By the Edmonton Oilers from the London Knights in 1993, 1st round, 16th overall.

Career Junior, NHL and World Junior Statistics

	GP	G	A	PTS	PIM
OHL Regular Season 1990-94	233	58	125	183	217
OHL Playoffs	34	5	17	22	30
NHL Regular Season 1995-96	2	0	0	0	4
NHL Playoffs	0	0	0	0	0
Canada 1994 World Juniors *in Czech Republic*	7	1	4	5	8

Junior Highlights

Won Gold Medal at World Junior Championships in 1994
OHL First All-Star Team in 1994

Around the Rink

Stajduhar played both of his NHL games with the Edmonton Oilers. Retired in 2001 after playing four seasons in the minors with ten different teams.

Staniowski, Ed

Born: July 7, 1955 in Moose Jaw, Saskatchewan
Drafted: By the St. Louis Blues from the Regina Pats in 1975, 2nd round, 27th overall.
Also Drafted by the Cleveland Crusaders (WHA) in 1975, 3rd round, 35th overall.

Career Junior, NHL and World Junior Statistics

(WHL W-L-T Incomplete)	GP	W	L	T	SO	AVG
WHL Regular Season 1971-75	206	39	12	9	7	3.56
WHL Playoffs	32	Not Available			1	3.33
Memorial Cup 1974 and 1975	3	2	1	0	1	3.00
NHL Regular Season 1975-85	219	67	104	21	2	4.06
NHL Playoffs	8	1	6	0	0	3.93
Canada 1975 World Juniors *in Manitoba*	2	2	0	0	1	1.50

Junior Highlights

Won Silver Medal at World Junior Championships in 1974
Won Memorial Cup in 1974
WHL First All-Star Team in 1975
Canadian Major Junior Player of the Year in 1975

Around the Rink

Staniowski traded to Winnipeg by St. Louis with Bryan Maxwell and Paul MacLean for Scott Campbell and John Markell, July 3, 1981. Traded to Hartford by Winnipeg for Mike Veisor, November 10, 1983. Retired from playing in 1985. Assistant Coach with Moose Jaw (WHL) in 1987-88.

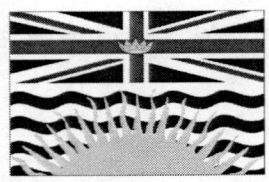

Stevenson, Turner

Born: May 18, 1972 in Prince George, B.C.
Drafted: By the Montreal Canadiens from the Seattle Thunderbirds in 1990, 1st round, 12th overall.

Career Junior, NHL and World Junior Statistics

	GP	**G**	**A**	**PTS**	**PIM**
WHL Regular Season 1988-92	246	100	103	203	886
WHL Playoffs	38	13	10	23	110
Memorial Cup 1992	4	2	0	2	18
NHL Regular Season 1992-Present	552	60	99	159	848
NHL Playoffs	53	5	11	16	48
Canada 1992 World Juniors *in Germany*	7	0	2	2	14

Junior Highlights

WHL West First All-Star Team in 1992
Memorial Cup All-Star Team in 1992

Around the Rink

Stevenson was selected by Columbus from Montreal in Expansion Draft, June 23, 2000. Traded to New Jersey by Columbus to complete transaction that sent Krzysztof Oliwa (June 12, 2000) and Deron Quint (June 23, 2000) to Columbus, June 23, 2000. Missed majority of 2001-02 season recovering from knee injury suffered in game versus Vancouver, December 29, 2001.

Stoll, Jarret

Born: June 24, 1982 in Saskatoon, Saskatchewan
Drafted: By the Calgary Flames from the Kootenay Ice in 2000, 2nd round, 46th overall.
Also Drafted by the Edmonton Oilers in 2002, 2nd round, 36th overall.

Career Junior, NHL and World Junior Statistics

	GP	G	A	PTS	PIM
WHL Regular Season 1997-02	245	124	162	286	275
WHL Playoffs	57	18	31	49	73
Memorial Cup 2000 and 2002	7	0	7	7	0
NHL Regular Season 2003-Present	4	0	1	1	0
NHL Playoffs	4	0	2	2	4
Canada 2001 World Juniors *in Russia*	7	0	2	2	6
Canada 2002 World Juniors *in Czech Republic*	7	2	4	6	4
Canada Totals	**14**	**2**	**6**	**8**	**10**

Junior Highlights

Won Bronze Medal at World Junior Championships in 2001
Won Silver Medal at World Junior Championships in 2002
Won Memorial Cup in 2002

Around the Rink

Stoll did not sign with Calgary after being drafted, therefore he went back into the NHL after two years. Played his first NHL game on January 29, 2003 against Minnesota, he also recorded his first NHL point in that game with an assist on Edmonton's first goal.

Storr, Jamie

Born: December 28, 1975 in Brampton, Ontario
Drafted: By the Los Angeles Kings from the Owen Sound Platers in 1994, 1st round, 7th overall.

Career Junior, NHL and World Junior Statistics

	GP	W	L	T	SO	AVG
OHL Regular Season 1991-95	131	60	54	7	2	4.10
OHL Playoffs	32	15	16	0	1	4.64
NHL Regular Season 1994-Present	205	85	78	21	16	2.52
NHL Playoffs	5	0	3	0	0	3.65
Canada 1994 World Juniors *in Czech Rep.*	4	4	0	0	0	3.50
Canada 1995 World Juniors *in Alberta*	4	3	0	1	0	2.50
Canada Totals	**8**	**7**	**0**	**1**	**0**	**3.00**

Junior Highlights

OHL All-Rookie Team in 1992
Won Gold Medal at World Junior Championships in 1994 and 1995
Named Best Goaltender at World Junior Championships in 1994
OHL First All-Star Team in 1994

Around the Rink

Storr was traded by Owen Sound to Windsor early on in the 1994-95 season. Has played all of his NHL games with Los Angeles. Made his NHL debut on January 25, 1995 against Dallas. Won his first game on January 28, 1995 versus Winnipeg.

Strueby, Todd

Born: June 15, 1963 in Lanigan, Saskatchewan
Drafted: By the Edmonton Oilers from the Regina Pats in 1981, 2nd round, 29th overall.

Career Junior, NHL and World Junior Statistics

	GP	G	A	PTS	PIM
WHL Regular Season 1980-83	197	118	155	273	378
WHL Playoffs	22	8	11	19	44
NHL Regular Season 1981-84	5	0	1	1	2
NHL Playoffs	0	0	0	0	0
Canada 1982 World Juniors *in United States*	7	0	5	5	4

Junior Highlights

Won Gold Medal at World Junior Championships in 1982
WHL First All-Star Team in 1982
WHL Second All-Star Team in 1983

Around the Rink

Strueby was traded by Regina to the Saskatoon Blades prior to the 1981-82 season. Traded to the New York Rangers by Edmonton with Larry Melnyk for Mike Rogers, December 20, 1985. Played all of his NHL games with Edmonton. Retired in 1993 after splitting nine seasons between playing in Germany, the IHL and AHL and the Canadian National Team.

Stuart, Brad

Born: November 6, 1979 in Rocky Mountain House, Alberta
Drafted: By the San Jose Sharks from the Regina Pats in 1998, 1st round, 3rd overall.

Career Junior, NHL and World Junior Statistics

	GP	**G**	**A**	**PTS**	**PIM**
WHL Regular Season 1995-99	191	48	122	170	209
WHL Playoffs	35	11	23	34	83
Memorial Cup 1999	2	0	2	2	8
NHL Regular Season 1999-Present	7	0	1	1	2
NHL Playoffs	29	2	3	5	14
Canada 1999 World Juniors *in Winnipeg*	7	0	1	1	2

Junior Highlights

WHL East Second All-Star Team in 1998
Won Silver Medal at World Junior Championships in 1999
WHL East First All-Star Team in 1999
Canadian Major Junior First All-Star Team in 1999
Canadian Major Junior Defenseman of the Year in 1999

Around the Rink

Stuart was traded to Calgary (WHL) by Regina (WHL) for Donald Choukalos and Ryan Geremia, January 15, 1999. Played his first NHL game on October 2, 1999 against Calgary, he also recorded his first NHL goal in that game.

Sutherby, Brian

Born: March 1, 1982 in Edmonton, Alberta
Drafted: By the Washington Capitals from the Moose Jaw Warriors in 2000, 1st round, 26th overall.

Career Junior, NHL and World Junior Statistics

	GP	G	A	PTS	PIM
WHL Regular Season 1998-02	208	79	99	178	362
WHL Playoffs	31	10	8	18	55
NHL Regular Season 2001-Present	79	2	9	11	95
NHL Playoffs	5	0	0	0	10
Canada 2002 World Juniors *in Czech Republic*	7	3	3	6	2

Junior Highlights

Won Silver Medal at World Junior Championships in 2002

Around the Rink

Sutherby was returned to Moose Jaw (WHL) by Washington, October 22, 2001.
Played his first NHL game on October 6, 2001 versus New Jersey.

Sutter, Brian

Born: October 7, 1956 in Viking, Alberta
Drafted: By the St. Louis Blues from the Lethbridge Broncos in 1976, 2nd round, 20th overall. Also Drafted by the Edmonton Oilers (WHA) in 1976, 3rd round, 36th overall.

Career Junior, NHL and World Junior Statistics

	GP	G	A	PTS	PIM
WHL Regular Season 1974-76	127	70	103	173	367
WHL Playoffs	13	3	5	8	84
NHL Regular Season 1976-88	779	303	333	636	1786
NHL Playoffs	65	21	21	42	249
Canada 1975 World Juniors *in Manitoba*	5	1	4	5	2

Junior Highlights

Won Silver Medal at World Junior Championships in 1975

Around the Rink

Sutter played all of his NHL games with St. Louis. Head Coach of St. Louis from 1988-92. Head Coach of Boston from 1992-95. Head Coach of Calgary from 1997-00. Head Coach of Chicago from 2001 to Present.

Sydor, Darryl

Born: May 13, 1972 in Edmonton, Alberta
Drafted: By the Los Angeles Kings from the Kamloops Blazers in 1990, 1st round, 7th overall.

Career Junior, NHL and World Junior Statistics

	GP	G	A	PTS	PIM
WHL Regular Season 1988-92	227	77	197	274	346
WHL Playoffs	61	9	50	59	75
Memorial Cup 1990 and 1992	8	4	2	6	8
NHL Regular Season 1991-Present	863	82	323	405	598
NHL Playoffs	116	8	39	47	58
Canada 1992 World Juniors *in Germany*	7	3	1	4	4

Junior Highlights

WHL West First All-Star Team in 1990, 1991 and 1992
Won Memorial Cup in 1992

Around the Rink

Sydor was traded to Dallas by the L.A. Kings with the L.A. Kings' 5th round choice (Ryan Christie) in 1996 Entry Draft for Shane Churla and Doug Zmolek, February 17, 1996. Made NHL debut on October 6, 1991 against Edmonton.

Tambellini, Steve

Born: May 14, 1958 in Trail, B.C.
Drafted: By the New York Islanders from the Lethbridge Broncos in 1978, 1st round, 15th overall.

Career Junior, NHL and World Junior Statistics

	GP	**G**	**A**	**PTS**	**PIM**
WHL Regular Season 1975-78	193	155	181	336	97
WHL Playoffs	30	23	22	55	7
NHL Regular Season 1978-88	553	160	150	310	105
NHL Playoffs	2	0	1	1	0
Canada 1978 World Juniors *in Montreal*	6	2	2	4	0

Junior Highlights

WHL Rookie of the Year in 1976
Won Bronze Medal at World Junior Championships in 1978

Around the Rink

Tambellini was traded to Colorado by the New York Islanders with Glenn Resch for Mike McEwen and Jari Kaarela, March 10, 1981. Transferred to New Jersey after Colorado franchise relocated, June 30, 1982. Traded to Calgary by New Jersey with Joel Quenneville for Mel Bridgman and Phil Russell, June 20, 1983. Signed as a free agent by Vancouver, August 28, 1985. Retired from playing in 1990 after two seasons in Europe. General Manager of Gold Medal Winning Team Canada at 2003 World Championships.

Tanguay, Alex

Born: November 21, 1979 in Ste. Justine, Quebec
Drafted: By the Colorado Avalanche from the Halifax Mooseheads in 1998, 1st round, 12th overall.

Career Junior, NHL and World Junior Statistics

	GP	G	A	PTS	PIM
QMJHL Regular Season 1996-99	152	101	113	214	112
QMJHL Playoffs	22	13	16	29	14
NHL Regular Season 1999-Present	310	83	160	243	131
NHL Playoffs	66	14	26	40	14
Canada 1998 World Juniors *in Finland*	7	2	1	3	2

Junior Highlights

QMJHL All-Rookie Team in 1997

Around the Rink

Tanguay played his first NHL game on October 5, 1999 against Nashville. He scored his first NHL goal a few days later on October 8 versus Pittsburgh.

Tanti, Tony

Born: September 7, 1963 in Toronto, Ontario
Drafted: By the Chicago Black Hawks from the Oshawa Generals in 1981, 1st round, 12th overall.

Career Junior, NHL and World Junior Statistics

	GP	G	A	PTS	PIM
OHL Regular Season 1980-83	154	177	161	338	370
OHL Playoffs	23	21	20	41	56
NHL Regular Season 1981-92	697	287	273	560	661
NHL Playoffs	30	3	12	15	27
Canada 1984 World Juniors *in Sweden*	7	0	4	4	0

Junior Highlights

OHL First All-Star Team in 1981
OHL Rookie of the Year in 1981
OHL Second All-Star Team in 1982

Around the Rink

Tanti was traded to Vancouver by Chicago for Curt Fraser, January 6, 1983. Traded to Pittsburgh by Vancouver with Rod Buskas and Barry Pederson for Dave Capuano, Andrew McBain and Dan Quinn, January 8, 1990. Traded to Buffalo by Pittsburgh for Ken Priestlay, March 5, 1991. Played six seasons in Germany before retiring in 1998.

Theodore, Jose

Born: September 13, 1976 in Laval, Quebec
Drafted: By the Montreal Canadiens from the St. Jean Lynx in 1994, 2nd round, 44th overall.

Career Junior, NHL and World Junior Statistics

	GP	W	L	T	SO	AVG
QMJHL Regular Season 1992-86	197	97	78	12	5	3.53
QMJHL Playoffs	34	18	15	0	1	3.18
Memorial Cup 1995	3	0	3	0	0	5.20
NHL Regular Season 1995-Present	248	91	115	25	17	2.59
NHL Playoffs	17	7	8	0	0	2.65
Canada 1996 World Juniors *in U.S.A.*	4	4	0	0	0	1.65

Junior Highlights

QMJHL Second All-Star Team in 1995 and 1996
Won Gold Medal at World Junior Championships in 1996
World Junior Championships All-Star Team in 1996
Named Best Goaltender at World Junior Championships in 1996

Around the Rink

Theodore was traded by the St. Jean Lynx to the Hull Olympiques after fifteen games in the 1994-95 season. Made his NHL debut against Hartford on February 26, 1996. Won his first NHL game on November 6, 1996 versus Anaheim. Recorded first career shutout against Carolina on April 7, 1999. Scored a goal versus the New York Islanders, January 2, 2001.

Thornton, Joe

Born: July 2, 1979 in London, Ontario
Drafted: By the Boston Bruins from the Sault Ste. Marie Greyhounds in 1997, 1st round, 1st overall.

Career Junior, NHL and World Junior Statistics

	GP	G	A	PTS	PIM
OHL Regular Season 1995-97	125	71	127	198	176
OHL Playoffs	15	12	9	21	35
NHL Regular Season 1997-Present	432	137	211	348	513
NHL Playoffs	28	6	12	18	27
Canada 1997 World Juniors *in Switzerland*	7	2	2	4	0

Junior Highlights

OHL All-Rookie Team in 1996
OHL Rookie of the Year in 1996
Canadian Major Junior Rookie of the Year in 1996
Won Gold Medal at World Junior Championships in 1997
OHL Second All-Star Team in 1997

Around the Rink

Thornton made his NHL debut on October 8, 1997 against Phoenix. Recorded his first NHL goal nearly two months later on December 3 versus Philadelphia.

Thornton, Scott

Born: January 9, 1971 in London, Ontario
Drafted: By the Toronto Maple Leafs from the Belleville Bulls in 1989, 1st round, 3rd overall.

Career Junior, NHL and World Junior Statistics

	GP	G	A	PTS	PIM
OHL Regular Season 1987-91	171	62	82	144	250
OHL Playoffs	28	3	19	22	37
NHL Regular Season 1990-Present	685	109	107	216	1167
NHL Playoffs	56	9	12	21	54
Canada 1991 World Juniors *in Saskatoon*	7	3	1	4	0

Junior Highlights

Won Gold Medal at World Junior Championships in 1991

Around the Rink

Thornton was traded to Edmonton by Toronto with Vincent Damphousse, Peter Ing and Luke Richardson for Grant Fuhr, Glenn Anderson and Craig Berube, September 19, 1991. Traded to Montreal by Edmonton for Andrei Kovalenko, September 6, 1996. Traded to Dallas by Montreal for Juha Lind, January 22, 2000. Signed as a free agent by San Jose, July 1, 2000.

Tkaczuk, Daniel

Born: June 10, 1979 in Toronto, Ontario
Drafted: By the Calgary Flames from the Barrie Colts in 1997, 1st round, 6th overall.

Career Junior, NHL and World Junior Statistics

	GP	G	A	PTS	PIM
OHL Regular Season 1995-99	238	145	189	334	183
OHL Playoffs	34	17	15	32	28
NHL Regular Season 2000-01	19	4	7	11	14
NHL Playoffs	0	0	0	0	0
Canada 1998 World Juniors *in Finland*	7	2	1	3	4
Canada 1999 World Juniors *in Winnipeg*	7	6	4	10	10
Canada Totals	**14**	**8**	**5**	**13**	**14**

Junior Highlights

Won Silver Medal at World Junior Championships in 1999
World Junior Championships All-Star Team in 1999
OHL First All-Star Team in 1999

Around the Rink

Tkaczuk played all of his NHL games with Calgary. Traded to St. Louis by Calgary with Fred Brathwaite, Sergei Varlamov and Calgary's 9th round choice (Grant Jacobsen) in 2001 Entry Draft for Roman Turek and St. Louis' 4th round choice (Yegor Shastin) in 2001 Entry Draft, June 23, 2001. Has played the last two seasons in the AHL.

Torres, Raffi

Born: October 8, 1981 in Toronto, Ontario
Drafted: By the New York Islanders from the Brampton Battalion in 2000, 1st round, 5th overall.

Career Junior, NHL and World Junior Statistics

	GP	G	A	PTS	PIM
OHL Regular Season 1998-01	185	111	112	223	148
OHL Playoffs	14	12	6	18	42
NHL Regular Season 2001-Present	31	0	6	6	12
NHL Playoffs	0	0	0	0	0
Canada 2001 World Juniors *in Russia*	7	3	2	5	10

Junior Highlights

OHL All-Rookie Team in 1999
OHL Second All-Star Team in 2000 and 2001
Won Bronze Medal at World Junior Championships in 2001

Around the Rink

Torres made his NHL debut with the New York Islanders against Anaheim on November 24, 2001. Traded by the New York Islanders with Brad Isbister to Edmonton for Janne Niinimaa and the Oilers 2003 entry draft 2nd round pick, March 11, 2003.

Trader, Larry

Born: July 7, 1963 in Barry's Bay, Ontario
Drafted: By the Detroit Red Wings from the London Knights in 1981, 5th round, 86th overall.

Career Junior, NHL and World Junior Statistics

	GP	G	A	PTS	PIM
OHL Regular Season 1980-83	175	40	88	128	360
OHL Playoffs	7	0	2	2	12
NHL Regular Season 1982-88	91	5	13	18	74
NHL Playoffs	3	0	0	0	0
Canada 1983 World Juniors *in Russia*	7	2	3	5	8

Junior Highlights

Won Bronze Medal at World Junior Championships in 1983

Around the Rink

Trader was traded to St. Louis by Detroit for Lee Norwood, August 7, 1986. Traded to Montreal by St. Louis with St. Louis' 3rd round choice (Pierre Sevigny) in 1989 Entry Draft for Gaston Gingras and Montreal's 3rd round choice (later traded to Winnipeg Winnipeg selected Kris Draper) in 1989 Entry Draft, October 13, 1987. Signed as a free agent by Hartford, August 3, 1988. Finished his playing career in 1994 after his fourth season in Italy. Head Coach of the Brantford Smoke of the Colonial League from 1995-98.

Trottier, Bryan

Hockey Hall of Famer, Inducted 1997
Born: July 17, 1956 in Val Marie, Saskatchewan
Drafted: By the New York Islanders from the Swift Current Broncos in 1974, 2nd round, 22nd overall. Also Drafted by the Cincinnati Stingers in 1974, 2nd round, 18th overall.

Career Junior, NHL and World Junior Statistics

	GP	G	A	PTS	PIM
WHL Regular Season 1972-75	202	103	198	301	189
WHL Playoffs	19	9	13	22	22
NHL Regular Season 1975-94	1279	524	901	1425	912
NHL Playoffs	221	71	113	184	277
Canada 1975 World Juniors *in Manitoba*	7	4	2	6	4

Junior Highlights

Won Silver Medal at World Junior Championships in 1975

Around the Rink

Trottier signed as a free agent by Pittsburgh, July 20, 1990. Did not play 1992-93. Signed as a free agent by Pittsburgh, June 22, 1993. Played with the Pittsburgh Phantoms (roller Hockey) 1993-94 (9-9-13-22-2). Retired from playing in 1994. Assistant Coach with Pittsburgh from 1993-97. Head Coach of Portland Pirates (AHL) 1997-98. Assistant Coach with the Colorado Avalanche from 1998-2002. Head Coach of the New York Rangers for 54 games in 2002-03. Fired by New York on January 29, 2003.

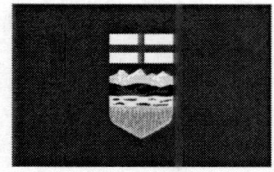

Tucker, Darcy

Born: March 15, 1975 in Castor, Alberta
Drafted: By the Montreal Canadiens from the Kamloops Blazers in 1993, 6th round, 151st overall.

Career Junior, NHL and World Junior Statistics

	GP	G	A	PTS	PIM
WHL Regular Season 1991-95	223	150	229	379	434
WHL Playoffs	62	32	40	72	112
Memorial Cup 1992, 1994 and 1995	14	6	7	13	6
NHL Regular Season 1995-Present	545	106	160	266	947
NHL Playoffs	50	8	11	19	65
Canada 1995 World Juniors *in Alberta*	7	0	4	4	0

Junior Highlights

Won Memorial Cup in 1992, 1994 and 1995
WHL West First All-Star Team in 1994 and 1995
Canadian Major Junior First All-Star Team in 1994
Memorial Cup All-Star Team in 1994 and 1995
Won Stafford Smythe Memorial Trophy (Memorial Cup MVP) in 1994
Won Gold Medal at World Junior Championships in 1995

Around the Rink

Tucker was traded to Tampa Bay by Montreal with Stephane Richer and David Wilkie for Patrick Poulin, Mick Vukota and Igor Ulanov, January 15, 1998. Traded to Toronto by Tampa Bay with Tampa Bay's 4th round choice (Miguel Delisle) in 2000 Entry Draft and future considerations for Mike Johnson, Marek Posmyk, Toronto's 5th (Pavel Sedov) and 6th (Aaron Gionet) round choices in 2000 Entry Draft and future considerations, February 9, 2000.

Turgeon, Pierre

Born: August 28, 1969 in Rouyn, Quebec
Drafted: By the Buffalo Sabres from the Granby Bisons in 1987, 1st round, 1st overall.

Career Junior, NHL and World Junior Statistics

	GP	G	A	PTS	PIM
Canadian National Team 1985-86	11	2	4	6	2
QMJHL Regular Season 1985-87	127	116	152	268	39
QMJHL Playoffs	7	9	6	15	15
NHL Regular Season 1987-Present	1139	480	754	1234	390
NHL Playoffs	99	34	57	91	28
Canada 1987 World Juniors *in Czech Republic*	6	3	0	3	2

Junior Highlights

QMJHL Offensive Rookie of the Year in 1986

Around the Rink

Turgeon was traded to the New York Islanders by Buffalo with Uwe Krupp, Benoit Hogue and Dave McLlwain for Pat LaFontaine, Randy Hillier, Randy Wood and the Islanders' 4th round choice (Dean Melanson) in 1992 Entry Draft, October 25, 1991. Traded to Montreal by the New York Islanders with Vladimir Malakhov for Kirk Muller, Mathieu Schneider and Craig Darby, April 5, 1995. Traded to St. Louis by Montreal with Rory Fitzpatrick and Craig Conroy for Murray Baron, Shayne Corson and St. Louis' 5th round choice (Gennady Razin) in 1997 Entry Draft, October 29, 1996. Signed as a free agent by Dallas, July 1, 2001. Placed on waivers by Dallas, May 16, 2003.

Turgeon, Sylvain

Born: January 17, 1965 in Rouyn, Quebec
Drafted: By the Hartford Whalers from the Hull Olympiques in 1983, 1st round, 2nd overall.

Career Junior, NHL and World Junior Statistics

	GP	G	A	PTS	PIM
QMJHL Regular Season 1981-83	124	87	149	236	181
QMJHL Playoffs	21	19	18	37	26
NHL Regular Season 1983-95	669	269	225	494	691
NHL Playoffs	36	4	7	11	22
Canada 1983 World Juniors *in Russia*	7	4	2	6	8

Junior Highlights

QMJHL Offensive Rookie of the Year in 1982
Won Bronze Medal at World Junior Championships in 1983
QMJHL First All-Star Team in 1983

Around the Rink

Turgeon was traded to New Jersey by Hartford for Pat Verbeek, June 17, 1989. Missed majority of 1990-91 season recovering from hernia surgery (August 23, 1990) and kneecap injury suffered in game vs. Chicago, February 6, 1991. Traded to Montreal by New Jersey for Claude Lemieux, September 4, 1990. Claimed by Ottawa from Montreal in Expansion Draft, June 18, 1992. Retired in 2001 after playing in Europe for five seasons.

Upshall, Scottie

Born: October 7, 1983 in Fort McMurray, Alberta
Drafted: By the Nashville Predators from the Kamloops Blazers in 2002, 1st round, 6th overall.

Career Junior, NHL and World Junior Statistics

	GP	G	A	PTS	PIM
WHL Regular Season 2000-02	131	74	96	170	250
WHL Playoffs	8	1	4	5	31
NHL Regular Season 2002-Present	8	1	0	1	0
NHL Playoffs	0	0	0	0	0
Canada 2002 World Juniors *in Czech Republic*	6	4	1	5	18
Canada 2003 World Juniors *in Nova Scotia*	7	3	3	6	10
Canada Totals	**13**	**7**	**4**	**11**	**28**

Junior Highlights

CHL and WHL Rookie of the Year in 2001
CHL and WHL All Rookie Team in 2001
Won Silver Medal at World Junior Championships in 2002 and 2003-05-20
WHL West Second Team All Star in 2002
Played in CHL Top Prospects Game in 2002

Around the Rink

Upshall played his first NHL game on October 15, 2002 against the New York Islanders. Scored his first NHL goal and point versus the New York Rangers on October 19, 2002.

Vaive, Rick

Born: May 14, 1959 in Ottawa, Ontario
Drafted: By the Vancouver Canucks from the Sherbrooke Beavers in 1979, 1st round, 5th overall.

Career Junior, NHL and World Junior Statistics

	GP	G	A	PTS	PIM
QMJHL Regular Season 1976-78	135	127	138	265	290
QMJHL Playoffs	27	18	17	35	116
NHL Regular Season 1979-92	876	441	347	788	1445
NHL Playoffs	54	27	16	43	111
Canada 1978 World Juniors *in Montreal*	6	3	0	3	4

Junior Highlights

QMJHL Rookie of the Year in 1977
Won Bronze Medal at World Junior Championships in 1978

Around the Rink

Vaive signed as an underage free agent by Birmingham (WHA), May 1978 and played one season. Traded to Toronto by Vancouver with Bill Derlago for Tiger Williams and Jerry Butler, February 18, 1980. Traded to Chicago by Toronto with Steve Thomas and Bob McGill for Al Secord and Ed Olczyk, September 3, 1987. Traded to Buffalo by Chicago for Adam Creighton, December 26, 1988. Signed as a free agent by Vancouver, September 2, 1992. Retired from playing in 1993 after half of a season in the minors. Head Coach of the South Carolina Stingrays (ECHL) from 1993-98. Head Coach of the St. John Flames, 1997-99. Named Head Coach of Mississauga (OHL), July 20, 2000. Fired by Mississauga after the 2000-01 season.

Van Ryn, Mike

Born: May 14, 1979 in London, Ontario
Drafted: By the New Jersey Devils from the University of Michigan in 1998, 1st round, 26th overall.

Career Junior, NHL and World Junior Statistics

	GP	G	A	PTS	PIM
NCAA 1997-99	75	14	27	41	96
OHL Regular Season 1999-00	61	6	35	41	34
OHL Playoffs	7	0	5	5	4
NHL Regular Season 2000-Present	69	2	11	13	26
NHL Playoffs	9	0	0	0	0
Canada 1998 World Juniors *in Finland*	7	0	0	0	4
Canada 1999 World Juniors *in Winnipeg*	7	0	1	1	4
Canada Totals	**14**	**0**	**1**	**1**	**8**

Junior Highlights

Won Silver Medal at World Junior Championships in 1999

Around the Rink

Van Ryn left the University of Michigan after two seasons and signed as a free agent with the Sarnia Sting. Although drafted by New Jersey he never played a game for the Devils. Signed as a free agent by St. Louis, June 30, 2000. Missed majority of 2000-01 season recovering from shoulder injury suffered in game versus Phoenix, October 5, 2000. Traded by St. Louis to Florida for Valeri Bure and a conditional 2004 draft pick, March 11, 2003.

Vaydik, Greg

Born: October 9, 1955 in Yellowknife, NWT
Drafted: By the Chicago Black Hawks from the Medicine Hat Tigers in 1975, 1st round, 7th overall. Also Drafted by the Phoenix Roadrunners (WHA) in 1975, 1st round, 9th overall.

Career Junior, NHL and World Junior Statistics

	GP	G	A	PTS	PIM
WHL Regular Season 1972-75	167	93	95	188	67
WHL Playoffs	28	8	11	19	11
NHL Regular Season 1976-77	5	0	0	0	0
NHL Playoffs	0	0	0	0	0
Canada 1975 World Juniors *in Manitoba*	3	0	1	1	0

Junior Highlights

Won Silver Medal at World Junior Championships in 1975

Around the Rink

Vaydik missed the majority of 1975-76 season recovering from knee injury suffered in practice, November 24, 1975. Played all five of his NHL games with Chicago. Retired in 1982 after five straight seasons in the minors.

Verbeek, Pat

Born: May 24, 1964 in Sarnia, Ontario
Drafted: By the New Jersey Devils from the Sudbury Wolves in 1982, 3rd round, 43rd overall.

Career Junior, NHL and World Junior Statistics

	GP	G	A	PTS	PIM
OHL Regular Season 1981-83	127	77	118	195	364
OHL Playoffs	0	0	0	0	0
NHL Regular Season 1982-2002	1424	522	541	1063	2905
NHL Playoffs	117	26	36	62	225
Canada 1983 World Juniors *in Russia*	7	2	2	4	6

Verbeek, Pat Continued

Junior Highlights

OHL Rookie of the Year in 1982
Won Bronze Medal at World Junior Championships in 1983

Around the Rink

Verbeek was traded to Hartford by New Jersey for Sylvain Turgeon, June 17, 1989. Traded to the New York Rangers by Hartford for Glen Featherstone, Michael Stewart, New York Rangers' 1st round choice (Jean-Sebastien Giguere) in 1995 Entry Draft and 4th round choice (Steve Wasylko) in 1996 Entry Draft, March 23, 1995. Signed as a free agent by Dallas, August 21, 1996. Signed as a free agent by Detroit, November 11, 1999. Signed as a free agent by Dallas, August 31, 2001. Unsigned free agent in 2002-03 and missed the entire season. Retired from playing, April 23, 2003.

Vernon, Mike

Born: February 24, 1963 in Calgary, Alberta
Drafted: By the Calgary Flames from the Calgary Wranglers in 1981, 3rd round, 56th overall.

Career Junior, NHL and World Junior Statistics

	GP	W	L	T	SO	AVG
WHL Regular Season 1980-83	151	84	49	5	7	3.56
WHL Playoffs	47	28	19	0	1	3.79
Memorial Cup 1982 and 1983	6	4	2	0	0	5.12
NHL Regular Season 1982-02	781	385	273	92	27	2.97
NHL Playoffs	138	77	56	0	6	2.68
Canada 1983 World Juniors *in Russia*	4	3	0	0	1	3.33

Junior Highlights

WHL First All-Star Team in 1982 and 1983
WHL MVP in 1982 and 1983
Won Bronze Medal at World Junior Championships in 1983
Won Hap Emms Memorial Trophy (Memorial Cup Top Goaltender) in 1983

Around the Rink

Vernon was traded to Detroit by Calgary for Steve Chiasson, June 29, 1994. Traded to San Jose by Detroit with Detroit's 5th round choice (later traded back to Detroit - Detroit selected Andrei Maximenko) in 1999 Entry Draft for San Jose's 2nd round choice (later traded to St. Louis - St. Louis selected Maxim Linnik) in 1998 Entry Draft and San Jose's 2nd round choice (later traded to Tampa Bay - Tampa Bay selected Sheldon Keefe) in 1999 Entry Draft, August 18, 1997. Traded to Florida by San Jose with San Jose's 3rd round choice (Sean O'Connor) in 2000 Entry Draft for Radek Dvorak, December 30, 1999. Selected by Minnesota from Florida in Expansion Draft, June 23, 2000. Traded to Calgary by Minnesota for the rights to Dan Cavanaugh and Calgary's 8th round choice (Jake Riddle) in 2001 Entry Draft, June 23, 2000. Retired from playing on September 13, 2002.

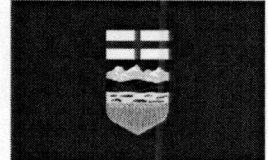

Viveiros, Emanuel

Born: January 8, 1966 in St. Albert, Alberta
Drafted: By the Edmonton Oilers from the Prince Albert Raiders in 1984, 6th round, 106th overall.

Career Junior, NHL and World Junior Statistics

	GP	G	A	PTS	PIM
WHL Regular Season 1982-86	251	60	261	321	227
WHL Playoffs	35	6	36	42	24
Memorial Cup 1985	5	2	6	8	4
NHL Regular Season 1985-88	29	1	11	12	6
NHL Playoffs	0	0	0	0	0
Canada 1986 World Juniors *in Hamilton*	7	1	1	2	2

Junior Highlights

WHL East Second All-Star Team in 1985
Won Silver Medal at World Junior Championships in 1986
WHL East First All-Star Team in 1986
WHL East MVP in 1986

Around the Rink

Viveiros played all of his NHL games with Minnesota. Traded to Minnesota by Edmonton with Marc Habscheid and Don Barber for Gord Sherven and Don Biggs, December 20, 1985. Signed as a free agent by Hartford, February 9, 1990. Has played in Europe since 1992.

Waite, Jimmy

Born: April 15, 1969 in Sherbrooke, Quebec
Drafted: By the Chicago Black Hawks from the Chicoutimi Sagueneens in 1987, 1st round, 8th overall.

Career Junior, NHL and World Junior Statistics

	GP	W	L	T	SO	AVG
QMJHL Regular Season 1986-88	86	40	33	4	2	4.71
QMJHL Playoffs	15	5	8	0	1	5.33
NHL Regular Season 1988-99	106	28	41	12	4	3.35
NHL Playoffs	6	0	3	0	0	3.98
Canada 1987 World Juniors *in Czech Rep.*	3	2	0	0	0	3.75
Canada 1988 World Juniors *in Russia*	7	6	0	1	0	2.29
Canada Totals	**10**	**8**	**0**	**1**	**0**	**2.69**

Junior Highlights

QMJHL Second All-Star Team in 1987
QMJHL Defensive Rookie of the Year in 1987
Won Gold Medal at World Junior Championships in 1988
World Junior Championships All-Star Team in 1988
Named Best Goaltender at World Junior Championships in 1988

Around the Rink

Waite was traded to San Jose by Chicago for future considerations (Neil Wilkinson, July 9, 1993), June 18, 1993. Traded to Chicago by San Jose for Chicago's 4th round choice (later traded to the New York Rangers – New York Rangers selected Tomi Kallarsson) in 1997 Entry Draft, February 5, 1995. Claimed by Phoenix from Chicago in NHL Waiver Draft, September 28, 1997. Signed as a free agent by Toronto, August 19, 1999 but never played a game for the Leafs. Played in the AHL from 1999-01. Signed as a free agent with Essen of the German league in 2001.

Wallin, Jesse

Born: October 30, 1978 in Saskatoon, Saskatchewan
Drafted: By the Detroit Red Wings from the Red Deer Rebels in 1996, 1st round, 26th overall.

Career Junior, NHL and World Junior Statistics

	GP	G	A	PTS	PIM
WHL Regular Season 1994-98	215	16	94	110	220
WHL Playoffs	30	1	8	9	16
NHL Regular Season 1999-Present	49	0	2	2	34
NHL Playoffs	0	0	0	0	0
Canada 1997 World Juniors *in Switzerland*	7	0	0	0	6
Canada 1998 World Juniors *in Finland*	4	0	0	0	4
Canada Totals	**11**	**0**	**0**	**0**	**10**

Junior Highlights

Won Gold Medal at World Junior Championships in 1997
Canadian Major Junior Humanitarian Player of the Year in 1997

Around the Rink

Wallin missed majority of the 1997-98 season recovering from arm injury suffered in automobile accident (September 10, 1997) and foot injury suffered in game versus Germany, December 30, 1997 Missed majority of 2001-02 season recovering from groin injury suffered in training camp, October 1, 2001. Made NHL debut versus Colorado on April 9, 2000. Recorded first NHL point with an assist against Colorado on February 4, 2002.

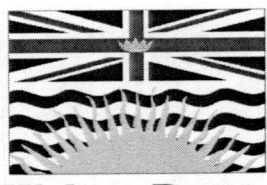

Walter, Ryan

Born: April 23, 1958 in New Westminster, B.C.
Drafted: By the Washington Capitals from the Seattle Breakers in 1978, 1st round, 2nd overall.

Career Junior, NHL and World Junior Statistics

	GP	G	A	PTS	PIM
WHL Regular Season 1973-79	218	138	183	321	346
WHL Playoffs	19	5	13	18	23
NHL Regular Season 1978-93	1003	264	382	646	946
NHL Playoffs	113	16	35	51	62
Canada 1978 World Juniors *in Montreal*	6	5	3	8	4

Junior Highlights

Won Bronze Medal at World Junior Championships in 1978
WHL First All-Star Team in 1978
WHL MVP in 1978

Around the Rink

Walter played his first four seasons of junior with the Kamloops Chiefs before being dealt to the Seattle Breakers prior to the 1977-78 season. Traded by Seattle to the Calgary Wranglers before the 1978-79 season. Traded to Montreal by Washington with Rick Green for Rod Langway, Brian Engblom, Doug Jarvis and Craig Laughlin, September 9, 1982. Missed majority of 1990-91 season recovering from wrist injury suffered in game versus Hartford, October 13, 1990. Signed as a free agent by Vancouver, July 26, 1991. Retired from playing in 1993 having never played a game in the minors.

Walz, Wes

Born: May 15, 1970 in Calgary Alberta
Drafted: By the Boston Bruins from the Lethbridge Hurricanes in 1989, 3rd round, 57th overall.

Career Junior, NHL and World Junior Statistics

	GP	G	A	PTS	PIM
WHL Regular Season 1987-90	120	84	162	246	101
WHL Playoffs	17	14	29	43	39
NHL Regular Season 1989-Present	395	68	102	170	214
NHL Playoffs	26	10	6	16	16
Canada 1990 World Juniors *in Finland*	7	2	3	5	0

Junior Highlights

WHL Rookie of the Year in 1989
Won Gold Medal at World Junior Championships in 1990
WHL East First All-Star Team in 1990

Around the Rink

Walz played his first season of junior with the Prince Albert Raiders in 1987-88, he was dealt to Lethrbidge before the start of the 1988-89 season. Traded to Philadelphia by Boston with Garry Galley and Boston's 3rd round choice (Milos Holan) in 1993 entry draft for Gord Murphy, Brian Dobbin, Philadelphia's 3rd round choice (Sergei Zholtok) in 1992 entry draft and 4th round choice (Charles Paquette) in 1993 entry draft, January 2, 1992. Signed as a free agent by Calgary, August 26, 1993. Signed as a free agent by Detroit, September 6, 1995. Signed as a free agent with Zug in the Swiss league in 1996. Signed as a free agent by Long Beach (IHL), October 12, 1999. Signed as a free agent by Minnesota, June 28, 2000.

Ward, Jason

Born: January 16, 1979 in Chapleau, Ontario
Drafted: By the Montreal Canadiens from the Erie Otters in 1997, 1st round, 11th overall.

Career Junior, NHL and World Junior Statistics

	GP	G	A	PTS	PIM
OHL Regular Season 1995-99	204	88	134	222	405
OHL Playoffs	26	13	14	27	37
NHL Regular Season 1999-Present	52	5	3	8	27
NHL Playoffs	4	1	1	2	6
Canada 1998 World Juniors *in Finland*	7	1	0	1	2
Canada 1999 World Juniors *in Winnipeg*	7	1	1	2	8
Canada Totals	**14**	**2**	**1**	**3**	**10**

Junior Highlights.

Won Silver Medal at World Junior Championships in 1999

Around the Rink

Ward's rights were transferred by Niagara Falls to Erie when franchise relocated at the end of the 1995-96 season. Traded to Windsor (OHL) by Erie (OHL) for Michael Rupp, January 6, 1998. Traded to Plymouth (OHL) by Windsor (OHL) for Kyle Chapman and Maxim Linnik, January 10, 1999. Scored his first NHL goal on his first NHL shift against the New York Rangers on December 3, 1999. Missed majority of 2000-01 season recovering from knee injury suffered in game versus Carolina, January 16, 2001.

Ware, Jeff

Born: May 19, 1977 in Toronto, Ontario
Drafted: By the Toronto Maple Leafs from the Oshawa Generals in 1995, 1st round, 15th overall.

Career Junior, NHL and World Junior Statistics

	GP	G	A	PTS	PIM
OHL Regular Season 1994-97	141	7	40	47	252
OHL Playoffs	25	1	5	6	48
Memorial Cup 1997	4	0	0	0	39
NHL Regular Season 1996-99	21	0	1	1	12
NHL Playoffs	0	0	0	0	0
Canada 1997 World Juniors *in Switzerland*	7	0	0	0	6

Junior Highlights

OHL All-Rookie Team in 1995
Won Gold Medal at World Junior Championships in 1997

Around the Rink

Ware was traded to Florida by Toronto for David Nemirovsky, February 17, 1999. Signed as a free agent by Columbus, May 31, 2001 but never played a game for the Blue Jackets. Officially announced retirement, January 25, 2002.

Warrener, Rhett

Born: January 27, 1976 in Shaunavon, Saskatchewan
Drafted: By the Forida Panthers from the Saskatoon Blades in 1994, 2nd round, 27th overall.

Career Junior, NHL and World Junior Statistics

	GP	G	A	PTS	PIM
WHL Regular Season 1991-95	197	22	62	84	368
WHL Playoffs	35	0	8	8	53
NHL Regular Season 1995-Present	483	13	56	69	660
NHL Playoffs	64	1	8	9	48
Canada 1996 World Juniors *in United States*	6	0	0	0	4

Junior Highlights

Won Gold Medal at World Junior Championships in 1996

Around the Rink

Warrener played his first NHL game against New Jersey on October 7, 1997. Scored first NHL goal versus Boston, January 23, 1998. Traded to Buffalo by Florida with Florida's 5th round choice (Ryan Miller) in 1999 Entry Draft for Mike Wilson, March 23, 1999.

Watt, Mike

Born: March 31, 1976 in Seaforth, Ontario
Drafted: By the Edmonton Oilers from Michigan State University in 1994, 2nd round, 32nd overall.

Career Junior, NHL and World Junior Statistics

	GP	G	A	PTS	PIM
NCAA 1994-97	115	53	45	98	233
NHL Regular Season 1997-Present	157	15	26	41	41
NHL Playoffs	0	0	0	0	0
Canada 1996 World Juniors *in United States*	6	1	2	3	6

Junior Highlights

Won Gold Medal at World Junior Championships in 1996

Around the Rink

Watt was traded to the New York Islanders by Edmonton for Eric Fichaud, June 18, 1998. Claimed on waivers by Nashville from the New York Islanders, May 23, 2000. Traded to Philadelphia by Nashville for Mikhail Chernov, May 24, 2001. Signed as a free agent by Carolina, August 7, 2002.

Weiss, Stephen

Born: April 3, 1983 in Markham, Ontario
Drafted: By the Florida Panthers from the Plymouth Whalers in 2001, 1st round, 4th overall.

Career Junior, NHL and World Junior Statistics

	GP	G	A	PTS	PIM
OHL Regular Season 1999-02	172	89	134	223	149
OHL Playoffs	47	17	41	58	41
NHL Regular Season 2002-Present	84	7	16	23	17
NHL Playoffs	0	0	0	0	0
Canada 2002 World Juniors *in Czech Republic*	6	3	1	4	6

Junior Highlights

OHL All-Rookie Team in 2000
Won Silver Medal at World Junior Championships in 2002

Around the Rink

Weiss was returned to Plymouth (OHL) by Florida, October 21, 2001, after sitting out the first three weeks of the NHL season. Made NHL debut on April 3, 2002 against Pittsburgh, recording his first NHL goal in that game.

Wesley, Glen

Born: October 2, 1968 in Red Deer, Alberta
Drafted: By the Boston Bruins from the Portland Winter Hawks in 1987, 1st round, 3rd overall.

Career Junior, NHL and World Junior Statistics

	GP	G	A	PTS	PIM
WHL Regular Season 1983-87	202	49	175	224	244
WHL Playoffs	41	12	35	47	64
Memorial Cup 1986	4	0	2	2	4
NHL Regular Season 1987-Present	1173	124	376	500	859
NHL Playoffs	144	15	36	51	125
Canada 1987 World Juniors *in Czech Republic*	6	2	1	3	4

Junior Highlights

WHL West First All-Star Team in 1986 and 1987

Around the Rink

Wesley was traded to Hartford by Boston for Hartford's 1st round choices in 1995 (Kyle McLaren), 1996 (Johnathan Aitken) and 1997 (Sergei Samsonov) entry drafts, August 26, 1994. Transferred to Carolina after Hartford franchise relocated, June 25, 1997. Traded by Carolina to Toronto for Toronto's 2nd round pick in 2004 entry draft, March 9, 2003.

Whitfield, Trent

Born: June 17, 1977 in Alameda, Saskatchewan
Drafted: By the Boston Bruins from the Spokane Chiefs in 1996, 4th round, 100th overall.

Career Junior, NHL and World Junior Statistics

	GP	G	A	PTS	PIM
WHL Regular Season 1993-98	248	114	155	269	272
WHL Playoffs	56	29	33	62	40
NHL Regular Season 2000-Present	100	3	6	9	69
NHL Playoffs	14	0	0	0	12
Canada 1997 World Juniors *in Switzerland*	7	1	0	1	4

Junior Highlights

Won Gold Medal at World Junior Championships in 1997
WHL West First All-Star Team in 1997
WHL West Second All-Star Team in 1998

Around the Rink

Whitfield signed as a free agent by Washington, September 1, 1998. Scored first NHL goal against the New York Rangers, March 9, 2001. Claimed on waivers by the New York Rangers from Washington, January 16, 2002. Claimed on waivers by Washington from the New York Rangers, February 1, 2002.

Wiemer, Jim

Born: January 9, 1961 in Sudbury, Ontario
Drafted: By the Buffalo Sabres from the Peterborough Petes in 1980, 4th round, 83rd overall.

Career Junior, NHL and World Junior Statistics

	GP	G	A	PTS	PIM
OHL Regular Season 1978-81	181	73	98	171	215
OHL Playoffs	32	10	13	23	34
Memorial Cup 1979 and 1980	10	2	1	3	6
NHL Regular Season 1982-94	325	29	72	101	378
NHL Playoffs	62	5	8	13	63
Canada 1980 World Juniors *in Finland*	5	2	2	4	2

Junior Highlights

Won Memorial Cup in 1979

Around the Rink

Wiemer was traded to the New York Rangers by Buffalo with Steve Patrick for Dave Maloney and Chris Renaud, December 6, 1984. Traded to Edmonton by the New York Rangers with Reijo Ruotsalainen. Clark Donatelli, Ville Kentala for Don Jackson, Mike Golden, Miloslav Horova and future considerations (Stu Kulak, March 10, 1987), October 23, 1986. Traded to the L.A. Kings by Edmonton with Alan May for Brian Wilks and John English, March 7, 1989. Signed as a free agent by Boston, July 6, 1989. Retired from playing in 1995 after a season in the minors.

Willis, Shane

Born: June 13, 1977 in Edmonton, Alberta

Drafted: By the Tampa Bay Lightning from the Prince Albert Raiders in 1995, 3rd round, 56th overall. Also Drafted by the Carolina Hurricanes from the Lethbridge Hurricanes in 1997, 4th round, 88th overall.

Career Junior, NHL and World Junior Statistics

	GP	G	A	PTS	PIM
WHL Regular Season 1994-98	265	159	152	311	249
WHL Playoffs	54	29	28	57	50
Memorial Cup 1997	5	2	2	4	4
NHL Regular Season 1998-Present	162	31	37	68	75
NHL Playoffs	2	0	0	0	0
Canada 1997 World Juniors *in Switzerland*	7	0	0	0	0

Junior Highlights

Won Gold Medal at World Junior Championships in 1997
WHL East First All-Star Team in 1997 and 1998

Around the Rink

Willis was traded to Lethbridge by Prince Albert midway through the 1996-97 season. Willis did not sign with Tampa after being drafted, therefore after two years he went back into the NHL draft and was selected by Carolina. Made NHL debut against Washington, February 5, 1999. Traded to Tampa Bay by Carolina with Chris Dingman for Kevin Weekes, March 5, 2002.

Willsie, Brian

Born: March 16, 1978 in London, Ontario
Drafted: By the Colorado Avalanche from the Guelph Storm in 1996, 6th round, 146th overall.

Career Junior, NHL and World Junior Statistics

	GP	G	A	PTS	PIM
OHL Regular Season 1995-98	186	95	83	178	96
OHL Playoffs	46	28	11	39	34
NHL Regular Season 1999-Present	69	7	8	15	29
NHL Playoffs	10	1	1	2	4
Canada 1998 World Juniors *in Finland*	7	0	2	2	4

Junior Highlights

OHL First All-Star Team in 1998

Around the Rink

Willsie played his first NHL game against Chicago on January 9, 2000. Recorded his first NHL point and goal on October 23, 2001 versus Carolina. Registered his first assist ion New Years Day 2002 against Nashville.

Wilson, Carey

Born: May 19, 1962 in Winnipeg, Manitoba
Drafted: By the Chicago Black Hawks from Dartmouth College in 1980, 4th round, 67th overall.

Career Junior, NHL and World Junior Statistics

	GP	G	A	PTS	PIM
Finnish Elite League 1981-83	65	31	41	72	120
NCAA 1979-81	55	25	35	60	72
WHL Regular Season 1978-79	5	1	1	2	0
WHL Playoffs	0	0	0	0	0
NHL Regular Season 1983-93	552	169	258	427	314
NHL Playoffs	52	11	13	24	14
Canada 1982 World Juniors *in United States*	7	4	1	5	6

Junior Highlights

Won Gold Medal at World Junior Championships in 1982

Around the Rink

Wilson left the Calgary Wranglers to play at Dartmouth. After two years of college hockey Wilson continued his junior career in Helsinki, Finland. Rights traded to Calgary by Chicago for Denis Cyr, November 8, 1982. Traded to Hartford by Calgary with Neil Sheehy and rights to Lane MacDonald for Dana Murzyn and Shane Churla, January 3, 1988. Traded to the New York Rangers by Hartford with Hartford's 5th round choice (Lubos Rob) in 1990 entry draft for Brian Lawton, Norm MacIver and Don Maloney, December 26, 1988. Traded to Hartford by the New York Rangers with the Rangers' 3rd round choice (Michael Nylander) in 1991 Entry Draft for Jody Hull, July 9, 1990. Traded to Calgary by Hartford for Mark Hunter, March 5, 1991. Suffered eventual career-ending knee injury in game versus St. Louis, December 4, 1992. Made a brief comeback with Manitoba of the IHL in 1996-97 for seven games and retired for good.

Witt, Brendan

Born: February 20, 1975 in Humboldt, Saskatchewan
Drafted: By the Washington Capitals from the Seattle Thunderbirds in 1993, 1st round, 11th overall.

Career Junior, NHL and World Junior Statistics

	GP	G	A	PTS	PIM
WHL Regular Season 1991-94	193	13	66	79	686
WHL Playoffs	30	5	11	16	137
Memorial Cup 1992	4	0	1	1	11
NHL Regular Season 1995-Present	496	17	43	60	771
NHL Playoffs	31	4	0	4	26
Canada 1994 World Juniors *in Czech Republic*	7	0	0	0	6

Junior Highlights

WHL West First All-Star Team in 1993 and 1994
Won Gold Medal at World Junior Championships in 1994
Canadian Major Junior First All-Star Team in 1994

Around the Rink

Witt missed the entire 1994-95 season after failing to come to contract terms with Washington. Played his first NHL game on October 7, 1995 against St. Louis. Scored his first NHL goal nearly three weeks later on October 26 versus Boston.

Wregget, Ken

Born: March 25, 1964 in Brandon, Manitoba
Drafted: By the Toronto Maple Leafs from the Lethbridge Broncos in 1982, 3rd round, 45th overall.

Career Junior, NHL and World Junior Statistics

	GP	W	L	T	SO	AVG
WHL Regular Season 1981-84	137	77	49	1	1	3.50
WHL Playoffs	27	17	8	0	1	3.27
NHL Regular Season 1983-00	575	225	248	53	9	3.63
NHL Playoffs	56	28	25	0	3	2.87
Canada 1984 World Juniors *in Sweden*	5	2	2	1	1	2.80

Junior Highlights

WHL East First All-Star Team in 1984

Around the Rink

Wregget was traded to Philadelphia by Toronto for Philadelphia's 1st round choice (Rob Pearson) and Calgary's 1st round choice (previously acquired, Toronto selected Steve Bancroft) in 1989 entry draft, March 6, 1989. Traded to Pittsburgh by Philadelphia with Rick Tocchet, Kjell Samuelsson and Philadelphia's 3rd round choice (Dave Roche) in 1993 entry draft for Mark Recchi, Brian Benning and Los Angeles' 1st round choice (previously acquired, Philadelphia selected Jason Bowen) in 1992 entry draft, February 19, 1992. Traded to Calgary by Pittsburgh with Dave Roche for German Titov and Todd Hlushko, June 17, 1998. Signed as a free agent by Detroit, July 23, 1999. Retired from playing in 2001 after a season in the IHL with the Manitoba Moose.

Wright, Jamie

Born: May 13, 1976 in Kitchener, Ontario
Drafted: By the Dallas Stars from the Guelph Storm in 1994, 4th round, 98th overall.

Career Junior, NHL and World Junior Statistics

	GP	G	A	PTS	PIM
OHL Regular Season 1993-96	185	90	90	180	115
OHL Playoffs	38	18	21	39	51
NHL Regular Season 1997-Present	124	12	20	32	54
NHL Playoffs	5	0	0	0	0
Canada 1996 World Juniors *in United States*	6	1	2	3	2

Junior Highlights

Won Gold Medal at World Junior Championships in 1996

Around the Rink

Wright played his first NHL game on November 16, 1997 against Anaheim. He scored his first NHL goal versus Detroit, January 9, 1998. Signed as a free agent by Calgary, August 2, 2001. Traded by Calgary to Philadelphia for future considerations, January 22, 2003.

Wright, Tyler

Born: April 6, 1973 in Canora, Saskatchewan
Drafted: By the Edmonton Oilers from the Swift Current Broncos in 1991, 1st round, 12th overall.

Career Junior, NHL and World Junior Statistics

	GP	G	A	PTS	PIM
WHL Regular Season 1989-93	233	115	211	326	647
WHL Playoffs	32	11	22	33	83
Memorial Cup 1993	4	1	3	4	6
NHL Regular Season 1992-Present	502	68	55	123	740
NHL Playoffs	30	3	2	5	40
Canada 1992 World Juniors in Germany	7	1	0	1	16
Canada 1993 World Juniors in Sweden	7	3	3	6	6
Canada Totals	**14**	**4**	**3**	**7**	**22**

Junior Highlights

Won Gold Medal at World Junior Championships in 1993

Around the Rink

Wright played his first NHL game with Edmonton on October 10, 1992 against Vancouver, he also scored his first NHL goal in that game. Traded to Pittsburgh by Edmonton for Pittsburgh's 7th round choice (Brandon Lafrance) in 1996 entry draft, June 22, 1996. Selected by Columbus from Pittsburgh in expansion draft, June 23, 2000.

Young, Brian

Born: October 10, 1958 in Jasper, Alberta
Drafted: By the Chicago Black Hawks from the New Westminster Bruins in 1978, 4th round, 63rd overall.

Career Junior, NHL and World Junior Statistics

	GP	G	A	PTS	PIM
WHL Regular Season 1975-78	204	25	109	134	222
WHL Playoffs	50	7	36	43	72
Memorial Cup 1976, 1977 and 1978	14	2	4	6	24
NHL Regular Season 1980-81	8	0	2	2	6
NHL Playoffs	0	0	0	0	0
Canada 1978 World Juniors *in Montreal*	7	0	2	2	2

Junior Highlights

Won Memorial Cup in 1977 and 1978
Won Bronze Medal at World Junior Championships in 1978
WHL Second All-Star Team in 1978
Memorial Cup All-Star Team in 1978

Around the Rink

Young played all of his NHL games with the Chicago Black Hawks. After a brief stint in the AHL in 1981-82, Young went to Germany where he played for six seasons. In 1987 he left Germany for Switzerland where he played until his retirement until 1990.

Yzerman, Steve

Born: May 9, 1965 in Cranbrook, B.C. – Raised in Nepean, Ontario
Drafted: By the Detroit Red Wings from the Peterborough Petes in 1983, 1st round, 4th overall.

Career Junior, NHL and World Junior Statistics

	GP	G	A	PTS	PIM
OHL Regular Season 1981-83	114	63	92	155	98
OHL Playoffs	10	1	5	6	16
NHL Regular Season 1983-Present	1378	660	1010	1670	860
NHL Playoffs	181	67	109	176	80
Canada 1983 World Juniors *in Russia*	7	2	3	5	2

Junior Highlights

Won Bronze Medal at World Junior Championships in 1983

Around the Rink

Yzerman is the longest serving Captain in NHL history, being named in 1984. Played his first NHL game on October 5, 1983 against Winnipeg, he also scored his first NHL goal in that game beating Doug Soetaert. Yzermans first Hat Trick came as an early Christmas present in 1983 when he scored three on Leafs goalie Mike Palmateer on December 23, 1983. Missed most of 2002-03 recovering from knee surgery.

Zigomanis, Mike

Born: January 17, 1981 in North York, Ontario
Drafted: By the Buffalo Sabres from the Kingston Frontenacs in 1999, 3rd round, 64th overall. Also Drafted by the Carolina Hurricanes in 2001, 2nd round, 46th overall.

Career Junior, NHL and World Junior Statistics

	GP	G	A	PTS	PIM
OHL Regular Season 1997-01	240	132	198	330	159
OHL Playoffs	22	2	17	19	4
NHL Regular Season 2003-Present	19	2	1	3	0
NHL Playoffs	0	0	0	0	0
Canada 2001 World Juniors *in Russia*	7	2	2	4	0

Junior Highlights

Won Bronze Medal at World Junior Championships in 2001

Around the Rink

Zigomanis was unsigned by the Buffalo Sabres for two years after the 1999 entry draft, therefore he re-entered the draft in 2001 where he was selected by Carolina. Scored in his NHL debut against Phoenix on February 26, 2003, he tallied a power play goal with 1:29 left in the third period in a 4-2 Carolina win. Recorded his first assist on April 2, 2003 versus Pittsburgh.

Photo Gallery Part Three

"All Photos are Courtesy of the Hockey Hall of Fame Collection"

Picture One is of Chris Pronger 1993 jpeg 27

Picture Two is of Mike Peca 1994 jpeg28

Picture Three is of Jason Botterill 1994 jpeg29

Picture Four is of Adrian Aucoin 1993 jpeg 30

Picture Five is of Martin Lapointe 1993 jpeg 31

Picture One is of Chris Pronger 1993

CHRIS PRONGER D

WORLD JUNIORS SWEDEN 93 CHAMPIONSHIPS

Picture Two is of Mike Peca 1994

Picture Three is of Jason Botterill 1994

Picture Four is of Adrian Aucoin 1993

Picture Five is of Martin Lapointe 1993

Where They`ve Won. Canada`s Medals By Country of Where Tournament Was Held

Tournaments	Gold	Silver	Bronze	Other
Canada 7	2	4	1	
Finland 5	2	1	0	2
Russia 4	1	0	3	
Czech Republic 4	1	2	0	DQ
Sweden 4	1	0	1	2
U.S.A. 3	2	0	0	1
Germany 2	0	0	0	2
Switzerland 1	1	0	0	0
Totals 30	10	7	5	8

Where the Players Were Born

Ontario	175
Alberta	**73**
Quebec	66
Sask.	**38**
B.C.	37
Manitoba	**17**
Foreign	11
NFLD.	**5**
N.B.	4
N.S.	**3**
NWT	1
Total	**430**

Leader Board

Most Points in One Tournament
18 - Dale McCourt in 1977
17 - Wayne Gretzky in 1978
17 – Eric Lindros in 1991
15 – John Anderson in 1977
15 – Marty Murray in 1995
15 – Jason Allison in 1995

Most Goals in One Tournament
11 – John Anderson in 1977
10 – Dale McCourt in 1977
9 - Brian Bradley in 1985
9 - Dave Chyzowski in 1990
8 – Wayne Gretzky in 1978

Most Assists in One Tournament
12 – Jason Allison in 1995
11 – Eric Lindros in 1991
10 – Joe Murphy in 1986
10 – Marty Murray in 1995

Penalty Minutes in One Tournament
G – Marc Denis
38 – Joe Contini in 1977
37 – Jason Doig in 1997
27 – Alexandre Daigle in 1993

Most Wins By A Goalie in One Tournament
6 – Manny Legace in 1993
6 – Jimmy Waite in 1988
5 – Marc Denis in 1997
5 – Al Jensen in 1977
5 – Stephane Fiset in 1989

Most Shutouts By A Goalie in One Tournament
2 - Pascal Leclaire in 2002
2 – Mathieu Garon in 1998

Most Points All Time
31 – Eric Lindros 1990/91/92
24 – Jason Allison 1994/95
19 – Shayne Corson 1985/86
19– Marty Murray 1994/95

Most Wins By A Goalie All Time
8 – Jimmy Waite 1987/88
8 – Stephane Fiset 1989/90
7 – Marc Denis 1996/97
7 – Maxime Ouellet 2000/01
7 – Jamie Storr 1994/95

Authors First All-Star Team
G – Manny Legace
D – Greg Hawgood
D – Gary Leeman
F – Dale McCourt
F – Wayne Gretzky
F – Eric Lindros

Authors Second All-Star Most Team

D – Patrice Brisebois
D – Paul Boutillier
F – John Anderson
F – Jason Allison
F – Dale Hawerchuk

Allen	Bryan	Calder	Kyle	Devereaux	Boyd
Allison	Jason	Campbell	Brian	Diduck	Gerald
Allison	Ray	Cammalleri	Mike	DiMaio	Rob
Anderson	John	Caprice	Frank	Doig	Jason
Andreychuk	Dave	Carkner	Terry	Dollas	Bobby
Armstrong	Chris	Carter	Anson	Domenichelli	Hnat
Arniel	Scott	Carter	Ron	Donovan	Shean
Arthur	Fred	Cassles	Andrew	Douris	Peter
Aucoin	Adrian	Cassidy	Bruce	Draper	Kris
Auld	Alex	Cassolato	Tony	Druken	Harold
Aulin	Jared	Chiasson	Steve	Dube	Christian
Babe	Warren	Chicoine	Daniel	Duguay	Ron
Babych	Wayne	Chimera	Jason	Dumont	JP
Bannister	Drew	Chouinard	Eric	Dykhuis	Karl
Barnes	Stu	Chyzowski	Dave	Eagles	Mike
Bassen	Bob	Ciccarelli	Dino	Eakin	Bruce
Baumgartner	Nolan	Cimetta	Rob	Eatough	Jeff
Beaudoin	Yves	Cirella	Joe	Elynuik	Pat
Begin	Steve	Clark	Wendel	Eminger	Steve
Belanger	Alain	Cloutier	Dan	Evans	Paul
Bell	Mark	Colaiacovo	Carlo	Evason	Dean
Bernhardt	Tim	Conroy	Al	Falloon	Pat
Berry	Brad	Contini	Joe	Fata	Rico
Bester	Allan	Convery	Brandon	Fenyves	David
Betts	Blair	Cooke	Matt	Ference	Andrew
Beukeboom	Jeff	Corriveau	Yvon	Ference	Brad
Billington	Craig	Corso	Daniel	Finley	Brian
Biron	Martin	Corson	Shayne	Fiset	Stephane
Biron	Mathieu	Cote	Alain	Flatley	Pat
Blight	Rick	Cote	Sylvain	Fleury	Theo
Boimistruck	Fred	Courteau	Yves	Flockhart	Rob
Bombardir	Brad	Courtnall	Russ	Forbes	Mike
Botterill	Jason	Courville	Larry	Foster	Corey
Bouchard	Joel	Craig	Mike	Foster	Dwight
Bouchard	P.M.	Craigwell	Dale	Foster	Norm
Bouck	Tyler	Crawford	Marc	Fountain	Mike
Boutillier	Paul	Creighton	Adam	Fox	Jim
Bouwmeester	Jay	Crossman	Doug	Fraser	Curt
Bradley	Brian	Cullimore	Jassen	Friesen	Jeff
Bradley	Matt	Currie	Dan	Gagne	Simon
Brewer	Eric	Cyr	Dennis	Gagner	Dave
Bridgman	Mel	Cyr	Paul	Gardner	Bill
Briere	Daniel	Daigle	Alexandre	Garon	Mathieu
Brind'Amour	Rod	Daigneault	JJ	Gartner	Mike
Brisebois	Patrice	Daley	Pat	Gaulin	JM
Brown	Curtis	Daniels	Kimbi	Gauthier	Denis
Brown	Keith	Dawe	Jason	Gavey	Aaron
Brown	Rob	Daze	Eric	Gelinas	Martin
Burke	Sean	Delorme	Gilbert	Gendron	Martin
Buthcer	Garth	Denis	Marc	Gillis	Jere
Byers	Lyndon	DeRouville	Phillipe	Gilmour	Doug
Calder	Eric	Desjardins	Eric	Gordon	Robb

Gosselin	Mario	Kidd	Trevor	McCrimmon	Brad
Gratton	Chris	Kitchen	Bill	McDonald	Terry
Gratton	Dan	Klassen	Ralph	McIntosh	Paul
Graves	Adam	Kluzak	Gord	McIntyre	John
Greenlaw	Jeff	Kobasew	Chuck	McKegney	Tony
Gretzky	Wayne	Komarniski	Zenith	McLean	Brett
Habscheid	Marc	LaFayette	Nathan	McLlwain	Dave
Hackett	Jeff	LaFerriere	Rick	Melanson	Roland
Haller	Kevin	Lambert	Dan	Mellanby	Scott
Halward	Doug	Langkow	Daymond	Melnyk	Larry
Harlock	David	Lanz	Rick	Metcalfe	Scott
Hartsburg	Craig	Lapointe	Martin	Micalef	Corrado
Harvey	Todd	Lapointe	Rick	Michaud	Olivier
Hawerchuk	Dale	Larsen	Brad	Mills	Craig
Hawgood	Greg	Latta	Dave	Miner	John
Hay	Dwayne	Laxdal	Derek	Moffat	Mike
Hazlett	Steve	Leach	Jamie	Moller	Mike
Heath	Randy	Leblanc	Fern	Moller	Randy
Heatley	Dany	Lecavalier	Vincent	Morrison	David
Herter	Jason	Leeb	Brad	Morrison	Mark
Hidi	Andre	Leeman	Gary	Morrow	Brendan
Hodgson	Dan	Legace	Manny	Muller	Kirk
Hodgson	Rick	Lemay	Moe	Murphy	Joe
Holden	Josh	Lemieux	Claude	Murphy	Larry
Holland	Jason	Lemieux	Mario	Murphy	Rob
Huber	Willie	Letowski	Trevor	Murray	Marty
Huffman	Kerry	Linden	Trevor	Murray	Troy
Hughes	Ryan	Lindros	Eric	Nash	Rick
Hull	Jody	Loewen	Darcy	Needham	Mike
Hunter	Dave	Lundmark	Jamie	Nelson	Jeff
Iginla	Jarome	Luongo	Roberto	Nemeth	Steve
Intranuovo	Ralph	Lupul	Gary	Niedermayer	Rob
Isbister	Brad	MacKenzie	Derek	Niedermayer	Scott
Jackmann	Barret	MacLean	John	Nielsen	Chris
Jackmann	Rick	Mair	Adam	Nieuwendyk	Joe
Jackson	Jeff	Malgunas	Stewart	Norris	Dwayne
Jarvis	Doug	Malhotra	Manny	Nylund	Gary
Jaspers	Jason	Manderville	Kent	O'Neill	Jeff
Jensen	Al	Mann	Cameron	Odelein	Selmar
Johansen	Trevor	Marsh	Brad	Ogrodnick	John
Johnson	Greg	Marsh	Peter	Orleski	Dave
Johnston	Greg	Marshall	Jason	Ott	Steve
Joly	Yvan	Matvichuk	Richard	Ouellet	Maxime
Jonathan	Stan	Maxwell	Bryan	Pachal	Clayton
Joseph	Chris	May	Brad	Paterson	Mark
Jovanovski	Ed	McAmmond	Dean	Paterson	Rick
Junker	Steve	McBean	Wayne	Patrick	James
Kariya	Paul	McCabe	Bryan	Peca	Mike
Keane	Mike	McCarthy	Kevin	Pederson	Denis
Keating	Mike	McCarthy	Steve	Pederson	Mark
Kelly	JP	McCauley	Alyn	Pellerin	Scott
Kennedy	Sheldon	McCourt	Dale	Penney	Chad

Pettinger	Matt	Secord	Al	Thornton	Scott		
Phillips	Chris	Seiling	Ric	Tkaczuk	Daniel		
Plantery	Mark	Sevigny	Pierre	Torres	Raffi		
Plavsic	Adrien	Sevigny	Richard	Trader	Larry		
Podollan	Jason	Shanahan	Brendan	Trottier	Bryan		
Potvin	Felix	Shannon	Darin	Tucker	Darcy		
Poulin	Patrick	Shantz	Jeff	Turgeon	Pierre		
Pronger	Chris	Shaw	Brad	Turgeon	Sylvain		
Propp	Brian	Sherven	Gord	Upshall	Scott		
Racine	Yves	Sillinger	Mike	Vaive	Rick		
Ramage	Rob	Slaney	John	Van Ryn	Mike		
Rathje	Mike	Smith	Barry	Vaydik	Greg		
Ratushny	Dan	Smith	Bobby	Verbeek	Pat		
Rausse	Errol	Smith	Geoff	Vernon	Mike		
Redden	Wade	Smith	Jason	Viveiros	Emanuel		
Recchi	Mark	Smith	Stuart	Waite	Jimmy		
Reeds	Mark	Smyl	Stan	Wallin	Jesse		
Regehr	Robin	Smyth	Ryan	Walter	Ryan		
Reid	Brandon	Snell	Chris	Walz	Wes		
Ribeiro	Mike	Soetaert	Doug	Ward	Jason		
Ricci	Mike	Sorochan	Lee	Ware	Jeff		
Rice	Steve	Spezza	Jason	Warrener	Rhett		
Richardson	Luke	Stajan	Matt	Watt	Mike		
Richer	Stephane	Stajduhar	Nick	Weiss	Stephen		
Rioux	Pierre	Staniowski	Ed	Wesley	Glen		
Rivers	Jamie	Stevenson	Turner	Whitfield	Trent		
Roberts	Gary	Stoll	Jarrett	Wiemer	Jim		
Robitaille	Luc	Storr	Jamie	Willis	Shane		
Rossiter	Kyle	Strueby	Todd	Willsie	Brian		
Sakic	Joe	Stuart	Brad	Wilson	Carey		
Sandlak	Jim	Sutherby	Brian	Witt	Brendan		
Sands	Mike	Sutter	Brian	Wregget	Ken		
Sanipass	Everett	Sydor	Daryl	Wright	Jamie		
Sarich	Cory	Tambellini	Steve	Wright	Tyler		
Savage	Reggie	Tanguay	Alex	Young	Brian		
Scamurra	Peter	Tanti	Tony	Yzerman	Steve		
Schneider	Andy	Theodore	Jose	Zigomanis	Mike		
Schultz	Nick	Thornton	Joe				

The End

Researched and Written By Kevin Gibson, Edited by Ben Fournier and Kevin Gibson.

Contact the Author
KevinGibson@Rogers.com
thefanswriter@hotmail.com

ISBN 1412001625